Contents

Acknowledgements

General Editor's acknowledgements

Although the ecological accounts of species described in this book are based largely on the contributors' own field observations, they would like to acknowledge the studies of other dragonfly workers which have been drawn on to amplify these accounts. In particular, reference was made to the work of Drs U Norling, H Dumont, H Wildermuth, S Gorb, H Beutler, S Blois, C Utzeri, J Waringer, N Michiels, A Dhondt, R Buchwald, J Phillips, F Kaiser, S Ormerod, L Frantsevich, F Johansson and J Convey.

I am grateful to Andrew Ross, Department of Palaeontology, Natural History Museum, London, who made helpful suggestions for the improvement of the section about the dragonfly fossil record.

I also acknowledge with affection the patience my wife, Ann, has exercised during the long development time of this book. Without her support it would not have been completed.

Steve Brooks

Artist's acknowledgements

The illustrations were made using a combination of museum specimens and photographs of living insects. I would like to thank the following individuals and institutions for supplying me with invaluable reference material: S Cham, G Giles, A McGeeney, S Brooks, Natural History Museum, London, and G McGavin, Hope Entomological Collections, Oxford University Museum.

I am grateful to Andrew Branson and British Wildlife Publishing for the great care taken in the production of such a demanding book.

To my wife, Georgina, and daughter, Alexandra, thanks for their companionship on our forays into the countryside looking at dragonflies.

Richard Lewington

Publisher's acknowledgements

This guide is the product of an excellent team effort, ably co-ordinated by Steve Brooks of the Natural History Museum, London, who in addition to providing many of the descriptions also wrote the introductory sections, including the keys. We would like to thank the contributors to the various sections (credited at the end of each description or regional guide), namely Steve Cham, David Clarke, Philip Corbet, Bob Kemp, Andrew McGeeney, the late Peter Miller, Steve Moon, Norman Moore, Brian Nelson, Mike Parr, Val Perrin, Mike Siva-Jothy, Betty and Bob Smith, Dave Thompson, Graham Vick and Dave Winsland. The photographs, including the superb ones of larvae, were supplied by Robert Thompson, with additional photographs from Ann Brooks, Andy Harmer and Andrew McGeeney. The maps were produced by Carte Blanche. We gratefully acknowledge the *Atlas of the dragonflies of Britain and Ireland* (see page 158 for details) produced by the Environmental Information Centre (Biological Records Centre, ITE, Monks Wood) which was used together with other sources to compile the references for the maps. Lastly, we must thank Richard Lewington, whose unrivalled artwork first inspired us to propose the project.

Andrew Branson, British Wildlife Publishing

Photographs All photographs by Robert Thompson with the exception of Ann Brooks, 20, 22, 36, 57 (top); Andy Harmer, 9, 19; Andrew McGeeney, 26, 37, 39.

Introduction

Male Common Darter resting on Heather.

DRAGONFLIES ARE the essence of summer. There can be few more enjoyable ways of spending a summer's day than strolling along the bank of a meandering river, or sitting quietly at the edge of a pond, watching the activities of dragonflies as they flutter and dart among the fringing plants. Dragonflies are fascinating insects with complex behavioural traits that are often easy to observe. This guide will help you to understand and interpret their behaviour while you watch them in the field. Some dragonflies are widely distributed in Britain, while others are restricted to very specific habitats, or occur in just a small part of the country. Another aim of the guide is to explain what governs these distributions and to detail some of the best places to watch dragonflies. Of course, it is essential to be able to identify dragonfly species when you see them, and detailed and accurate illustrations and descriptions are provided of all the species that occur in Great Britain and Ireland. Many of the country's leading dragonfly experts have contributed descriptions of species that they have studied for many years. But the study of dragonflies will never be complete. There will always be puzzling aspects of their behaviour that need to be investigated and resolved by anyone prepared to commit himself or herself to patient and careful observation.

Adult dragonflies are among the largest and most spectacular insects alive today, and their beautiful colours, phenomenal aerobatic skills and habit of flying only in warm, sunny weather make them very conspicuous. They are a fascinating and rewarding group of animals to study. Because they are large and day-flying they are easy to observe. The highly coloured body markings are diagnostic for most species, so, with a little practice, they are relatively easy to identify. The British dragonfly fauna is not large, so it does not take long to become familiar with most of the species. Armed with these identification skills, useful studies can be made mapping the distribution of the British species to help establish which are common or rare, declining or increasing.

The behaviour of dragonflies is complex and many exciting discoveries can be made by just sitting at the side of a pond or river making careful notes about the interactions. The larvae of all the British species live in standing or running freshwater and are simple to keep alive in aquaria. This provides an opportunity to observe an important part of a dragonfly's life history that is normally hidden from sight. Witnessing the awe-inspiring transformation from larva to adult is an unforgettable experience.

Dragonflies are harmless to humans, they have no sting and will not attack or bite, although some species appear inquisitive and may approach closely to investigate a human intruder. By feeding on many insect pests, they are beneficial, although their true worth is aesthetic and so is priceless. Unfortunately, humans are harmful to dragonflies and some species are now threatened in Britain as never before in their long history. The ponds and rivers in which they breed are being destroyed by human activities at an unprecedented rate. Hopefully, as more people become interested in dragonflies and value them for their beauty and fascinating lifestyles, this seemingly inexorable trend may be halted.

What are dragonflies?

Dragonflies belong to the insect order called Odonata, which means 'toothed jaws'. Adult dragonflies can be recognised by their large eyes and two pairs of large wings, which have a dense network of veins. There are about 5,300 species of dragonfly in the world today. Most of them live in the tropics, but about 120 occur in Europe and 38 species breed in Great Britain and Ireland.

The Odonata are divided into three groups, or suborders, comprising Zygoptera (damselflies), Anisoptera (dragonflies) and the Anisozygoptera (a primitive group now almost extinct). It is rather confusing that the English name 'dragonfly' is used both for the Odonata and for the Anisoptera. For this reason, when the name 'dragonfly' is used in this book it will refer to the entire order of Odonata. When the suborder is being discussed, it will be referred to as 'anisopteran dragonfly'.

Damselflies (Zygoptera) are delicate-looking insects. The head of the adult is rectangular, with large eyes on each side. The front and back wings are the same shape (the Greek word *zygoptera* means 'paired wings') and, when the insect is at rest, they are usually held closed over the top of the abdomen. They have a weak, fluttering flight and are often present in large numbers among vegetation at the waterside. Damselfly larvae have a long slender body and at the tip of the abdomen are three paddle-shaped appendages called caudal lamellae.

Anisopteran dragonflies have a much more robust appearance than damselflies. The head is spherical and almost entirely covered by a pair of large eyes. The front and back wings are dissimilar in shape (the Greek word *anisoptera* means 'different wings'); the front wings are narrower than the back pair and, when the insect is at rest, both pairs are held wide open. Anisopteran dragonflies are powerful fliers and are usually less plentiful at water than damselflies. Some Anisoptera characteristically perch on twigs or plants emerging from the water, while others fly restlessly, quartering a pond or river. Anisopteran dragonfly larvae are torpedo-shaped or rather spider-like in appearance and, instead of having caudal lamellae, have five short spines at the tip of the abdomen.

The fossil record

Dragonflies belong to the Palaeoptera, the most ancient group of winged insects, which also includes mayflies. The ancestors of dragonflies, the Protodonata, flew above the warm Carboniferous forests 300 million years ago and are among the largest flying insects ever to have existed. The wingspan of one group, the Meganeuridae, reached a colossal 70cm, making these the largest flying creatures of their time. These giant insects resembled modern dragonflies, but there were important differences in the structure of the wings. In particular, there was no notch, or node, near the middle of the leading edge of the wing, and the pterostigma was also absent. These two features distinguish all modern dragonflies, and their absence in the Protodonata shows that they were only distantly related.

We know very little about the shape of the bodies of Protodonata, since most are known only from their fossilised wings.

No-one can be sure what triggered the appearance of gigantic dragonflies or why they became extinct. Changing atmospheric conditions may have been responsible. Insect respiration is based on diffusion, so an increase in the oxygen content of air during the Carboniferous would have suited large insects. A subsequent 20% decline in oxygen levels may have led to the extinction of the giant protodonates. Alternatively, perhaps, the thin Carboniferous air encouraged the evolution of dragonflies with a large wing area. Another theory is that the giant dragonflies became easy prey for the rapidly evolving reptiles.

The first insects that can be recognised as true dragonflies appeared in the fossil record during the Permian, 250 million years ago, and many of the modern dragonfly families were already present by this time. The fossil record shows that dragonflies were once much more diverse than now.

All the world's dragonflies

About 5,300 species of dragonfly are known in the world. Of these, about 2,720 are anisopteran dragonflies and 2,580 are damselflies. These are divided among 29 families. A large majority of the species occur in the tropics. Colder regions support fewer species, but a few dragonfly groups include more species in temperate, mountainous or arctic regions than in the tropics. The bodies of these species are often darkly coloured to help to absorb heat, or they are covered in downy hairs for insulation.

Dragonflies breed in almost every conceivable aquatic habitat. A few breed in marine rock-pools, and several species breed in brackish estuaries or coastal saltmarshes. Some species live in semi-desert regions, breeding in temporary pools or streams. Their larvae develop quickly in the warm, shallow waters and emerge as adults before the pools dry. They then move on, tracking the weather fronts to arrive at the next location shortly after the rains, or alternatively surviving the dry season as eggs or dormant aestivating adults. Most species breed in permanent freshwater ponds and lakes, and some even specialise in water-filled rot-holes in trees. Running-water habitats also support dragonflies; these range from shallow seepages and runnels among forest leaf-litter or peat bogs, to torrential streams or even the moss-covered faces of waterfalls. A few tropical rain-forest species even have terrestrial larvae.

Dragonfly senses

In order to make sense of the behaviour of dragonflies, it is necessary to understand something of the basic behaviour, body form and physiology common to all species. With that in mind, I

A close-up of the head of a Common Hawker showing the enormous compound eyes.

have attempted to summarise the most important aspects. For a more detailed and thorough account, the reader should consult the books by Philip Corbet and Peter Miller on dragonfly biology listed in the bibliography.

A dragonfly's world is one of light. The perception of its surroundings overwhelmingly comes from its massive eyes. All adult dragonflies have very short, seven-segmented antennae which provide useful close-range tactile or olfactory information, for example when consuming prey. But for the other important activities, especially prey capture and mate recognition, keen eyesight plays a crucial role.

The eyes of adult dragonflies are the largest among insects. Because the eyes surround the head, dragonflies are able to see in front, to the side and behind all at the same time. Like most other insects, dragonflies have compound eyes. These are so called because each eye is made up of a large number of smaller facets called ommatidia. Each ommatidium has a lens on the surface and a second, conical lens just below. The more ommatidia there are, the more sensitive is the eye. The compound eye of an American emperor dragonfly, the Common Green Darner (*Anax junius*), is made up of 28,672 individual ommatidia. The ommatidia are not distributed evenly over the surface of the eye. Those in the upper part, looking forward, are larger and more numerous than the lower ones. In some darter dragonflies this differentiation is plainly visible and the eye is often a darker colour above than below. The size difference means that a dragonfly is better able to see subtle detail and movement from the front or above than from below. For this reason, dragonflies often approach their prey, mates or rivals from below and behind. A perched dragonfly is also extremely aware of approaching danger. One or more black spots or pseudopupils are visible in the centre of a dragonfly's eye. In this region, none of the light is being reflected; it is all absorbed, and corresponds to the part of the eye with the greatest visual acuity. The size of the pseudopupil appears to change when different parts of the eye are viewed; the larger the pseudopupil, the greater is the visual power of that section of eye.

Dragonflies have excellent colour vision, which is to be expected considering the colourful and complex markings of many species. They can also see ultraviolet light, and this enables them to detect light reflected from the surface of water. The species with the largest eyes belong to a group of hawker dragonflies (Aeshnidae: Acanthagynini) that live in shady tropical rain forests. They are active by day only in the gloomiest parts of the forest, but most of their flight activity is reserved for the evening or early morning while it is still quite dark. This type of behaviour is called crepuscular. A few British species, especially the Southern Hawker and Brown Hawker, will fly well into dusk on warm summer evenings, but in temperate countries it is often too cool to allow dragonflies to continue being active after dark.

On top of the head, dragonflies have a set of three additional eyes arranged in a triangle with the apex pointing forwards. These are simple eyes, or ocelli, made up of a single lens. They have poor visual acuity but are very sensitive to light intensity. They are particularly important in informing the dragonfly of its attitude in flight, and nerves connect the ocelli directly to the flight muscles. If the insect starts to dive or roll, the level of the horizon will change and with it the quality of light received by the ocelli.

Dragonfly larvae also have compound eyes. Larvae living among aquatic plants near the water surface have short antennae and rely principally on sight to detect the movements of their prey. However, many larvae live in or on the bottom sediments, where light intensities can be low. Vision is not so effective, so these larvae tend to have smaller eyes but longer antennae and legs. Larvae in these habitats locate their prey by touch.

Flight

Dragonflies are among the fastest and most manoeuvrable flying insects. It has been calculated that the giant fossil dragonflies would have needed to fly at 69km/hour just to stay airborne. Modern hawker dragonflies have a top speed of about 36km/hour and damselflies about 10km/hour. They owe this speed to the enormous flight muscles, which are firmly attached to the walls of the thorax at one end and to the base of the wings at the other, and can flap the wings at about 30 beats per second. Compared with other insects, this rate is quite slow and

Male Brown Hawker coming in to land.

is not fast enough to produce an audible hum or buzz. The noise that usually accompanies a dragonfly in flight is the rustling or clattering produced when the wing membranes clash together or against vegetation.

The wings are attached to the top of the synthorax, the fore wings to the mesothorax and the hind wings to the metathorax, by a narrow flexible joint. This allows the wings to twist in flight and gives a dragonfly great manoeuvrability, enabling it closely to pursue dodging prey or rivals, and to outfly predators. The wings have a stiff transparent membrane and a complex reticulation of wing-veins. They stiffen the wing but, because they are hollow, add little weight. The pattern of the wing-veins can often provide useful clues about the relationships between different species of dragonfly. At the tip of the wing is a dark brown or yellow pigmented area of membrane called the pterostigma.

The wings of dragonflies are not flat. The longitudinal wing-veins are arranged in a corrugated fashion, with the thick vein on the leading edge (costa) raised and the next vein (subcosta) lowered and so on back to the trailing edge in a series of ridges and furrows. This helps to provide rigidity and lift when the insect is in flight. Because the veins become thinner towards the trailing edge, this part of the wing is more flexible and allows the wing to twist and adapt its shape to aerodynamic forces.

In order to achieve forward movement, each wing is first swept forwards and downwards. At the end of this stroke the wing is twisted about its long axis and pulled upwards and backwards. The wing thus describes a figure-of-eight during each beat. The pterostigma at the tip of the leading edge is thought to act as a counterweight, promoting wing-twisting and wing-tip rigidity. The wings beat independently of each other.

As well as forward flight, dragonflies are able to fly sideways and backwards, and to change the direction and speed of flight rapidly. They are also capable of sustained hovering and gliding. Gliding flight is facilitated by a broad basal area of the hind wing. This is particularly well developed in some libellulids such as the Globe Skimmer (*Pantala flavescens*), which undertakes long migratory flights across the world's tropical oceans. Gliding presumably helps to conserve energy on these long-distance flights. The wings of most damselflies (except demoiselles) are too narrow to enable hovering. Hovering flight is employed when dragonflies are searching for food or mates, because vision is improved when the head is held still.

Life history

Male Large Red Damselfly resting on a horsetail.

INSECTS FALL into two developmental groups. The most primitive insects, including dragonflies (Odonata), mayflies (Ephemeroptera), grasshoppers (Orthoptera) and bugs (Hemiptera), all undergo incomplete metamorphosis. They are termed hemimetabolous. The other group is holometabolous; it has complete metamorphosis, and includes the more recently evolved insect orders such as flies (Diptera), beetles (Coleoptera), and butterflies and moths (Lepidoptera).

Holometabolous insects have four distinct stages to the life cycle: egg, larva, pupa, and adult. Each stage is completely distinct from the previous one. In contrast, hemimetabolous insects have a three-stage life cycle, with no pupal stage. In addition, the larval stage is rather similar in appearance to the adult. Like the adult, the larva has fully segmented legs, compound eyes, and mouthparts that function in a similar way to those of the adult. For this reason, adult and larva often feed on similar food and may even compete with each other for a food source. Although the larva does not have functioning wings, wing buds are evident, protruding from the thorax. With each progressive larval stage the wing buds grow longer. The larva does not have functioning reproductive organs, but these organs are present and gradually develop as the larva grows. It is quite easy to tell the sex of a dragonfly larva by carefully looking for the signs of a developing ovipositor underneath the eighth abdominal segment in a female larva, while secondary genitalia below the second abdominal segment indicate a male larva. It is impossible to sex a holometabolous insect larva. Hemimetabolous insect larvae undergo a large and variable number of moults and, when fully developed, the adult simply emerges after the final moult.

The difference in body form between dragonfly larvae and adults appears greater than in many other hemimetabolous insects because the larvae are aquatic and therefore have several adaptations for this environment that are not carried through to the adult stage. A major adaptive advantage in having an aquatic larva is that there is no direct competition between the larva and adult.

Egg

Dragonfly eggs have two principal shapes. Those eggs that are laid endophytically (into plant tissue) are elongate, while eggs that are laid directly into water are spheroid. Eggs laid endophytically, by damselflies and hawker dragonflies, are laid individually. They are protected from casual predators and drought by the plant tissue that surrounds them. Living plants are rarely seriously damaged by endophytic oviposition, but occasionally they are killed if the frequency of oviposition is very high.

Eggs laid directly into the water by darter dragonflies and emerald dragonflies are held together by a sticky gelatinous substance, rather like frog-spawn. The jelly is hygroscopic and so it rapidly absorbs water on contact and expands. The sticky jelly helps to protect the eggs from predators and extremes of weather, but also allows the eggs to adhere to plants. This prevents them sinking into too deep water or being washed into unsuitable, shaded habitats, where colder water may retard egg development.

Larvae usually hatch after 2-5 weeks, but hatching rate is temperature-dependent and varies between species. As temperatures increase, the development time of the eggs decreases. This is especially important in species that develop in temporary habitats and must complete larval development before the habitat dries out. Temperature optima for the maximum number of larvae successfully hatching is, however, usually between 15°C and 20°C, depending on species. Larvae from the same clutch of eggs may hatch over a period of several days, which probably helps to reduce cannibalism.

Although the eggs of most of the British species hatch within a few weeks, the development of eggs laid in late summer by emerald damselflies and some hawker and darter dragonflies is arrested after oviposition, and the eggs enter a diapause during the winter months. At the onset of spring, with higher temperatures, the eggs at last begin to develop and the larvae hatch a few weeks later.

Larvae

The cuticle of an insect is tough and waterproof but, because it is not very elastic, the insect cannot grow within it. Therefore, if a larva is to grow, the cuticle must be shed. Each time the larva passes through a moult it is said to enter a new stadium (formerly known as an instar). Like most other hemimetabolous insects, dragonfly larvae go through a variable number of stadia, from eight to eighteen depending on species and conditions, before development is complete. Prior to moulting (ecdysis), the larva pumps fluid into the thoracic region, causing it to swell. The skin then splits along a line of weakness running down the middle of the upper surface of the thorax, across the back of the head, splitting into a Y-shape next to the eyes. The larva then pushes itself through this hole. The newly ecdysed larva is whitish as the new cuticle has not taken on any pigmentation, and is therefore highly visible and vulnerable to predation. The new cuticle is also quite soft and elastic so that the larva can expand into it. After a few hours the cuticle darkens and hardens. Another important function of moulting is to allow the replacement of lost limbs or caudal lamellae, which can be gradually regenerated during larval growth.

Early stadium of a Brown Hawker. This larva has just moulted and its pigment has not darkened.

Larval development

When a larva first hatches from an egg, it is enclosed within a membrane. This stage is termed the prolarva. Almost as soon as the prolarva comes into contact with water, the membrane splits and the first larval stadium emerges. In species in which the eggs are laid below water, the prolarva stage is therefore of very short duration. Some species, however, lay their eggs above the water-line, in plants or rotten wood overhanging the water, in muddy depressions, or among plant roots near the water's edge. In these species, the function of the prolarva is to reach the water. It does this by flexing the body and performing a series of prodigious leaps until it comes to rest in the pond or river.

Apart from those species that overwinter in the egg stage, all species of British dragonfly pass at least one winter in the larval stage. In most species, development is completed within one or two years, but some hawker dragonflies may take three years and the Golden-ringed Dragonfly may take five years or more to reach the adult stage.

Development time is mainly temperature-dependent. The colder the water temperature, the slower the metabolism of a larva, and the longer it takes to develop. Larvae of the Golden-ringed Dragonfly often develop in cold upland streams and this, together with the large size of the species, accounts for its prolonged period of development. Similarly, larvae of the Blue-tailed Damselfly take two years to develop in northern Britain, and only one year in southern England, but in southern France the species may complete two or even three generations in one year.

Larval body form and habitats

The appearance of dragonfly larvae differs widely from one family to another. These different forms have evolved to adapt larvae to specific habitats. This helps to reduce competition between larvae of different species, since they can occupy subtly different aquatic habitats or different micro-habitats of the same waterbody, enabling them to exploit different food sources.

The body shape of both chaser and emerald dragonfly larvae is rather short, squat and flattened. These larvae have long legs, long antennae and small eyes, and the legs and upper surface of the body are covered in long hairs, called setae. This body plan makes them well suited to live among the sediments and rotting plant debris at the bottom of ponds and slow-flowing rivers. Fine particles of silt and mud get trapped in the body setae and help to conceal the larvae. The long legs and flattened body spread the weight of the larva and prevent it from sinking below the surface of the soft sediments. There is often no oxygen below the surface of the mud, so larvae would not be able to survive if they could not remain near the top of the sediments. The long legs also help the larvae to burrow quickly into soft sediments. The legs are drawn up underneath the body and then quickly pushed outwards to displace sediments beneath the larvae. Within a few seconds they can be hidden below a fine covering of silt. The flattened body enables larvae to squeeze between leaves and other debris, where they can lie in wait for prey and be concealed from predators. Demoiselle larvae are also bottom-dwellers and characteristically have longer legs and antennae than other damselfly species which live among submerged plants.

Since the bottom of a pond or river is often rather murky, it may not be possible to locate prey visually. The long legs and antennae and the clothing of fine setae over the body are all sensitive to movement, and enable a larva to locate most prey by touch. Most of the potential prey at the bottom of a pond or river are rather slow-moving, so keen eyesight to locate fast-swimming prey is unnecessary. Typical prey items might include water-lice (*Asellus*), midge larvae (Chironomidae), alderfly larvae (*Sialis*), leeches and tubifex worms.

The nature of the substrate has an influence on the species of dragonfly larvae that are likely to occur. For example, a bare gravelly substrate is an ideal habitat for larvae of the Golden-ringed Dragonfly. Coarse, unrotted leaf-litter is where the larvae of the Downy Emerald occur, whereas larvae of the Broad-bodied Chaser are more common in areas where the leaf-litter is finer and more decomposed. By utilising slightly different habitats, which may all occur in the same pond, different species avoid competing with each other. The concentration of oxygen dissolved in the water in each micro-habitat is also likely to be different, and species may have a different threshold below which it cannot survive.

In contrast to the body shapes of bottom-living larvae, the body of hawker dragonflies appears much more streamlined. Rather than being flattened, it is narrow and torpedo-shaped. The legs and antennae are shorter, the eyes larger, and the body is not covered in setae. These larvae are adapted to living in clear water, among submerged plants near the water's surface. Their streamlined body enables them to move quickly through the water in pursuit of fast-swimming prey, which they locate visually rather than by touch. The head of these larvae is extremely mobile – they track potential prey as it swims through the water and will turn towards it. The large eyes are wrapped around the front of the head, giving the larvae stereoscopic vision and enabling them to estimate strike-distance with great accuracy. They are able to see clearly for a considerable distance, and I have noticed hungry larvae move to the side of an aquarium in anticipation of a meal as I entered the room several feet away.

While habitat architecture (type of substrate, quantity of plants, the amount of shade caused by overhanging trees) is likely to be the most important factor governing the distribution of dragonfly larvae in a pond, other environmental variables can also be significant. Waters seriously affected by organic pollution, which causes nutrient enrichment or eutrophication (usually as a result of silage or fertiliser run-off from farms or sewage pollution), do not support rich dragonfly faunas. Highly eutrophic waters are usually low in oxygen, because the excess nutrients promote the growth of algae and bacteria. The bacteria use up oxygen as they break down the huge quantities of dead plant matter. With less oxygen available, most dragonfly larvae find it difficult to survive. Planktonic and filamentous algae also cause a problem for dragonfly larvae. Planktonic algae increase the turbidity of the water, so restricting the depth to which light can penetrate the water column and making conditions less suitable for submerged aquatic plants. Similarly, filamentous algae grow over aquatic plants in thick, blanketing clumps and also prevent light from reaching the leaves of the plants, and so kill them. A thick surface coating of algae can even be a hazard for ovipositing adults because, when the insects settle on the surface, their legs become entangled and they eventually drown.

The acidity (pH) of the water can also influence which species of dragonfly occur there. In general, dragonflies appear to be quite tolerant of acidic conditions. In lakes affected by acid rain, dragonflies are among the last creatures to disappear as the water becomes increasingly acidified. The pH of water has a strong influence on the plant communities, which in turn affects the architecture of the aquatic habitat. This, together with the lack of fish, may be an important factor governing which dragonfly species occur in acid waters.

Feeding

Dragonfly larvae are essentially ambush predators. They either lie concealed among silt or plant debris at the bottom of ponds, waiting for prey to stumble past, or lurk in the leaves of submerged plants waiting for a meal to swim past. Dragonfly larvae will catch only moving prey, which they sense either by touch or sight. They feed on insect larvae, water-fleas, snails, small fish and tadpoles, the larger larvae taking the largest prey. Prey is caught with the modified lower lip (the labium), the form of which is unique to Odonata. The labium has a pair of sharp, sideways-hinging spines (modified palps) at the tip, used to impale prey, and is hinged and folded double below the head. When prey moves within range, the larva suddenly strikes, extending the labium with lightning speed. This movement is so fast that the larva often has a chance to strike several times if the first attempt is unsuccessful. The force of the strike is enough to cause the larva to recoil. In the Golden-ringed Dragonfly, darter dragonfly and emerald dragonfly larvae, the palps completely cover the lower half of the front of the face, like a mask. In damselflies, Club-tailed Dragonflies and hawker dragonflies, the labium is flat and covers the bottom of the head only. If a large prey is caught, anisopteran dragonfly larvae will attempt to subdue their struggling victim by stabbing it with the array of spines at the tip of the abdomen. The prey, securely held by the labium, is offered up to the fearsomely sharp mandibles, which make short work of insect cuticle and rapidly devour the soft flesh of vertebrates.

Dragonfly larvae are cryptically coloured, and between moults are capable of changing colour to suit their current background. Bottom-dwelling larvae are generally dark brown with paler brown mottling, while plant-dwelling larvae tend to be various shades of green. Damselfly larvae and hawker dragonfly larvae typically remain motionless, gripping the stems of submerged plants, behind which their narrow, cylindrical body is perfectly concealed. Because

Late-stadium Brown Hawker larva attacking a stickleback.

of their cryptic behaviour and camouflaged body, they rarely fall prey to larger predators, such as fish, although, in ponds in which fish stocks are kept artificially high, hungry fish will seek them out. Probably the major predators of dragonfly larvae are larger dragonfly larvae. Although dragonflies usually remain still, hungry larvae will stalk prey. At night, larvae are more active and hunt for prey.

Respiration

Insects evolved on land. All are primarily air-breathers. Species that have secondarily adopted an aquatic lifestyle have to solve the problem of breathing while underwater. Dragonfly larvae are able to remain underwater all the time by using gills. This means that they need not make the dangerous journey to the surface every few minutes. Gills are thin-walled outgrowths of the body membrane that have a dense network of hollow tubes, called tracheae, near the gill surface. Oxygen, dissolved in the water, diffuses across the gill membrane and into the tracheal system, from where it is transported throughout the insect's body by diffusion and the pumping action of the abdomen. The water surrounding the gills soon becomes depleted of oxygen, so a current of water moving over the gill surface must be maintained to bring a constant supply of oxygenated water to the insect. This is no problem in flowing water, but in standing water the insect must create a current itself. Damselfly larvae do this by periodically waving the abdomen from side to side, or by flexing the legs as if they are doing press-ups, thus causing a current of water to flow down the length of the body and across the caudal lamellae. These three leaf-like appendages at the tip of the abdomen have a dense branching network of tracheae, and so function as gills. Damselfly larvae can also take up oxygen across the entire body surface, but only in water with high concentrations of dissolved oxygen.

Anisopteran dragonfly larvae do not have caudal lamellae; instead, they have two rows of 30-40 gills inside the rectal chamber of the abdomen. By contracting its abdominal muscles a larva can draw water through the rectum and extract oxygen as it passes over the gills. Larvae can cope with low oxygen concentrations simply by pumping the water through more rapidly. In water that has very low oxygen concentrations, dragonfly larvae may breathe oxygen directly from the air: both damselfly and anisopteran dragonfly larvae reverse up emergent plant stems until the caudal lamellae or the tip of the abdomen is protruding through the surface of the water into the air.

Larval interactions

Dragonfly larvae are aggressive predators and will attempt to drive off other dragonfly larvae, particularly those of the same species, that approach them. This is not territorial behaviour, but serves to space out individuals within a habitat and reduces the risk of cannibalism. If a damselfly larva is approached by another larva of similar size, it will turn to face it. The larvae will remain stationary, staring at each other until one, usually the interloper, backs off. One larva may swing the abdomen to display the caudal lamellae and persuade the other to leave. Occasionally, a duel will be fought and the larvae may strike at each other with the labium. This may result in some injuries being inflicted, such as the loss of a caudal lamella or leg, but this is rarely serious as these appendages can be regenerated during successive moults. In a confrontation between anisopteran dragonfly larvae, each may swing its abdomen in an attempt to stab the other with the spines at the tip of the abdomen.

Movement

Dragonfly larvae spend most of the time concealed among plants or silt. During the night, or when very hungry, they may walk around, hunting prey. Larvae may also attempt to escape from large predators by swimming. Damselfly larvae use the caudal lamellae as paddles and flex the abdomen from side to side in order to swim. The legs are held splayed out to balance the insects in the water, but they swim rather slowly and it is not an effective way of avoiding fast-moving predators such as fish or predatory beetles.

Anisopteran dragonfly larvae employ a mode of jet-propulsion to escape predators. During respiration, water is drawn into the rectal chamber by pumping the abdominal muscles. If these muscles are suddenly contracted, the water is expelled to jet the larva along. The streamlined body offers little water resistance and, to reduce this still further, the legs are held back flat against the body.

Diapause

Adult dragonflies are relatively short-lived; most do not survive for more than a few weeks. It is important therefore that the adults have the best possible chance of meeting the opposite sex. One way is to synchronise emergence. This ensures that the entire adult population of a species is on the wing at the same time of year, but it has the disadvantage that adverse weather can seriously affect mating success. A second strategy is to prolong the emergence period so that adults are on the wing throughout summer. The population is less likely to suffer as a result of poor weather, but it means that fewer adults will be on the wing at any one time.

Dragonflies that emerge early in the season adopt synchronised emergence, while summer-emerging dragonflies have a long emergence period. To achieve synchronised emergence, spring species undergo a resting stage, or diapause. Diapause is triggered by changes in daylength during the summer of the year preceding emergence. Development is halted in larvae entering the final or penultimate stadium after a critical date. This ensures that most of the population overwinter in the same stadium, and are ready to emerge together the following spring. A few precocious larvae which enter the final stadium before the threshold date will, however, emerge in the summer of the same year, with the effect of prolonging the adult flight season.

Metamorphosis

Metamorphosis is triggered by changes in daylength and rising spring temperatures. Once a threshold has been crossed, the entire larval population begins to metamorphose and synchronised emergence occurs a few weeks later, with most of the adults emerging within a few days of each other. In summer-emerging species, there is no diapause in the final stadium, larval growth continues unchecked, and larvae begin metamorphosis as soon as they are ready. Since the eggs are laid in late summer, most will have overwintered as early-stadium larvae. Development continues rapidly but at slightly different rates, depending on availability of food, during spring and summer, and the emergence period is spread over several weeks.

The most important changes that occur during metamorphosis are the switch-over from gill-

Stages in an emerging female Hairy Dragonfly.

breathing to air-breathing, an expansion of the compound eyes, and the retraction of the larval labium. During the last few days of metamorphosis, the larvae are unable to feed and must breathe directly from the air. Metamorphosing larvae migrate to the water margin in preparation for emergence, and often cling to emergent plants just below the surface of the water. The thoracic spiracles, which are sealed during larval growth, are now opened and the larvae sit with head and thorax protruding above the water-line, breathing air directly.

Emergence

The last apparent act of the larva is in reality the first act of the adult, for, when the dragonfly finally leaves the water, a fully formed adult is already present inside the cuticle of the final larval stadium. Emergence is hazardous for a dragonfly. For an hour or more the insect is exposed, unable to escape, and the cuticle is soft. To minimise predation, especially from birds, hawker dragonflies emerge during the night. Damselflies and the other families of anisopteran dragonflies emerge during the early morning. At this time they are vulnerable to bird predation, but temperatures are higher and emergence can be completed more quickly. Emerging dragonflies are also vulnerable to other predators, including ants, spiders and slugs.

Most fully metamorphosed larvae leave the water by climbing up emergent plants at the water's edge. Other larvae may climb up the bank and out of the water to emerge in terrestrial vegetation surrounding the pond or river. Some may walk several tens of metres away from the water margin before selecting an emergence support, and this behaviour may help to reduce predation by dispersing the vulnerable adults over a wide area. Most emerge vertically, but a few species emerge horizontally on bare ground, on rocks protruding from the water, or on the surface of the floating leaves of aquatic plants such as water-lilies or pondweeds (*Potamogeton*). Once the larva has selected an emergence support, it ensures that it has a secure grip by flexing its legs and violently flicking the abdomen. This behaviour also helps to establish that there are no obstructions close by that may prevent the wings from expanding properly. Occasionally, a larva may fall back into the water and is liable to drown, because the spiracles are fully open and the insect must breathe air directly.

Emergence of the adult follows the same pattern as ecdysis in any of the larval stadia. The adult, within the larval cuticle, pumps body fluids into the thoracic region, causing it to swell. The larval cuticle splits along the line of weakness down the mid upper surface of the thorax and behind the eyes. Through this hole the adult begins to push itself. (Sometimes the larval skin does not split enough and the adult is unable to extract itself, which results in death.) To begin with, the thorax, head, legs and first few abdominal segments emerge. The portion of the abdomen that remains inside the larval cuticle secures the partially enclosed adult and prevents it from falling to the ground, from where it would be unable to complete emergence successfully. Then follows a period of quiescence while the legs harden. In damselflies and Club-tailed Dragonflies, the upper part of the body that has already emerged is held above the larval case, facing forwards. In most anisopteran dragonflies, however, the partially emerged adult hangs backwards, reflexed over the top of the abdomen.

Once the legs have hardened, the dragonfly grasps the emergence support and withdraws the rest of the abdomen from the larval skin. The shed larval skin is known as an exuvia. Body fluids are pumped through the wing-veins to expand the wings, which have been compressed into the larval wing buds. The wings have a greenish appearance at this stage, imparted by the colour of the body fluids, and are soft and easily damaged. They can be punctured by raindrops or by other larvae climbing over the emerging adult, or they may become snagged on nearby plants. If this happens, the fluids leak out and harden on the wing surface. This prevents the adult from flying. Sometimes the wing does not fully expand owing to an external obstruction or because of a blockage in a wing-vein. Usually this is fatal, but if only the wing tip is affected the adult may still be able to fly on the crippled wing. Throughout expansion the wings are held closed.

When the wings are fully expanded, the fluids are withdrawn from them and are pumped into the abdomen, which begins to expand. Usually this proceeds without a hitch, but if the lengthening abdomen meets an obstruction it may become bent out of shape. This may not be fatal, and it is not uncommon to see adult damselflies with kinked abdomens, but it must adversely affect their ability to fly and to mate.

The emergence process takes 2-3 hours in hawker dragonflies, but is usually completed within an hour in other species. Hawker dragonflies must wait until morning to make their maiden flight. Once the thoracic muscles have warmed up, the wings are flicked open and the adult takes to the air. Newly emerged dragonflies are called tenerals. They can be recognised by the shiny appearance of the wings and the drab coloration of the body. Teneral dragonflies are not sexually mature. The maturation process can take another week following emergence.

During the maiden flight the adult dragonfly usually flies vertically upwards towards the tree-tops and then away from the pond. During the immature phase dragonflies actively avoid water. Waterbodies are a meeting place for aggressive, sexually active males, which may easily damage soft-bodied tenerals. So, instead, immatures seek the shelter of trees or long grass, where they can feed in peace and become sexually mature. The immature phase is the disper-sive phase.

Migration and dispersal

Animals that live in standing water are usually good at dispersing. They have to be. Ponds and lakes gradually fill with silt, washed in from streams or from the surrounding land by rain. They fill up with leaves from bankside plants and are slowly encroached upon first by emergent plants and finally by trees. Not all freshwater habitats, however, are quite so temporary. Peat bogs, which often form over old lake basins, and rivers and streams are relatively permanent. Consequently, the dragonfly species that specialise in these habitats tend to be quite sedentary.

Many species of dragonfly are powerful fliers and will disperse over wide areas in search of new breeding sites. It is not unusual to see lone males or females far from water. Even species with seemingly weak flight, such as the Scarce Blue-tailed Damselfly which breeds in shallow temporary seepages, can disperse over many miles by flying high into the sky to be carried by wind currents. Dragonflies also respond to changing weather patterns and, following the spate of unusually warm summers during the late 1980s and 1990s, the Emperor Dragonfly, Southern Hawker, Migrant Hawker, Hairy Dragonfly, Broad-bodied Chaser and Ruddy Darter have been expanding their British ranges.

Some species will also willingly cross the sea to disperse, and populations of resident British species, such as Four-spotted Chaser, Migrant Hawker, Ruddy Darter and Common Darter, are increased by migrants from Europe. The British dragonfly fauna is also regularly supplemented by more exotic species from Europe and North Africa which occasionally arrive in their thou-sands, but which rarely establish breeding colonies that survive for more than a few years.

Following strong south-westerly winds in July and August, large numbers of Red-veined Darters, accompanied by a few Lesser Emperors, may appear along the south coasts of England and Wales and gradually make their way further inland. Strong south-easterlies may bring migrants from eastern Europe, such as Yellow-winged Darter and Vagrant Darter. Other species may also arrive, and in the last few years the Lesser Emperor, Globe Skimmer, Banded Darter, Scarlet Dragonfly and Southern Emerald Damselfly have all been seen for the first time in Britain. This may be in response to climate change or as a result of increasing numbers of drag-onfly-watchers.

Three other species have been confirmed as migrants to this country: the Southern Migrant Hawker, collected in Kent in August 1952; the Yellow-legged Clubtail (*Gomphus flavipes*), taken in Sussex in August 1818; and the Willow Emerald Damselfly, confirmed from an exuvia found in Kent in 1992. There are also doubtful old records of the Southern Darter.

Finding a mate

The maturation period may take just a few days or several weeks, depending on air tempera-ture, but, once it is complete, the sexually mature adult dragonfly is ready to return to water. It has attained full adult coloration and is ready for the business of finding a mate.

The most important thing in the life a male dragonfly is to maximise the number of eggs laid that have been fertilised by him. He must ensure that he mates with many different females and that these females succeed in laying 'his' eggs. Several different mating strategies have evolved. The first step is to optimise the chances of meeting a female. Females can be found widely dispersed around the hinterland of ponds and rivers, feeding and developing eggs. Eventually they must come to water to oviposit, so it makes sense for a male to wait for females to arrive at the water, where large numbers will be concentrated in a relatively small area. However, most other males have the same plan and large numbers of male dragonflies quickly congregate at the water-side during the summer. Success in finding a mate thus becomes a rather chancy business.

One way to improve the odds is to drive away other males from the water. This tactic is employed by demoiselles and most anisopteran dragonflies. Male demoiselles and libellulids adopt a perch overlooking the water as a vantage point from which to spot females and to attack rival males. Hawkers,

Male Banded Demoiselles competing for a favourable perch.

Golden-ringed Dragonflies and emerald dragonflies patrol a section of the bank and drive away intruding males. As the number of males at the water's edge increases, so the size of territory that the resident male can successfully defend gets smaller. Eventually, a maximum capacity will be reached and no more males will be able to establish a territory for themselves. Different tactics will then be adopted. Males without territories will search the hinterland and mate with females before they arrive at the water, or they may arrive at the water late in the day when pressure for space is reduced owing to falling temperatures and lessened female activity.

Mate recognition

In demoiselles, the males adopt an elaborate courtship display using their distinctly coloured wings to persuade females to mate with them. But in other dragonflies, males recognise their mates principally by their characteristic markings, flight and behaviour as they oviposit at the water's edge. Mistakes can sometimes happen, however, and not infrequently males attempt to mate with other males, with females of different species or even different genera or families, and sometimes even with dead females caught in spiders' webs, on plants or on the water's surface. Such behaviour often occurs during periods of high population densities, when the mating urge of frustrated males is at its peak.

The females of many damselflies occur in several colour forms. Explanations for female poly-morphism are still in doubt, but it has been suggested that male-like females avoid excessive male harassment at high densities, but risk not mating at low densities and may also suffer from increased predation.

Keeping a mate

As soon as a male notices a female, he will attempt to grasp her thorax with his legs. If the female is not receptive, she will try to escape by flying quickly away and curving her abdomen down as if to mimic oviposition movements. At the tip of the male's abdomen are the anal appendages: a set of hook-shaped claspers. The superior appendages are paired; the inferior ones are also paired in damselflies, but in Anisoptera there is a single inferior appendage. In damselflies, the male uses the claspers to grasp the female on the pronotum, which is often sculptured with grooves and projections. The male's claspers have minute teeth, the shape and number of which differ according to species and help to ensure that a secure grip is achieved only between males and females of the same species. In anisopteran dragonflies, the male anal

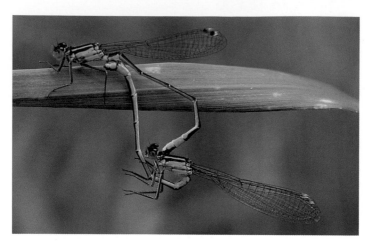

appendages grasp the female around the top of the head, the superior appendages hooking over the back of the head and eyes, and the inferior appendage grasping the vertex. The male appendages of each species are shaped to fit closely to the contours of the female's head or into grooves and notches, which helps to minimise interspecific pairings. Occasionally the hooked appendages may damage the eyes of the female, leaving a scar. The pair is now in the tandem position. Other males may attempt to dislodge the first male from the tandem, and sometimes two males will hold a single female or form a train of three dragonflies: female-male-male. But generally, so long as a male holds a female in tandem, he can prevent another male from mating with her.

Mating

Prior to mating the male must pass a packet of sperm (spermatophore), which is produced in the primary genitalia below the eighth abdominal segment, up to the secondary genitalia located below the second abdominal segment. The secondary genitalia are composed of paired lateral hooks (hamules) and, within an opening underneath the abdomen, the flexible finger-like penis. These structures are used in sperm transfer. The male will try to induce the female to mate by swinging his abdomen forwards to bring her reproductive organs, located below the eighth abdominal segment, into contact with his secondary genitalia, forming the characteristic 'wheel' copulatory position. Male dragonflies are unique in having secondary genitalia, so the wheel position is not adopted by any other insect group during mating. After a few attempts the female usually complies, but sometimes she is unreceptive and the pair breaks up. The female may assist in maintaining the wheel position by gripping the base of the male's abdomen with her legs. To facilitate this, the base of the hind wing in most male hawker, club-tail, emerald and golden-ringed dragonflies is cut away at an angle. In chaser and skimmer dragonflies, the abdomen of mature males is covered in a powdery blue, waxy secretion called pruinescence. This wax is often rubbed off by the female's legs during copulation to reveal the darker coloration of the abdomen beneath.

The duration of copulation is dependent on the mating tactics of the male. In most libellulids copulation lasts just a few seconds, but in some coenagrionid damselflies the wheel position may be maintained for six hours or more. The tip of the penis in some libellulids is club-shaped, and, as it enters the female spermatheca, it pushes aside any sperm that may have already been introduced by other males. The last male then places his own sperm on top of the pile. By using this tactic, a male libellulid can ensure that most, but not all, of the eggs laid have been fertilised by himself. On the other hand, because mating is brief, he has plenty of time to mate with other females and so to maximise his mating opportunities.

The tip of the penis in some coenagrionid damselflies is whip-like and equipped with short spines. For the majority of the time that the pair is copulating, the male penis scrapes out the

A Common
Hawker
ovipositing in
a small
mountain
stream.

female spermatheca and removes any stored sperm that was derived from previous matings. Towards the end of copulation the male finally introduces his own sperm. In this way, the male again ensures that virtually all of the eggs that are subsequently laid have been fertilised by himself, although the time available for other matings is curtailed. Other species adopt strategies part-way between these two extremes.

This behaviour is termed 'sperm competition' and has been intensively studied in some species of dragonfly. A detailed description of sperm competition is provided in the book on dragonflies by Peter Miller.

Oviposition

Shortly after mating, the search for an oviposition site begins. In most hawker, club-tail, emerald and golden-ringed dragonflies the female oviposits alone, but in damselflies and libellulid dragonflies the female is usually accompanied by the male during oviposition. By guarding his mate, the male can prevent rival males from mating with the female and displacing his own sperm. Non-contact guarding is usually adopted by species in which the male is territorial, since this allows him to drive off other males. In non-territorial males, however, oviposition is usually carried out in tandem.

The ovipositor is located beneath abdominal segments 8-10. In damselflies and hawkers it consists of a curved blade especially adapted for cutting a small slit in plant tissue. It is formed of a sheath (the valve) which opens down the middle to reveal the ovipositor itself. A single egg is placed inside each slit, so protecting the egg against predators or desiccation. The female may spend a considerable time ovipositing among a group of plants, and the eggs are laid in a characteristic pattern which varies between species, either in a spiral configuration or in line across the stem. Typically, the eggs are laid in the stems of emergent plants, under the leaves of floating-leafed plants or in submerged plants close to the water surface. Some species also lay in rotten wood. Damselflies often climb down the plant stem during oviposition until they are submerged. They can stay underwater for 30 minutes or more, breathing air trapped between their wings. Oviposition into submerged vegetation increases the amount of oviposition substrate available and allows the female to avoid male harassment, but it exposes her to fish predation.

Damselflies usually maintain the tandem position throughout oviposition. The oviposition site, apparently chosen by the female, is often among submerged plants close to the water surface, away from the banks, in full sunshine. While the female is ovipositing, the male holds his body rigid and vertical. In this position not only does he prevent other males from mating with the female, but he is also in a good position to keep a vigilant lookout for predators. Fish are particularly menacing while the female is submerged, and the male can quickly pull his mate out of the water if danger threatens.

Sometimes females can become waterlogged while ovipositing underwater and cannot break free of the surface tension. In these instances the male may not be able to drag the female out of the water, and after repeated attempts the male will break the tandem. All is not lost, however, and the female, using her wings as paddles, can row to the water's edge or to emergent vegetation where she can climb free and dry out.

Female Golden-ringed Dragonflies have a long, straight ovipositor, extending beyond the tip of the abdomen, which they use to stab into soft mud and gravels in streambeds. Libellulids, club-tails and emerald dragonflies oviposit directly into shallow, open water or over submerged plants. They allow a ball of eggs to accumulate at the end of the chute-shaped ovipositor (called the vulvar scale) and then, hovering just above the water surface, repeatedly dip the tip of the abdomen into the water.

While a female chaser dragonfly is ovipositing, her mate hovers close by, ready to drive off any rival males that may approach and attempt to mate. He is usually successful but, when the density of males is high, a rival may sneak in and grasp the female while the male is chasing another rival. Darter and skimmer dragonflies often maintain the tandem throughout oviposition. The male selects the oviposition site and, hovering overhead, swings the female so that the tip of her abdomen grazes the water surface and the egg mass is washed off.

Feeding

The structure of a dragonfly's thorax greatly assists in the efficient capture of aerial prey. The prothorax is the first and smallest segment and is attached to the back of the head by a narrow, neck-like projection which allows the head great manoeuvrability – especially useful when tracking and manipulating prey. The front pair of legs is attached below the prothorax. The massive synthorax, which holds the mid and hind legs, is angled forwards, which means that the legs also project forwards. This prevents an adult dragonfly from walking, but makes the legs well suited for catching prey in flight and holding it up to the downward-facing mandibles. On the inner surfaces of the legs is a row of stout thorn-like bristles. When the legs are flexed, they function like a toothed trap and securely grip the prey. During feeding-flight, dragonflies hold their legs out in front of the head, the spines of the legs meshing together to form a basket to scoop their prey out of the sky.

Adult dragonflies prey on flying insects, especially small flies, midges and mosquitoes, although larger species such as the Emperor or the Black-tailed Skimmer will also take butterflies and smaller dragonflies. The mandibles, a large pair of strong and powerful jaws, are knife-edged and sharp-toothed; they hinge sideways, one sliding over the other, enabling them to hold, slice and crush the body of their prey with ease. The wings are bitten off and allowed

to spiral down to earth, but the rest of the body is eaten. Anisoptera usually consume their prey while in flight, but libellulids and damselflies often perch before eating. As well as catching flying prey, damselflies also snatch flies that have settled on the surface of leaves. Dragonflies consume about 20% of their body weight in food every day. Feeding continues throughout the day, but is less intensive in the middle of the day when reproductive activity is at its peak. Towards the evening, hawker and darter dragonflies often feed in large groups in woodland clearings, in the lee of hedges or, sometimes, under street lights that attract night-flying insect prey.

Male Hairy Dragonfly feeding on a male Large Red Damselfly.

Distribution

Climate

APPROXIMATELY 40 species of dragonfly are known to breed in Great Britain and Ireland today. Their survival, however, is by no means assured. Since 1945, three species that formerly bred in England have become extinct. Many other species are far less common now than they were 40 years ago. On the plus side, a new species was discovered to be breeding in Ireland in 1981. In addition, some species appear to have become more common in the last 20 years or so.

Local extinctions of species, contractions and expansions of distributional range, and colonisations of new sites are natural ecological processes that can result from climatic change. Immediately after the last ice age, about 14,000 years ago, there were probably no species of dragonfly living in the British Isles. As the glaciers retreated, dragonflies crossed into Britain via the land-bridge that connected England to continental Europe until about 8,500 years ago.

The distributions of the British species reveal the significance of climate in governing where species can survive. A few species, like the Common Blue Damselfly and the Blue-tailed Damselfly, are widespread throughout the British Isles. These species are eurytopic – they can tolerate a wide range of temperatures and habitat types.

Many other species have a more restricted distribution, and are said to be stenotopic. The Golden-ringed Dragonfly and the Keeled Skimmer occur throughout much of southern England, but also along the west coast of Britain into northern Scotland. These species appear unable to tolerate the more continental climate of eastern Britain, with cold winters and dry summers. The west coast is warmed by the Gulf Stream, and has an oceanic climate of wet summers and mild winters. The distributions of these species are further restricted by their habitat requirements: shallow streams for the Golden-ringed Dragonfly, and shallow bog pools and seepages for the Keeled Skimmer. Both habitats are susceptible to drought, so the warm, wet climate of western Britain is ideal. The Golden-ringed Dragonfly is absent from Ireland, which further suggests that its colonisation of Britain occurred after the disappearance of the Irish land-bridge, which was inundated before the European land-bridge. Even the Common Darter, which is widespread throughout most of Britain, is less common in the north-east. This is probably because it cannot tolerate the colder climate of this region, since otherwise it has broad habitat requirements.

Some species, such as the Black-tailed Skimmer and the Scarce Chaser, occur only in south-east England. These species appear to be unable to tolerate the cooler conditions of northern England. The Black-tailed Skimmer is further restricted to lakes in the early stages of succession, and the Scarce Chaser typically breeds in slow-flowing rivers.

The Migrant Hawker at present occurs roughly south-east of a line drawn between the Humber and the Severn estuaries. However, this species is a recent colonist from Europe. Only 40 years ago it was not even thought to be breeding in this country and was restricted to the extreme south-east of England. It is now rapidly expanding its range north and west, probably aided by continuing climatic amelioration.

The Brown Hawker has an intriguing distribution. It is absent from northern Britain, presumably because conditions are too cold. Although the species is also absent from Wales and south-west England, however, it is present in Ireland, so it is unlikely to be an unsuitable climate that is limiting its colonisation of western Britain.

A few species, such as the Northern Emerald and the Northern Damselfly, occur only in Scotland. These species are unable to complete their life cycle successfully in the warmer conditions of southern England. There may be several reasons for this, but the precise explanation for their restriction to northern regions is unknown. They may be marginalised to northern habitats that are suboptimum for other species because they are unable to compete with more vigorous species, egg mortality may be high in warm water, or the adults may be unable to become sexually mature in higher temperatures.

For the last ten years there has been a continuing trend of a northward and westward expansion of species that were formerly restricted to southern England. Simultaneously, there has been an increase in the frequency and abundance of migrants from continental Europe, together with the sustained appearance of species that were previously unrecorded from Britain (notably Lesser Emperor, Small Red-eyed Damselfly and Scarlet Darter). This would appear to be in response to the well-documented rise in average global temperatures, and the increasing number of record-breaking warm summers we have experienced in Britain during this period. We should anticipate that this trend will continue and perhaps that species restricted to northern and upland Britain will begin to contract their range.

Habitats

Many species will breed only in specific habitats, and this further restricts their distribution. Species such as the Small Red Damselfly and the White-faced Darter are largely restricted to acid bogs. This habitat is most plentiful in areas of high rainfall: Scotland, northern and western England and Wales. The White-faced Darter, however, has a predominantly northern distribution, whereas the Small Red Damselfly has a southern distribution, suggesting that climate is also a significant factor.

Some species are restricted to running water, and it is interesting to compare the distribution of the Banded Demoiselle with that of the Beautiful Demoiselle. Larvae of the Banded Demoiselle live in slow-flowing rivers but, in contrast, the larvae of the Beautiful Demoiselle live in faster-flowing water. Both species are apparently intolerant of extreme cold, since neither occurs in the Highlands of Scotland. The Banded Demoiselle occurs throughout England, Wales and Ireland, but its absence from southern Scotland may be as much to do with the absence of slow-flowing rivers in this region as with climatic reasons. The Beautiful Demoiselle is able to exploit the upland streams of western Scotland, where the climate is relatively mild, but it is not found in the colder regions of eastern Scotland. The absence of the species from the flat landscape of East Anglia, however, is probably due to the absence of fast-flowing streams rather than to an unsuitable climate.

Rare species

Species in Britain and Ireland that are on the edge of their climatic range and which are further restricted to a rare habitat are never going to be common, no matter how much is done to conserve them. The three species that have become extinct in the last 50 years, the Orange-spotted Emerald, Dainty Damselfly and Norfolk Damselfly, were always rare and had very restricted distributions. The Dainty Damselfly became extinct after the few ponds in which it bred on the Thames Marshes in Essex were inundated by seawater following severe storms. The Norfolk Damselfly disappeared after its breeding sites dried up, and the Orange-spotted Emerald was adversely affected by a pollution incident. These three species were vulnerable because they were restricted to a very few sites.

Species on the edge of their range in Britain are often restricted to one particular habitat, whereas in other parts of their range in Europe, where climatic conditions are optimal, they are less fastidious. For example, the Norfolk Hawker is widely distributed in the Mediterranean region and central Europe, and is rare in northern Europe. In Britain it occurs only in parts of Norfolk and Suffolk, where it breeds in ditches that contain Water Soldier (Stratiotes aloides), a semi-submerged aquatic plant. The Water Soldier itself is also rare in Britain and is largely restricted to unpolluted ditches in East Anglia. In Europe, however, the Norfolk Hawker will breed in a much wider range of aquatic habitats and is not associated with any particular species of plant.

Even in Britain a species may occupy different habitats in different parts of its range. Throughout most of the country, the Downy Emerald breeds in woodland ponds, but in the New Forest it frequently occurs in ponds in open heathland. In Europe, the species frequents bog pools. It is therefore not always possible to make generalisations about the habitat requirements of species that can be applied throughout their range, and this, of course, has implications for the conservation management of breeding sites.

Dragonfly habitats

THIS SECTION includes descriptions of key habitats for dragonflies. This, in conjunction with information on the national distribution of each species and their flight periods, will enable the observer to predict which species are most likely to be found when visiting a site.

Lowland rivers

Lowland rivers are a potentially rich dragonfly habitat. There are a few species which are restricted to this habitat, but slow-flowing rivers will support a large number of additional species that also breed in standing water. A mosaic of habitats is often the key to a diverse dragonfly fauna. A meandering river passing through unimproved water meadows, with luxuriant growths of submerged, emergent and floating-leaved plants, together with scattered bankside trees and blocks of woodland nearby, is ideal. The silty substrate will provide a habitat for the larvae of slow-river specialists like the Club-tailed Dragonfly and Scarce Chaser. Adjacent woodland will provide important feeding and roosting grounds for the Club-tail. Other specialists, such as Banded Demoiselles, will be attracted to the dappled shade provided by bankside trees and, where there is dense emergent vegetation, swarms of White-legged Damselflies will occur.

Lowland rivers are prone to flooding, so are frequently subjected to harsh management practices to speed water flow, including straightening, deepening, and the removal of aquatic plants and bankside trees. They frequently receive huge inputs of nutrients, washed in from intensively farmed fields or from sewage-works outfalls. This promotes blooms of algae and duckweeds, which smother other aquatic plants and cause the water to become turbid, shaded and deoxygenated. All this unfortunately means that large stretches of our rivers have a poor dragonfly fauna.

Streams and upland rivers

Fast-flowing streams and rivers are shunned by most species of dragonfly. The hard and stony substrate is unsuitable for the larvae of species which like to burrow into soft sediments. Also, there are often few submerged aquatic plants, so species with weed-dwelling larvae find them unfavourable. As the water is seldom warm, the rate of larval development is slow. Despite this, there are a few species that specialise in this habitat. The Golden-ringed Dragonfly is associated with small upland, heathland and moorland streams that are deeply cut and devoid of shading vegetation. The Southern Damselfly prefers unshaded, shallow, gravelly streams. The Beautiful Demoiselle is more likely to be found in the riffle sections of larger streams and rivers, where shallow water passes over a stony bed, and emergent vegetation, together with overhanging trees, provides a habitat of dappled shade which is attractive to males. Because upland streams are often remote from human habitation, they are not usually threatened by pollution or development. Nevertheless, the afforestation of upland moors with conifers can pose problems with shading and acidification.

Bogs, moorland and lowland wet heath

Acidic bog pools and seepages support the most diverse dragonfly assemblages of any habitat in Britain. Indeed, Britain's premier dragonfly locality, Thursley Common in Surrey, is wet heathland with shallow peat deposits, and supports 26 of the 38 British breeding species. Not only will many generalist species breed in bog pools but, in addition, there are about 11 species, among them some of our rarest, that specialise in this habitat. The continued existence of a large proportion of the British dragonfly fauna is therefore dependent on the conservation and careful management of bogs and wet heathland. Dragonflies do well in bog pools because their larvae are usually the top predators; the waters are too acidic for fish, so dragonfly larvae have few natural enemies. The shallow water of bog pools and seepages warms quickly, and, since there are few trees to shade them, egg and larval development can be rapid. Bogs and wet heathland that have a mosaic of different habitat types are likely to support the largest number of species.

Males of the Small Red Damselfly can be found hovering over even the smallest area of open water in mires in southern England and Wales, while larger pools are favoured by the Common Hawker and Black Darter. Small runnels and seepages trickling out of the soaked peat are patrolled by males of the Keeled Skimmer and the Scarce Blue-tailed Damselfly. One of England's rarest and most rapidly declining species, the White-faced Darter, is restricted to bog pools, and the rare Northern Emerald Dragonfly and Azure Hawker occur only in shallow bog pools in the Scottish Highlands.

Bogs and wet heaths are declining rapidly throughout Britain. Raised bogs are being destroyed in England and Ireland by large-scale, industrial peat-mining for fuel and the horticultural industry. About 95% of the original bogs have been destroyed. Small-scale hand-

cutting is actually beneficial for dragonflies, as it creates small ditches of open water (a pristine raised bog has little, if any, open water), but industrial-scale peat-mining destroys the bog by milling off the entire surface and cutting down to the mineral soil below. In Scotland, bogs and moorland are threatened by peat extraction and drainage prior to afforestation, which, in turn, can lead to acidification of streams and pools. The wet heaths of southern England are at risk from drainage and reclamation for agriculture, forestry, roads and building development.

Levels, fens and grazing marshes

The river floodplains of Somerset and southeast England and the fens of East Anglia epitomise the tranquil countryside of lowland England. They provide productive farmland for grazing cattle or raising arable crops. The sluggish rivers and ditches, rich in aquatic plants, which crisscross the fields also provide important dragonfly habitats. Typical species include the Hairy Dragonfly, Norfolk Hawker, Ruddy Darter, Scarce Emerald Damselfly and Variable Damselfly. Although these species have a restricted distribution in Britain, they

Excellent habitat for dragonflies in the form of a drainage dyke through grazing marshes in Suffolk, with a good variety of floating and emergent vegetation, including Yellow Water-lily.

can be common locally where habitat conditions are favourable. Levels and fenlands are intimately associated with farmland, and the dragonflies that they support are increasingly threatened by drainage, as arable fields become ever larger, as well as by run-off from excessive applications of fertilisers, herbicides and insecticides.

Ponds and gravel pits

Ordinary farm and garden ponds are where the commonest British dragonfly species breed. These species are common because ponds are numerous throughout the country. Potentially, farm ponds provide ideal dragonfly habitat: sheltered, but not shaded, by a scattering of bankside trees, with profuse growths of submerged, floating-leaved and emergent vegetation, stretches of the banks bare and poached by drinking cattle, and hedgerows and woodland blocks close by to provide shelter and feeding sites for dragonflies. Field ponds have been a feature of farmland ever since farmers domesticated livestock and needed to provide them with watering holes. Over the last 100 years, however, as farming has intensified, there has been a

75% decrease in ponds throughout the wider countryside. In addition, even where ponds are still present the quality of the habitat has declined through neglect, and they have become overshaded by trees and polluted by farm run-off. Many of the common dragonfly species are no longer as common as they were in rural Britain. On the credit side, the efforts of FWAG (Farming & Wildlife Action Group) have encouraged farmers to restore and re-create farm ponds. In urban areas, many people are digging ponds in their back gardens. This has encouraged species such as the Emperor Dragonfly, Southern Hawker and Common Darter to colonise the heart of even the largest conurbations in Britain.

While road-building, housing and industrial developments have undoubtedly destroyed many important dragonfly sites, the extraction of sand, gravel and clay (ironically to provide materials for these enterprises) has left many pits which have been rehabilitated as large lakes. When they are carefully landscaped for the benefit of wildlife, especially if the edges are left gently shelving to encourage marginal plants, they can provide excellent dragonfly habitats. Species that have benefited, and which are expanding their range as a result, include the Black-tailed Skimmer and the Migrant Hawker. Other typical species are the Broad-bodied Chaser, Red-eyed Damselfly, Common Blue Damselfly and Blue-tailed Damselfly.

Ponds in deciduous woodland, when they are not too heavily shaded by bankside trees and so support luxuriant aquatic plants, will attract a wide range of species, notably the Emerald Damselfly, Large Red Damselfly and Brown Hawker. Two species, the Brilliant Emerald Dragonfly and Downy Emerald Dragonfly, are virtually restricted to woodland ponds (at least in England) because their larvae live among leaf-litter.

Dragonflies and the law

RELATIVELY FEW insect species are directly protected under British law. Certain species of birds, mammals and plants have relatively small populations that can be vulnerable to the activities of collectors or hunters. In contrast, even rare insects may be locally abundant and have the potential to produce large numbers of offspring. To protect them from collectors is, therefore, usually inappropriate and can even hinder conservation efforts, since it is often necessary to collect insects in order to identify them and monitor their populations. Insects are best conserved by protecting the habitats in which they live.

The Norfolk Hawker and Southern Damselfly are currently the only species of dragonfly protected by law in Britain, and under the provisions of the Wildlife and Countryside Act (1981) it is illegal to collect these species. The Wildlife and Countryside Act also allows for the recognition of Sites of Special Scientific Interest (SSSIs). These are areas of countryside that have a high wildlife value, and legal restrictions are placed on agricultural, forestry or development activities which may damage the site. Unfortunately, the law has not always proved effective in protecting SSSIs.

As a result of the Biodiversity Convention, signed by the British Government in Rio de Janeiro in 1992, a top tier of SSSIs has now received the new status of proposed Special Areas of Conservation (SACs), to be included in a Europe-wide series of wildlife sites known as Natura 2000. In theory, these sites will receive better protection than current SSSIs.

Nevertheless, SSSIs, SACs and the many nature reserves owned or managed by government, local authorities and nature conservation organisations cover only a small fraction of the countryside, and we cannot therefore rely on these sites to conserve all our species indefinitely. It is essential that sites suitable for supporting a diversity of dragonfly species continue to be available throughout the wider countryside, and this can be ensured only by wise and sustainable land management.

Regional guides

This section highlights some of the best places in the country to look for dragonflies, but it is also rewarding to discover some dragonfly sites for yourself close to home. This will give you the opportunity to visit a site on several occasions throughout the season and in successive years. You will become acquainted with the dragonflies that live there, the ways species divide the site between them, and how the behaviour of the various species is adapted to suit the habitat. If you study the site over a long period you will begin to understand the population dynamics of the species and the reasons why some species are rare while others are common. You can build up a collection of larval exuviae and establish which species breed at the site and which are regular or occasional visitors. You can photograph the larvae and adult dragonflies that are present at the site, and submit records of the various species to your local biological recording centre.

Finding a dragonfly site

The best place to start looking for a site is on a 1:25,000 or 1:50,000 Ordnance Survey map of your area. Ponds, lakes and slow-flowing rivers usually support the richest assemblages. Sites in natural or semi-natural countryside are likely to be better than those in forestry plantations or intensively farmed areas. If the site is on privately owned land, make sure that you have the landowner's permission before you visit. Another way to get to know your area is to join the British Dragonfly Society and attend local walks or talks. Some of the Wildlife Trusts also have walks to look at dragonflies on local reserves.

It is best to time your first visit to coincide with maximum dragonfly activity. This way, you can quickly decide whether subsequent visits are going to be fruitful. June and August are probably the best months, because in June most of the spring species should be present as adults and by August most of the summer species should be on the wing. It is best to visit in optimal weather conditions, around the middle of a sunny day, with temperatures at least 20°C, and with no more than light winds.

Once you have found a hopeful site, your enjoyment of the dragonfly fauna can be enhanced by focusing your studies. There is still much that the amateur enthusiast can contribute to our knowledge of dragonflies. The distribution of species is quite well-known throughout most of England and Wales, but there is still a relative paucity of records from Ireland and Scotland. So simply recording what species are present at a site can provide useful information. Of more value are records of which species are breeding, since this information can be used to assess the local status of species and is essential if habitat management is being considered. Records also provide information on species' declines or range expansions. Your dragonfly records should be sent to the county recorder, who is likely to be based at the county museum, or to the National Recording Scheme, which is co-ordinated by the British Dragonfly Society. The latest atlas of British dragonflies, based on 10km squares, was published in 1996 and your records can be compared against these maps. There are also a number of county dragonfly atlases now available; these often show records at a higher resolution, based on the tetrad system (2km squares).

Studies of dragonfly behaviour can also be rewarding. It is surprising how little is known about the habitat requirements of even the commonest species. Yet, without this knowledge, habitat management and conservation can only be done by guesswork. So, make notes of the micro-habitat in which you find larvae. Are they in soft sediments, among leaf-litter or in aquatic plants, for example? Are different parts of the site used by different species and, if so, can these areas be characterised by the kind of plants growing there or by water chemistry? Do males and females of the same species use different parts of the site? Where do females oviposit and the males patrol? Are there particular parts of the site in which the adults feed when they are away from water? Is there a main breeding locality with smaller satellite populations in neighbouring sites? These are just a few questions that might need answering before a sensible management strategy could be put in place.

Other aspects of behaviour which do not have such a direct bearing on conservation can be equally fascinating. How do males recognise their mates or rivals? How do larvae avoid overcrowding? How long do males stay at the pond during the day? Do the same males come back day after day and do they use the same part of the site? Do the adults specialise on a specific prey item? How much food do they eat in one day? How long do the adults live?

Long-term monitoring of a site can also provide useful information about the dynamics of dragonfly populations and the impact that changes in land management, or the neglect of a site, have had on the populations of different species.

Equipment

All that is essential to study dragonflies is a keen pair of eyes, a notebook and pencil, and patience. A pair of close-focusing binoculars can be useful to assist in identification or to more closely observe behaviour.

An insect net is useful to catch adult dragonflies to confirm identifications. A standard 15in diameter butterfly net-frame, with a deep 1mm mesh net bag, should be used. A light, strong, non-flexible aluminium handle of about 1.5-2m is ideal, but extra screw-on lengths are useful if high-flying dragonflies need to be caught.

Flying dragonflies are most easily caught if the net is swung following the dragonfly. Perching dragonflies are best captured with a rapid upward swing from behind. Once the dragonfly is in the net the swing should be followed through until the dragonfly is in the toe of the net-bag, whereupon the swing should be rapidly reversed and the net flipped over so that the bag flops downwards and closes the opening. To remove the dragonfly you should carefully place your finger and thumb on either side of the wing base, thus closing the wings over the top of the abdomen, and slowly pull the insect out, ensuring that the claws are gently released from the bag. Providing that the wings are held securely closed at the wing base, the insect will not be damaged. However, on no account should freshly emerged dragonflies be caught, since their soft wings and bodies can easily be damaged irreparably. Tenerals can be recognised by their shiny wings. It is worth catching a few dragonflies so that their magnificent colours, eyes and intricate bodies can be examined in close detail. Photographs, paintings and distant views can never substitute for this.

Larvae can be collected using a sturdy pond net, swept through aquatic plants. The net bag should have a 1mm mesh and be securely attached to a strong, rigid metal square frame. This should be securely attached to a sturdy wooden handle of at least 1m. If you drop the net in the water, the wooden handle will ensure that it does not sink without trace. The net will experience considerable water resistance and may be snagged on submerged logs and branches, so it is essential that the net bag will not rot or tear and that the frame does not bend, especially at its attachment point to the pole. Larvae in leaf litter, silty or gravelly sediments or in *Sphagnum* moss are best collected by riddling with a sieve.

1 Bodmin Moor
2 Red River Valley
3 Tamar Valley
4 Dartmoor
5 Aylesbeare Common
6 West Sedgemoor
7 Avon Valley
8 Studland Heath NNR
9 The Rough (River Stour)
10 Moors Valley Country Park
11 Arne Peninsula
12 New Forest

13 Pamber Forest
14 Warren Heath
15 Bracknell area
16 Theale and Pingewood
17 Pangebourne
18 Basingstoke Canal
19 Thursley Common
20 Esher and Wimbledon Common
21 Amberley Wildbrooks
22 Epping Forest
23 Wicken Fen
24 Ouse Washes

25 Upton Fen
26 Strumpshaw Marsh
27 Thompson Common
28 Dersingham Bog
29 Castle Marsh
30 River Stour
31 River Severn
32 Whixall Moss NNR
33 Cotswold Water Park
34 Saltwells LNR
35 Catherton Common
36 Sefton Coast
37 Southern Lake District

38 Blyth and Wansbeck Rivers
39 North York Moors
40 Filey Dams
41 Pocklington Canal
42 Hornsea Mere
43 Anglesey mires and lakes
44 Mynydd Preselli
45 Kenfig NNR
46 Gwent Levels
47 Cosmeston Country Park
48 Ffrwd Farm Mire
49 Cors Caron NNR
50 Dowrog Common
51 Wye Valley
52 Loch Barean
53 Silver Flowes NNR
54 Lochan Dubh, Oban
55 Carsaig Mire
56 Abernethy
57 Dinnet NNR
58 Glen Affric
59 Loch Maree
60 Brackagh Bog NNR
61 Peatland Park
62 Killarney National Park
63 The Burren
64 Montiaghs Nature Reserve
65 Crom Estate
66 Castle Coole

Main sites mentioned in the regional guides

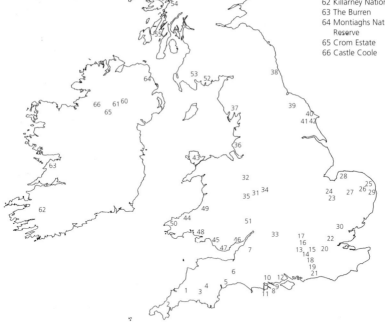

West Country

The West Country is a varied area including lowland rivers, high moorland, woodland, acid peatland, farmland and limestone hills. At least 31 species of dragonfly have been recorded in recent years.

Unfortunately, virtually all the lowland peaty areas have been subjected to gross changes resulting from peat extraction, drainage and re-seeding as 'improved' pastures. In many areas, removal of acidic peat has exposed the underlying alkaline clay. Despite the man-made changes in recent years, however, many dragonflies have adapted well to habitat disturbance and loss. Probably the chief casualty has been the Small Red Damselfly, which existed on at least one site in the Somerset Levels (Street Heath ST464393), but has now disappeared as a result of drainage and large-scale peat extraction.

Cornwall

Over 70 sites which are of conservation significance to dragonflies have been identified. These are key sites where at least one of the following species breeds: Scarce Blue-tailed, Small Red and Red-eyed Damselflies, and Ruddy Darter. A total of 28 dragonfly species had been recorded for Cornwall up to 1999. Of greatest importance perhaps is the area of **Bodmin Moor** (e.g. at SX2477 and SX2572) where 21 species were recently recorded. Of these, only the White-legged Damselfly, Banded Demoiselle and Black-tailed Skimmer are restricted in their distribution on the Moor. A good area with public access is Bowithick (SX 182826). Other good areas include the **ex-tin streaming areas of west Cornwall**, e.g. Red River Valley, near Camborne, and the **china-clay areas** of the mid-Cornwall moors, e.g. Menadew (SX 027593), both of which have nationally important populations of Scarce Blue-tailed and Small Red Damselfly and Keeled Skimmer. Concentrations of the Banded Demoiselle and White-legged Damselfly, in particular, are found along the **Tamar Valley** north of Gunnislake (15 species), with few sites elsewhere in the county.

Devon

About 31 dragonflies have been recorded for the county, including some of the rarer migrants. The area is dominated by **Dartmoor** and its fringes,

from a dragonfly point of view, and it is here that the national rarities, the Small Red and Scarce Blue-tailed Damselflies, are likely to be seen, together with the Keeled Skimmer and Black Darter (at e.g. SX5759). The White-legged Damselfly, Migrant Hawker and Emperor are more often encountered on lower ground away from Dartmoor. The pebble-bed commons of south-east Devon, such as **Aylesbeare Common** (SY057898), an RSPB reserve, have produced sites attractive to the Small Red and Southern Damselflies, where well-established but rather small colonies exist centred on seepages and small drainage runnels. The Downy Emerald has two sites at ball-clay pits in south Devon. The Scarce Blue-tailed Damselfly has been recorded at clay pits in the same part of the county. The Orange-spotted Emerald, which is believed to be extinct in Britain, is known to have once had a tenuous foothold on the borders of Devon and Cornwall, where it occurred on the **River Tamar**, above Gunnislake. Recent surveys have produced no evidence that the species still exists there. Much of the Tamar, however, is relatively unpolluted and it may be worthwhile to continue to make careful searches for it.

Somerset

About 28 species are recorded from Somerset, with some interesting and rare species occurring close to Bristol and Bath.

The extensive array of rivers, streams, drainage channels (rhynes) and peat pools of the **Somerset Levels** form a large area of interest, although some of the rarer species, such as the Scarce Blue-tailed, Southern and Small Red Damselflies, found

further west are apparently absent. The Levels are a stronghold for the White-legged, Variable and Banded Demoiselle Damselflies, Hairy Dragonfly, Black-tailed Skimmer and Ruddy Darter. The Hairy Dragonfly and Red-eyed Damselfly are two species that appear to be expanding their ranges and are locally common in suitable sites. The Hairy Dragonfly is particularly well represented on **Westmoor** and **West Sedgemoor** (ST3636) and **Huntspill and Brue Rivers** and other associated Levels in south Somerset. In parts of the Brue River valley, the Red-eyed Damselfly has shown its ability to survive as a breeding population in the temporary absence of water-lily leaves after dredging has denuded the riverbanks. Under these conditions, the Red-eye will perch on emergent reeds and grasses in the manner of other damselflies.

Although much of Somerset is intensively farmed, away from the Levels the rivers, lakes and ponds often support a rich dragonfly fauna.

The rarest dragonfly regularly breeding in Somerset is probably the Downy Emerald, which is known to occur at an upland peaty pool on **Mendip**, close to Priddy. The Black Darter is another scarce dragonfly in Somerset, occurring mainly in a few peaty ponds on Mendip, and is surprisingly absent from the main part of the Levels. The Common Hawker and Emerald Damselfly often occur with the Black Darter.

Further north, the **River Avon** close to the urban centres of Bath and Bristol is home for breeding populations of the Scarce Chaser and White-legged Damselfly. Here the Scarce Chaser is often associated with bur-reed and Yellow Water-lily growing along the river margins, especially where shallow silty inlets occur.

Mike Parr

Dorset

Dorset has an extremely varied geology, ranging from the acid Tertiary deposits of Bagshot Sands in the Poole Basin in the south-east, through a broad band of chalk, to the clays of the north and west. Other deposits of Gault and Greensand, Wealden and Purbeck Beds occur in smaller pockets. The species diversity of the dragonfly fauna is reflected in the geology, with maximum numbers around the Poole Basin, a marked decline upon reaching the chalk, and a slight increase in the extreme west of the county.

The Dorset heathlands were once very extensive and separated from those of the New Forest only by the floodplains of the Stour and Avon rivers. Since the latter half of the 19th century they have been systematically eroded through urbanisation and industrial development, and are now fragmented. We are fortunate that much of what is left is included in nature reserves.

Studland Heath NNR (SZ0384)

This heathland reserve lies immediately adjacent to the sea and forms the extreme eastern tip of Poole Harbour. It has a wealth of natural history interest. There are few natural ponds in the county, but Little Sea, a lake on Studland Heath, is one example. Here there are extensive beds of Common Reed and much of the immediate surrounding area is a marshy woodland supporting strong colonies of Hairy Dragonfly and Ruddy Darter. In total, 20 species have been recorded, including the Emperor, Common, Southern and Migrant Hawkers, Downy Emerald, Four-spotted and Broad-bodied Chasers, Black-tailed and Keeled Skimmers, Common and Black Darters and Scarce Blue-tailed Damselfly.

The Rough (River Stour) (SZ086966)

Dorset is a major stronghold of the Scarce Chaser and it is well distributed along the River Stour. The Rough is an area of disused meadows flanking the southern bank. There is some sallow incursion away from the river, which is of benefit as it contains discrete and sheltered glades of rough grassland with stands of umbellifers. It is in these areas that the Scarce Chaser basks and feeds while attaining maturity. The river itself has extensive beds of Common Club-rush. The river is managed for coarse fishing, and each fishing bay usually forms the territory of a male Scarce Chaser.

The White-legged Damselfly abounds here. When the weather prevents these insects from taking up residence on the river, they may be found sheltering in the lee of hedges.

Other species likely to be encountered include the Emperor Dragonfly, Southern Hawker, Broad-bodied Chaser and Blue-tailed, Large Red and Azure Damselflies.

Moors Valley Country Park (SU105062)

This recently established amenity park boasts three ponds and the Moors River. The river is relatively unproductive in this area, but the two major ponds are of great interest because they provide totally contrasting habitats. The larger of the two, constructed with the creation of the park, is fringed with sallow to the north and east and has access to the south and west. There is little in the way of emergent vegetation and this does restrict the number of species, but this is compensated for by the abundance of those that do occur. These include the Emperor, Southern Hawker, Brown Hawker and Black-tailed Skimmer. Common Blue Damselflies can occur in their thousands, accompanied by Large Red and Blue-tailed. The other semi-natural pond is acidic, fringed with rushes and sedges, and is notable for the densities that can be attained by Four-spotted Chasers. This can best be appreciated from the aerial walkway which crosses this pond. In addition to those also occurring on the large pond, Common and Black Darter dragonflies are found, with Common Emerald and Small Red Damselflies. The Scarce Blue-tailed Damselfly has also been recorded from the park.

Arne Peninsula (RSPB reserve) (SZ9788)

This is essentially another heathland site with most, if not all, of the ponds having been created artificially.

During the 1950s, Dr Norman Moore carried out a valuable project here in assessing population densities amongst a series of adjacent WW2 bomb craters. He was able to establish, by means of translocation, the optimum bank-length/surface areas required by the various species inhabiting the area. This has proved to be the standard

Hatchet Pond in the New Forest, Hampshire, 1990.

work in this field. Since that time numerous other ponds have been established, many of them as an aid to combating heathland fires. In spite of the fact that their location was not chosen for their suitability for dragonflies, they quickly became colonised. Eighteen species have been recorded at Arne over the years, and 16 are firmly established. These include the Emperor, Downy Emerald and Black-tailed and Keeled Skimmers.

David Winsland

Central Southern England

The New Forest

The New Forest is arguably the most valuable wildlife reservoir left in Britain today. It is the largest tract of semi-natural vegetation remaining in lowland western Europe and comprises pasture woodland, acid heath and valley mire, with the varying levels of drainage providing a rich mosaic of habitats. The total area is about 40,000ha, of which 20,000ha are unenclosed and heavily grazed by cattle, ponies and deer. Topographically, the Forest comprises a series of gravel terraces deeply eroded by river valleys; the terraces are highest in the north, but in the south much of the later deposits have been eroded, giving rise to a less rugged terrain. This erosion has removed much of the most acidic strata and exposed the more basally enriched Headon Beds. A watershed bisects the Forest from east to west and conveniently separates the northern and southern areas. This division is further enhanced by the fact that much of the southern slopes were afforested during the 19th century, and this acts as a barrier to the cooling north-east winds which are often prevalent in the spring. The warm climate of the southern heaths is enhanced by the sea breezes. These factors, when considered collectively, provide a significant climatic gradient, and the flowering of plants and the emergence of insects in spring in the south may be up to three weeks in advance of the northern part.

Twenty-eight species of dragonfly breed regularly each year in the New Forest (70% of the resident British population) and three of the migrants, the Yellow-winged Darter, the Red-winged Darter and the Vagrant Emperor, have been recorded during the past 15 years. It is the valley mires and the streams for which the New Forest is best known, and Victorian entomologists made annual pilgrimages here because of the rich diversity of species.

Hatchet Pond (SU3601)

This is a man-made pond constructed by building a causeway to dam Hatchet

Stream and flood a series of gravel and marl pits at the start of the 19th century. With the exception of a 4m-deep trench lying parallel to the causeway, the depth over the rest of the pond seldom exceeds 1m. Much of the pond is relatively devoid of dragonflies, with the interest being restricted to the extreme western end and the sheltered north-east corner. It is extremely shallow for at least 100m at the western end, and here vast swarms of Common Blue Damselflies may be found.

Immediately in the vicinity of the Hatchet Stream inflow, where sparse emergent vegetation occurs, the Scarce Blue-tailed Damselfly may often be found, sometimes accompanied by the Southern Damselfly, numerous other damselflies and usually by the Broad-bodied Chaser and the Emperor.

Whereas in the bulk of the pond the substrate is gravel, in the north-east corner this is replaced by clay, which encourages the growth of large beds of Bogbean. It is here that there is the greatest assemblage of species, with the Downy Emerald being the most notable. This species is seldom seen in large numbers here, but it may be found by searching along the north bank of the pond. The heathland habitat is atypical for this species.

Additional species of interest to be found in the north-east corner are: the Emperor, Southern and Migrant Hawkers, Black-tailed and Keeled Skimmers, Four-spotted and Broad-bodied Chasers, Common Darter, and Common Blue, Blue-tailed, Emerald and Azure Damselflies. There is a car park with facilities immediately adjacent to the pond.

Eyeworth Pond (SZ228146)

Constructed to provide a head of water for a gunpowder mill in the early part of the 18th century, Eyeworth Pond is in direct contrast with Hatchet Pond. With the exception of the south-east bank, a short section of the south-west bank and the most northerly tip, the entire circumference is ringed with mature trees and some sallow scrub. This topography makes it very sheltered, and although bankside access is limited it is well worth a visit, particularly early in the season. Downy Emeralds occur here in abundance and, before they are relegated to the margins by the appearance of the Emperor, they can form a spectacular display. This is also the home of Red-eyed Damselflies in the New Forest, where they have now recovered from their decline of recent decades. Other species which are recorded here are Four-spotted and Broad-bodied Chasers, Common Darter, and Blue-tailed, Common Blue and Emerald Damselflies.

Upper Crockford Stream (SZ3499)

From a dragonfly point of view this area is probably the most famous in the New Forest. It is the traditional home of the Southern Damselfly in a valley mire situated on the southern terraces in the Headon Beds. Actually, this site is but one segment in a complex of sites which occupy much of Beaulieu Heath.

Immediately to the north of Crockford Bridge is an extensive area of marl pits which, since ceasing to be used, have been largely overgrown with oak, thorn and sallow scrub. Upstream from this is typical open valley mire with, for the most part, a well-defined central watercourse. The Southern Damselfly may be found on those stretches which are neither too overgrown nor too open. The Beautiful Demoiselle, Golden-ringed Dragonfly, Keeled Skimmer and Common Darter are prevalent here, together with both Large and Small Red and Emerald Damselflies. Only rarely have Scarce Blue-tailed Damselflies been found. Some additional species such as the Emperor, Downy Emerald, Broad-bodied Chaser, Black Darter, and Azure, Common Blue and Blue-tailed Damselflies may be found on the more ponded areas, particularly those near the source.

Ober Water – Markway Bridge (SZ250038) to Puttles Bridge (SZ270028)

The Ober Water is a typical New Forest stream, with this section flowing gently between grassy lawns which are occasionally interrupted by groves of oak and thorn or by mires which empty their runnels into the main stream. It could be equated with the floodplain region of major rivers where silt is allowed to accumulate in the slower stretches, thus encouraging the growth of vegetation. This area was where the last record of the Club-tailed Dragonfly in any numbers was made, in 1967. Col. F C Fraser, an eminent naturalist of this century, had previously stated that 'more individuals could be seen in the New Forest in the course of a gentle stroll than in the whole of the rest of the country.' Sadly, the species is now considered extinct in the area. The White-legged Damselfly does still occur here, although not in the numbers in which it may be seen elsewhere. The varying flow-rates of the water encourage species not normally associated with running water, such as the Emperor, Broad-bodied Chaser and Common Blue Damselfly. These species occur particularly in the ponded regions. Throughout the area the Beautiful Demoiselle, Golden-ringed Dragonfly and Keeled Skimmer are common. Small Red Damselflies are restricted to areas in or adjacent to the mires, where Common Darters and Emerald Damselflies may also be common.

David Winsland

Hampshire and Berkshire borders

This area contains some of the best dragonfly habitat in Britain and 29 species breed here. On the sandy Bagshot Beds, with their associated plateau gravels of the southern edge of the London Basin, there are extensive areas of heath, oak woodland and pine plantations. There are many ornamental lakes and ponds, which hold some of the strongest populations of Brilliant and Downy Emeralds in the country, as well as Red-eyed Damselflies on those with water-lilies. There has been extensive extraction of gravel, and the pits in later stages of natural succession can support Common, Southern, Brown and Migrant Hawkers, while the Emperor and Black-tailed Skimmer move in and colonise the pools fairly soon after abandonment. Black and Ruddy Darters can be locally common and in boggy parts, where there is extensive *Sphagnum* moss, the Keeled Skimmer and Small Red Damselfly occur. On shady streams, the Golden-ringed Dragonfly and both demoiselles

breed. Recently, the Scarce Blue-tailed Damselfly has been recorded in the area, but colonies seem to be short-lived.

Pamber Forest, Hants
This mature oak woodland (SU186616) is an excellent site of abundant Golden-ringed Dragonfly and Beautiful Demoiselle, especially as the management team has worked so hard to open up the woodland, which had become far too dense. Just over the Berkshire border, there are many sites situated in the heathland and pine forests which lie to the north of Silchester. **Wasing Woods and Gravel Pits** (SU578635), **Decoy Heath** (SU613637) and **Benyon's Inclosure** (SU626633) all contain strong populations of the Brilliant and Downy Emeralds on the larger ponds and lakes, as well as most of the commoner species on the smaller ponds. The Keeled Skimmer is at Decoy Heath. The famous pond at **Wokefield Common** (SU652662) was used by Philip Corbet for his ground-breaking studies on the seasonal regulation of the Emperor Dragonfly, and it is still a fairly good site nearly 50 years later.

Hartley Wintney, Hants
The stream at **Warren Heath** (SU776586 to SU783588) contains strong populations of Small Red Damselfly on the boggy pool which forms its source; Keeled Skimmer and Golden-ringed Dragonfly occur further downstream. The stream flows into two man-made pools which are good places to see the Brilliant and Downy Emeralds. The Black-tailed Skimmer breeds in nearby gravel workings. There are other good ponds at **Heath Warren** and **Bramshill Common**, further to

the north.

Windsor and Bracknell, Berks
There are good populations of both Downy and Brilliant Emeralds at **Rapley Lake** (SU898646) and **Butter Bottom** (SU858640). The Golden-ringed Dragonfly breeds on many of the boggy streams, such as **Wishmoor Bottom** (SU878628). The Small Red Damselfly and the Keeled Skimmer occur on **Owlsmoor Bog** (SU846625 to SU849630), and the Scarce Blue-tailed Damselfly has also been recorded here recently.

Kennet Valley, Berks
Away from the more acid soils, gravel extraction has produced numerous ponds and lakes with higher nutrient levels, and the Variable Damselfly, a rare species in the area, breeds here, as well as a large number of the commoner species such as the Red-eyed Damselfly. Some of the best sites are in the complex of pools between **Theale** and **Pingewood** (SU661709 to SU690710).

River Thames, Berks/Oxon
The Club-tailed Dragonfly has one of its strongest colonies on the Thames, and there are weaker satellite populations on the **Kennet** (e.g. near Ufton Nervet) and the **Loddon** (including the **Whitewater/Blackwater** tributaries). The species is particularly easy to see during emergence in early May on the stretch of the Thames between **Streatley and Pangbourne** (SU624772), and mature adults can be seen near the railway viaduct over the river at **Goring** (SU604795). Another concentration occurs between **Wargrave** and **Remenham** and they can be

Pond at Wimbledon Common, 1988.

seen on the stretch used for the Henley Regatta, even during the Regatta! The White-legged Damselfly and Banded Demoiselle occur on these rivers in places where bank clearance has not been too vigorous.

Basingstoke Canal, Hants
This is an extremely rich dragonfly site of fairly base-rich water and, along with some of the associated pools, lakes and gravel pits, it holds most of the breeding species of the area. The two English emerald dragonflies occur, but what is regionally the rarest species here is the Hairy Dragonfly, which breeds both in the canal (especially around the 'flashes') and in adjacent waters.

Some of the best parts are near **Fleet**, at **Eelmoor** (SU842528), and **Ash Lock** (SU881518), just on the Surrey/Hants border. A walk along the towpath of the canal westwards from Ash Lock on a sunny day in early June will almost certainly produce sightings of the Hairy Dragonfly and Downy Emerald, and the Red-eyed Damselfly is particularly approachable here as the floating-leaved vegetation is confined to the bankside margins.
Graham Vick

South-east England

South-east England is the most densely populated part of Britain but, fortunately for dragonfly enthusiasts, it is also one of the richest parts of the country for dragonflies. This means that, although many of us do not have to travel far to see the majority of the dragonfly species that occur in Britain, many of the sites that support these species are under great pressure.

More species of dragonfly can be seen on the acid heaths of Surrey than anywhere else in Britain. Species such as Brilliant Emerald, Keeled Skimmer, Small Red Damselfly and Golden-ringed Dragonfly are locally abundant.

On the lowland rivers and water meadows of Sussex, the Variable Damselfly, White-legged Damselfly, Scarce Chaser and Club-tailed Dragonfly can be found.

In Essex and Kent, on the grazing marshes that border the River Thames, lies the English stronghold of the Scarce Emerald Damselfly, while a good range of species, such as the Ruddy Darter, Black-tailed Skimmer, Emperor Dragonfly and Red-eyed Damselfly can abound in the many flooded gravel pits in the region.

Thursley Common (SU905415)
This acid heathland, situated a few miles to the south-west of Guildford, is perhaps the premier dragonfly site in southern England and supports about 26 species. A car park is situated close to the tree-lined Moat Pond, from where good views of the Brilliant Emerald, Downy Emerald, Four-spotted Chaser and Red-eyed Damselfly are usually possible. Typical acid-water species will be seen during a short walk over duck boards crossing the bog immediately to the east of the pond. Here the Golden-ringed Dragonfly speeds down the narrow drainage ditches, while the Keeled Skimmer and Small Red Damselfly are usually present in large numbers over the numerous small bog pools. Thursley Common is also the sole remaining southern outpost of the White-faced Darter. Unfortunately, the species has become increasingly rare on the common. It is apparently restricted to one breeding pool which has deteriorated in recent years. In recent years none have been seen. The decline of the species may be associated with fires, drought, increasingly warm summers, or visitor pressure. This underlines the need for dragonfly-watchers to take the utmost care when searching for rare species, to ensure that they do not inadvertently damage the habitat.

Esher and Wimbledon Commons
Situated close to London, both these commons are fine examples of acid heathland and support a rich and varied dragonfly fauna. Esher Common has become drier in recent years, partly as a result of drainage

during the construction of the A3 road which bisects the common, but also because of encroachment of trees onto the boggy areas which has resulted in the disappearance of several small, unshaded bog pools. Small Red Damselflies used to breed here but have not been seen for several years. Nevertheless, the **Black Pond** (TQ128623) and the ponds on **Fairmile Common** (TQ127616), just south of the A3, still support many interesting species, including the Black Darter, Brilliant Emerald, Downy Emerald, Common Hawker and Four-spotted Chaser. The **River Mole** is just a short distance away (TQ122625), where typical riverine species such as the Banded Demoiselle and White-legged Damselfly can be seen.

Black Darters can also be found on Wimbledon Common, the species' nearest breeding site to central London being on the **Blue Pool** (TQ235718). Other species benefiting from the numerous well-vegetated ponds on the common include Common Hawkers, Emerald and Large Red Damselflies.

Amberley Wildbrooks and River Arun, Sussex
Overlooked by the South Downs and a few miles to the north-east of Bognor Regis, the Wild-brooks are an outstanding example of traditionally managed water meadow. The meadows are crisscrossed by numerous ditches, choked with a profusion of aquatic plants. On the western boundary of the site, the River Arun, tidal at this point, snakes its way through the floodplain.

During early summer, Variable Damselflies are often encountered sheltering in the hedges along the chalky drive that leads into the site from Amberley. Species typically associated with the drainage ditches include the Hairy Dragonfly, Four-spotted Chaser and Emperor, while the White-legged Damselfly, Club-tailed Dragonfly and Scarce Chaser may be found nearby in the fields bordering the River Arun or further upstream near **Pulborough** (TQ033181).

Epping Forest and Lea Valley
Just a few miles to the north-east of London, this area harbours over 20 species of dragonfly. The River Lea flows along the Hertfordshire/Essex border and is managed by the Lea Valley Park Authority. One of the best dragonfly sites in the Lea Valley is the **Cornmill Dragonfly Sanctuary**, near Waltham Abbey (TL381090). It is an area of water meadows, bounded on three sides by slow-flowing rivers with luxuriant aquatic plants. This is a good place to see White-legged Damselfly and Banded Demoiselle. Also common is the Red-eyed Damselfly, which may be seen perched on floating water-lily leaves. In recent years the Hairy Dragonfly has begun to make regular appearances.

A leaflet describing the dragonflies and where to see them is available from the Interpretation Centre.

Close by, there are many flooded gravel pits (**Fisher's Green** (TL375028) and **Rye House Marsh** (TL387106)) which support Black-tailed Skimmer, Broad-bodied Chaser and several other species of hawker.

A few miles to the east lies

Cornmill Dragonfly Sanctuary in the Lea Valley.

Epping Forest. Within this famous forest there are over 100 ponds that are managed by the Corporation of London. One of the best for dragonflies is the **Wake Valley Pond** (TQ421988), which supports at least 18 species, including Downy Emerald, Large Red Damselfly, Common Emerald Damselfly, Four-spotted Chaser and Ruddy Darter. In recent years, Black Darter and Scarce Emerald have also been recorded from some of the forest ponds.

Steve Brooks

East Anglia

East Anglia has a rich dragonfly fauna, despite the fact that five species have become extinct here since the end of the Second World War. Of the 26 species breeding in 1996, eight are very local, being recorded from fewer than 15 10km squares; two of these are confined to one site each. Of the remaining 18 species, 15 are common, occurring wherever suitable habitat occurs.

East Anglia is notable for its populations of three rare species – the Scarce Emerald Damselfly, the Norfolk Hawker and the Scarce Chaser – and for the relative abundance there of the Red-eyed Damselfly, the Variable Damselfly, the Brown Hawker, the Hairy Dragonfly and the Ruddy Darter.

Much of East Anglia consists of low hills covered by boulder clay. In this area, dragonflies are largely confined to farm ponds. Sadly, many ponds have become neglected and overgrown or have dried out owing to changes from mixed farming to arable farming in recent years, so they no longer provide habitats for dragonflies.

There are very few bodies of acid water left in East Anglia. That is why species such as the Common Hawker and Black Darter are so rare.

The area of impoverished glacial sands in Norfolk and Suffolk known as the Breck is of great ecological interest, although most of it has been planted with conifers. It includes the only natural lakes in the region – the Breckland meres – and still supports many dragonflies, including several populations of the Scarce Emerald Damselfly. These are small and very vulnerable, however, and the species is better observed in sites in Essex and Kent, where it is more abundant.

Most dragonflies in East Anglia live in the floodplains of the main rivers and in the vast area of reclaimed land lying just above or below sea level in the Fens and the Broads. Together, these areas include slowly moving, relatively unpolluted rivers, drainage dykes and ditches and numerous water-filled gravel and sand pits.

The following sections suggest some places which can be visited in the three East Anglian counties.

Cambridgeshire

This county includes the old counties of Cambridgeshire and Isle of Ely, Huntingdon and the Soke of Peterborough. It contains most of the East Anglian Fenland and one of the largest concentrations of gravel pits in Britain.

Newly dug gravel pits are quickly colonised by Common Blue Damselflies and Black-tailed Skimmers. Mature pits support a wide range of species, including Variable Damselflies and even Scarce Chasers. Brown Hawkers, Ruddy Darters and Red-eyed Damselflies are common insects in the Fens and gravel pits.

Two sites are especially recommended:

Wicken Fen (TL563705)
This property belongs to the National Trust and is Britain's oldest nature reserve. Eighteen species of dragonfly breed in its dykes, ditches and mere. They include good populations of the Variable Damselfly, Red-eyed Damselfly, Hairy Dragonfly and Ruddy Darter. A noticeboard gives information about local sightings. An entrance fee is charged for visitors who are not members of the National Trust. The boardwalk enables visitors in wheelchairs (and pushchairs) to visit dragonfly habitats.

Sutton Gault, Ouse Washes (TL425799)
A public footpath runs along the top of the bank between the Old Bedford River and its Counter Drain. Much of the adjoining washes is an RSPB reserve. The two watercourses together support a wealth of dragonfly species, including good populations of the Scarce Chaser, Hairy Dragonfly, Ruddy Darter and Red-eyed Damselfly. The Variable Damselfly also occurs.

Norfolk

As in Cambridgeshire, many farm ponds have been lost but water-filled sand and gravel pits have been gained. A number of lakes in private parks throughout the county provide good habitats for dragonflies. Most of the Broads and their associated rivers are rather disappointing places for dragonflies nowadays because they have lost most of their water plants owing to pollution. One or two isolated broads such as **Cockshoot Broad** (TG344155) are, however, being restored. The smaller unpolluted waterways and ditches in the Broadland area are very rich in dragonfly species.

The best places for dragonflies in Norfolk are the Breck and the heaths in the west of the county and the Broadland river valleys and marshes in the east. Four sites are especially recommended:

Upton Fen (TG385137)
This is a reserve belonging to the Norfolk Wildlife Trust. It borders Upton Broad. It supports 18 species of dragonfly, including the Norfolk Hawker.

Strumpshaw Marsh (TG341065)
This is an RSPB reserve in the Broads, noted for its birds and Swallowtail Butterflies. Twenty species of dragonfly have been recorded here, and 15 of these probably breed regularly. Brown Hawker, Hairy Dragonfly and Ruddy Darter are common. Norfolk Hawker breeds in those ditches which contain Water Soldier. Scarce Chasers visit parts of the reserve and may breed in it. Dragonflies can be watched from the many trails on the reserve.

Thompson Common (TL940965)
This is a Norfolk Wildlife Trust reserve in the Breck. It is noted for its pingoes, which are pools formed during the last ice age. Eighteen species of dragonfly breed in the pingoes, including Scarce Emerald and Variable Damselflies.

Dersingham Bog (TF662283)
A heathland nature reserve managed by English Nature. There are permitted paths and a

Dyke with Water Soldier at Upton Fen, Norfolk, June 1985.

boardwalk from which the Black Darter can be observed. This is one of the few places in eastern England where this acid-water species still occurs.

Suffolk
As in Cambridgeshire and Norfolk, many pond habitats have been lost but flooded gravel and sand pits gained. The best places for dragonflies in Suffolk are the river valleys, especially those which border Norfolk and Essex, the small area of fen and Breck in the north-west of the county and the coastal marshes. Two sites are especially recommended:

Castle Marsh, Barnby (TM475915)
This grazing marsh in the lower Waveney Valley is bordered on its west and north sides by public footpaths. The marsh itself is a Suffolk Wildlife Trust

reserve, and permission to visit it must be obtained from the Trust. The dykes and ditches of the reserve contain outstanding populations of Variable Damselfly, Hairy Dragonfly, Norfolk Hawker and Scarce Chaser.

River Stour between Bures (TL906340) and Stratford St Mary (TM042340)
This stretch of river is crossed by several minor roads, and several footpaths go to it, cross it or run beside it (for details consult OS map). This site is one of the very few places in East Anglia where one can see the White-legged Damselfly. The Red-eyed Damselfly, which is a scarce species in Suffolk, also occurs here. It is also found upstream and downstream of the stretch recommended.
Norman Moore

Catherton Common, Shropshire, 1991.

The Midlands

The Midland region of England is a very large area and to cover it comprehensively would require a book in its own right. Consequently, the selection of sites below is, by necessity, severely limited. Although rather biased towards the south and west, the selection has been chosen because the sites support a number of key species that are of interest within the region.

River Severn

This river still remains one of the least spoilt lowland rivers in the country. Above **Stourport-on-Severn** in Worcestershire, the river remains relatively undisturbed. Over considerable lengths of its course it passes close to extensive areas of semi-natural, ancient woodland such as the Wyre Forest and Ironbridge Gorge. As there is little boating activity and no locks etc above Stourport, the water flow is less regulated and as a result there is considerable variation from shallow riffles to slow, 'mill-pond'-like stretches.

Where there is plentiful emergent and submerged vegetation, the river supports large populations of the White-legged Damselfly and Banded Demoiselle. The Severn is well known for its large population of the Club-tailed Dragonfly. This species is best seen at the end of May to beginning of June, when the adults are emerging. At other times during the flight period adults are most often encountered in surrounding woodland. The stretch of river between **Bewdley, Worcestershire, and Ironbridge, Shropshire**, is particularly good. Wooded tributaries of the Severn, such as the **River Teme** (SO849543) or **Dowles Brook** (SO763768) in the **Wyre Forest**, support small populations of the Beautiful Demoiselle.

Whixall Moss, Shropshire (SJ490360)

This large area of lowland raised mire on the Welsh border, comprising Whixall, Fenns and Bettisfield Mosses, was acquired by the Nature Conservancy Council in 1991 and is now managed as a National Nature Reserve. Access to the site is by permit only and these can be acquired from English Nature. There are no public rights of way.

The site is composed of many acidic, nutrient-deficient pools, ditches and cuttings which have been maintained by peat-cutting activities over many years. As a result of this, and recent management to raise the water level, there are now many waterbodies at different stages of plant succession providing ideal conditions for breeding dragonflies.

The most notable species is the White-faced Darter, though there are good numbers of Common Hawker, Four-spotted Chaser, and Black and Common Darters. Damselflies include the Emerald, Large Red, Common Blue, Azure and Blue-tailed. Recently the Variable Damselfly has been seen also. Twenty-seven species of dragonfly have been recorded, but several are not resident breeding species.

Cotswold Water Park
(SU026597)

In the extreme south of the region, on the border of Gloucestershire and Wiltshire, gravel extraction (from the extensive, ancient bed of a much larger River Thames) has resulted in a large area of flooded gravel workings. The older workings containing shallow water are ideal for the dragonflies for which the park is well known. The water is relatively lime-rich and this has encouraged a rich and varied vegetation on many of the lakes and pools. The park supports strong populations of Black-tailed Skimmer, Broad-bodied and Four-spotted Chasers, Common and Ruddy Darters, the Emperor, and Brown and Migrant Hawkers. The park also has large numbers of Large Red, Common Blue, Blue-tailed and Azure Damselflies. Diligent observers may be lucky to find the Scarce Blue-tailed Damselfly, which is known to breed. A visitor centre is located on the spine road through the Ashton Keynes section of the park.

Saltwells Local Nature
Reserve, Dudley (SO935873)

Situated within the Black Country, on the edge of the West Midland Conurbation, the Saltwells LNR is an extremely good site to see dragonflies. The reserve lies 2 miles south of Dudley, between Brierley Hill and Netherton. It is composed of a mosaic of different habitats on land subjected to various industrial uses in the past, such as coal, clay and salt extraction. A canal, stream and several pools have been managed with dragonflies in mind. Over 18 species have been recorded, including Common, Brown, Migrant and Southern Hawkers,

the Emperor, Four-spotted and Broad-bodied Chasers, Black-tailed Skimmer, and Common, Black and Ruddy Darters. One of the pools in 1995 hosted several migrant Yellow-winged Darters. Of the damselflies, Banded Demoiselle and Emerald, Large Red, Blue-tailed, Azure and Common Damselflies are regularly found. With luck, the Variable Damselfly may also be found. The site has a visitor centre.

Catherton Common and the
Clee Hills, Shropshire
(SO649796)

Titterstone Clee and the Brown Clee are both distinctive south Shropshire hills that tower over the fertile lowlands of north Herefordshire, Worcestershire and the Teme Valley. Catherton Common, on the south-eastern flanks of Titterstone Clee Hill, is a large open area of unenclosed common land. It is an important area for wildlife, and is composed of dry and damp heathland with a spring-fed bog and is traversed by several small streams. Large areas of the Clees are covered with Bracken and gorse. However, numerous wet flushes and streams can be found nearer the summits. Brown Clee has several pools and a lake. On the lower slopes of Catherton Common, a spring-fed bog supports an isolated but thriving population of the Keeled Skimmer. In addition, the Golden-ringed Dragonfly, Four-spotted and Broad-bodied Chasers, and Common and Southern Hawkers are frequently seen.

Damselflies include Large Red, Common Blue, Azure and Emerald. Pools nearer the summit of each hill have good numbers of Black Darter.

Bob Kemp

Northern England

The country north of the Mersey and Humber can claim 23 dragonfly species, including populations of the following nationally scarce or important species: Variable Damselfly, Hairy Hawker, Downy Emerald, Keeled Skimmer, and White-faced Darter.

The great spine of the Pennines forms a natural east-west divide and much of this range, especially on the drier limestones, is not the best terrain for dragonflies. The lowlands on either side provide the bulk of Odonata interest. Cumbria, with its more oceanic climate, is an exception and has many important sites within hill massifs, most especially in the **Lake District**. The western coastal lowlands contain many high-quality dragonfly habitats – most notably within dune systems, and on peat mosses bordering some major estuaries. On the east side, the broad **Vale of York** forms an important corridor for northward movement of species, and local nature reserves include some good freshwater sites. Throughout the region a valuable range of waterbodies derives from use or re-use of industrial sites, from gravel pits, quarries and mine workings to factories and power stations.

Northern England has several species on the edge of their British range – currently the Brown Hawker, Migrant Hawker, Emperor Dragonfly, Broad-bodied Chaser, Ruddy Darter, Red-eyed Damselfly and Banded Demoiselle. The Ruddy Darter in particular has spread a long way north over the past decade. One consequence of the northerly latitude is that sites with ten or more breeding species, even in favourable locations, are relatively uncommon and thus always of conservation value. Whilst many important populations are within managed nature reserves, some vulnerable species, and sites, still remain relatively unprotected.

The number of species present in any one part of the area is greatly influenced by topography. There are strong populations of the widespread species of moorland and upland habitats: the Large Red, Common Blue and Emerald Damselflies, Common Hawker, Golden-ringed Dragonfly, Four-spotted Chaser and Black Darter. Increasing altitude and latitude generally results in a rapid decline in species numbers. Dependent upon aspect, sites above 300m usually support fewer than five species. The Common Hawker is one of the few hardy species to be found breeding on exposed tarns at 600m or more.

Selected sites

(* denotes access by permit)

Sefton Coast, Lancashire
The extensive dune systems in this coastal belt between Formby and Southport have much dragonfly interest, with 15 recorded species, of which 11 breed. There is a variety of waterbodies, from man-made scrapes and bomb craters to seasonally flooded dune slacks. The Local Nature Reserves of **Ainsdale/Birkdale Hills** have some good sites and are accessible on foot from the coast road between Southport and Ainsdale. **Wicks Lane Lake**, at Formby Point, is another good and accessible site. The Ruddy Darter has been regularly seen since its first occurrence in 1989, and this is a good area to look for other resident species expanding northwards. Emperor

Dragonfly and Broad-bodied Chaser are possible; the former already has a history of breeding in the area.

Lake District, Cumbria
The well-wooded area extending from Ambleside southwards contains an outstanding range of static waterbodies and streams and is generally very accessible. It holds at least 14 dragonfly species, including the only northern England population of the Downy Emerald. The species prefers large pools with deep water at some margins, near woodland. Among its many sites in the area are **Loughrigg Tarn** (NY3404) and **Wraymires Tarn** (SD3697). The latter is in the rocky afforested uplands of **Claife Heights**, between Lake Windermere and Esthwaite Water, which have a rich variety of mires, streams, pools and tarns. This area holds one of the few, fragile, English populations of the White-faced Darter. **Torver Common** (SD2892, etc), on the west side of Coniston Water, is a good place for species of flowing water, notably the Golden-ringed Dragonfly and Beautiful Demoiselle. The latter species is local in Cumbria and not found elsewhere in the north-west. The Keeled Skimmer may be encountered on boggy runnels in *Sphagnum* lawns at several sites in the general area, usually below 150m.

Northumbria rivers
The Banded Demoiselle has been recorded on some well-vegetated reaches of the rivers **Blyth** and **Wansbeck**, downstream of north-south gridline NZ00. These are the northernmost known populations in the country and were

discovered only recently. Potentially suitable areas are often best viewed from bridges, such as **Belasis Bridge** (NZ1977). Slow-flowing stretches on other rivers further north, such as the **Coquet**, **Aln** and **Till**, might repay investigation.

North York Moors and coast
The Beautiful Demoiselle occurs on some streams draining the eastern Moors, for example near **Goathland** (NZ8301) and **Langdale End** (SE9491). The Keeled Skimmer has been found on boggy flushes higher in the hill country of the **River Derwent** above **Harwood Dale**. These species are rarely found elsewhere to the east of the Pennines. Coastal sites, such as **Filey Dams*** (TA106708; Yorkshire Wildlife Trust [YWT]), are good places to look for migrant and colonising species.

Vale of York and Holderness
The Red-eyed Damselfly is known from eastern stretches of the **Pocklington Canal** (SE7844 etc) and the **Leven Canal** (TA1045 etc), which are at the northern edge of the species' range in Britain.

Nature reserves in the area having dragonfly interest include: **Fairburn Ings** (SE460278; RSPB); **Blacktoft Sands** (SE843232; RSPB); **Skipwith Common*** (SE669378-642374; YWT); **High Batts*** (SE300764); **Tophill Low** (TA071484; Yorkshire Water); **Hornsea Mere** (TA198473; RSPB).

In addition to the commoner species, there may be others such as the Migrant Hawker and Ruddy Darter which are relative newcomers to the area, and are now regularly recorded as far north as Ripon; Emperor Dragonfly, Broad-bodied Chaser and Black-tailed Skimmer are further possibilities.

David Clarke

Wales

William Condry, in his preface to *The Natural History of Wales*, was able to write: 'This is a preface to a book which itself is little more than a preface'. He was referring to the fact that the natural history of Wales is inexhaustible in its scope. The same conundrum faces the present writer: 33 species of dragonflies and damselflies are known to observers in Wales, no doubt a reflection of the diverse assemblage of habitats to be found in the Principality, but their abundance and distribution are but patchily known. The provisional and incomplete character of most maps of dragonfly distribution should stimulate enthusiasts to send records to the national biological records centres, and there is ample opportunity in Wales for genuine exploration and discovery, and the chance to add to the database!

There are a number of species for which Wales appears to hold a significant proportion of the British population. These include the Beautiful Demoiselle, the Southern Damselfly and the Golden-ringed Dragonfly, while both the Scarce Blue-tailed Damselfly and the Keeled Skimmer have a particularly Welsh bias in their distribution. It is worth noting here also that the only British record of *Sympetrum pedemontanum* was of a male at Trefil, above Merthyr Tydfil in South Wales, in 1995.

Any good freshwater habitat in the uplands of Wales has the potential to support a range of species. Most of the peat deposits in Wales lie in the hill

country, and they play a major part in the scenery as well as providing habitat for species adapted to acid, boggy conditions. Great spreads of Purple Moor-grass and Wiry Mat-grass are interspersed with areas of fescues, bents and Sweet Vernal-grass, and there are patches of heather, a habitat in decline through overgrazing. Dragonfly enthusiasts will find themselves floundering across a wilderness of heather, bilberry and bog mosses, searching the surface of the *Sphagnum*, and encountering a multitude of small waters, the obvious relics of glaciation lying in ice-scooped hollows.

These areas have the potential to support the Scarce Blue-tailed Damselfly, Keeled Skimmer, Common Hawker and Black Darter, with Golden-ringed Dragonfly along the streams and Beautiful Demoiselle lower down on the watercourses. The Keeled Skimmer is likely to be under-recorded, and may be much commoner than atlases suggest. Similarly, the Scarce Blue-tailed Damselfly is likely to be under-recorded, its habitats of acid flushes and seepages often being temporary or seasonal. It is also a species that is more often found in the west and south of Wales.

A number of species are limited to lowland habitats in south Wales, notably the Ruddy Darter and Black-tailed Skimmer, whilst the Emperor and Migrant Hawker also occur in other scattered sites as far north as Anglesey. The **Anglesey mires and lakes** (e.g. at **Cors Erddreiniog NNR** (SH470820) and **Cors Goch** (SH497813)) are especially important for the Hairy Dragonfly and Variable Damselfly, species which are rarely seen away from the

southern half of Wales.

The Southern Damselfly has a stronghold in west Wales, in particular on **Mynydd Preselli**, for example at **Brynberian Moor** (SN115345), with other populations on Gower and on Anglesey. Two species, the Red-eyed Damselfly and the Brown Hawker, are strangely absent from most of Wales, occurring only in a few sites in Montgomeryshire and the north-east. This is particularly difficult to explain in the case of the Brown Hawker, since it also occurs further west, in Ireland.

The patchy nature of data for dragonflies and damselflies in Wales means that observers all too readily migrate to well-known hot-spots. In the south, **Kenfig National Nature Reserve**, Bridgend (SS792808), has a total of 22 species on its list. Seventeen of these are breeding, including Hairy Dragonfly, Emperor Dragonfly and Ruddy Darter, and rare migrants include Red-veined and Yellow-winged Darter. However, there are many other excellent places for dragonflies along the South Wales coast. The **Gwent Levels** (e.g. **Magor Marsh** (Gwent Wildlife Trust reserve, ST425866)) has a good insect fauna which includes the Hairy Dragonfly and Variable Damselfly. **Cosmeston Country Park** (ST180693) and **Ffrwd Farm Mire** (Dyfed Wildlife Trust reserve, SN420026) are also good sites.

Further north, another honeypot is **Cors Caron National Nature Reserve**, Cardiganshire (SN690640), an inland raised mire. The three bogs that make up this nationally important site are home to the Keeled Skimmer, Four-spotted Chaser, Common Hawker and Black Darter. The

Golden-ringed Dragonfly is there, often beside clear running water, while other stream-loving species are the Beautiful and Banded Demoiselles and the Large Red Damselfly.

Some sites are important for isolated populations of scarce and declining species: the Small Red Damselfly occurs in valley bogs in Gwynedd and has a stronghold at **Dowrog Common**, Pembrokeshire (SM775273). River species such as the White-legged Damselfly and the Club-tailed Dragonfly are found on the slower-flowing sections of the **Dee**, **Severn** and **Wye**. The Downy Emerald has been discovered near Harlech and continues to survive at a forest lake in South Wales.

Wales contains a diverse geography, from mountain tops, crags and corries to small coastal peat mires, freshwater canals, dykes and ditches. There are sparkling stony lakes and shallow peaty ponds, moors, mires, rivers, and marshes, dunes and estuaries, native woodlands and conifers (of course!), and all have potential for supporting dragonflies and damselflies.

Good baseline data and recording have a fundamental function, apart from the enjoyment it gives to enthusiasts. It contributes to reference material for conservation. There are still many gaps in our knowledge and our coverage, and the more information that can be gathered about sites that may be threatened, or which may be worthy of greater protection, the better will be the decisions about planning issues relating to such sites.

Steve Moon

Scotland

Of the 21 species of dragonfly known to breed in Scotland, 11 are rare or local. Three of these (Azure Hawker, Northern Emerald and White-faced Darter) are bog-pool species; another three (Hairy Dragonfly, Brilliant Emerald and Downy Emerald) breed in sheltered lochans; and one (Northern Damselfly) is confined to three fairly compact but quite separate areas of partly overgrown ponds. The Southern Hawker, Keeled Skimmer and Variable Damselfly are southern species benefiting from the ameliorating warmth of the Atlantic Drift, mainly near the west coast. The Beautiful Demoiselle, formerly more widespread, is now confined to well-vegetated streams within a radius of 100km from Oban.

South-east Scotland

The area from Fife down to the border counties is poor for dragonflies. None of the scarce species occurs and even those species common elsewhere, such as Golden-ringed Dragonfly and Four-spotted Chaser, have not been recorded as breeding.

Silver Flowes National Nature Reserve, Galloway, Scotland, 1991.

South-west Scotland

A greater variety of habitats is found in the south-west. Where there are basic soils in Galloway many lochans are found where Variable Damselflies occur, while a few of the larger waters such as **Loch Barean** by Colvend (park at NX866546 and walk north) also have good populations of Hairy Dragonflies. The Golden-ringed Dragonfly is widespread, and a recent record of Keeled Skimmer in Ayrshire suggests that the species could be breeding in the area. Beautiful Demoiselle was noted 100 years ago and, in this under-recorded region, may yet be refound. On higher ground, the highly acidic bleak bog pools of the **Silver Flowes** (NX4783) are the breeding grounds of the Azure Hawker (walk 10km up a forestry road from the Southern Upland Way).

West Scotland

Western Scotland, northwards to the foot of the Great Glen, holds a concentration of the mainly southern species. There are tightly-packed groups of lochans in North Kintyre and in the **Oban** area (for example **Lochan Dubh** NM866319) where there are populations of Hairy Dragonflies. The Downy Emerald breeds close to Loch Lomond and at Lochan Dubh. The latter area has the most northerly known concentration of the Variable Damselfly in Britain. This is a long way from the strong Kirkcudbright population, and one wonders if there are other undiscovered colonies in between.

The western coastline, washed by the waters of the Atlantic Drift with its local but very effective winter warming, provides suitable conditions for almost the entire Scottish population of Keeled Skimmers, stretching for more than 200km, albeit in a very narrow band. A good example is at **Carsaig Mire** (NR739881). The numerous Beautiful Demoiselles and more local Southern Hawkers obviously benefit from the same phenomenon. There is another small population of the latter species on the coast of the **Moray Firth** at the north-east end of the Great Glen.

Central Scotland

Inland from Oban, one leaves the southern species for those associated with peat bogs. The Northern Emerald and the White-faced Darter are widespread in Central Scotland, with the former species recently discovered as far south as the **Trossachs** in Perthshire. Undoubtedly afforestation has wiped out many breeding areas for both species, and one has to go north to Speyside to find good numbers of White-faced Darters. Here, in the RSPB reserve at **Abernethy** (e.g. NH982175), the damming of ditches and creation of ponds allow the observer to look at this species and others close by the roadside or from the forest footpaths without disturbance to Ospreys or other breeding birds. This superb area of Old Caledonian Forest also holds a fine population of Northern Damselflies (e.g. NH954192), easily seen from one of the perimeter paths alongside a recently created marshy pool. This scarce species also occurs in Deeside, centred on the **Dinnet NNR** (e.g. NJ434011), and very locally in Perthshire.

Perthshire is the present northern limit of the Azure Damselfly, but there is a possibility of northward spread of this species. The elusive Azure Hawker reappears here particularly in the bleak **Rannoch** area but, like the other bog species, its numbers have suffered as a result of afforestation.

North-west Scotland

North and west of the Great Glen and away from the cultivated eastern strip there is more and more a feeling of wilderness, much modified though the landscape has been. **Glen Affric** is a superb place. Parking is easy (NH283283 for Coire Loch and NH198234) and the forest footpaths make numerous small lochans accessible. Brilliant and Downy Emeralds are common. White-faced Darters are on some of the lochans, and the *Sphagnum* moss-covered shallow bogs support Northern Emeralds (e.g. at NH197232) and, where the vegetation is suitable, Azure Hawkers. A major problem here is the weather. Long days of sunshine are the exception, as the hills create their own cloud cover. Glen Affric is a place to look for larvae and exuviae, a rewarding exercise with 14 breeding species.

A lot of dragonfly-recording has been done in Affric, but much primary recording is still required in other, less well-known glens. Could the known distribution of Brilliant and Downy Emerald be extended? Is there still a population of Northern Damselflies waiting to be re-discovered in Sutherland, as suggested by one old record?

Further to the west and north the situation is similar. New breeding sites for the Azure Hawker are being identified every year. **Loch Maree** is excellent for this species. A strip of old Scots Pine at the **Bridge of Grudie** (NG965678) gives a sheltered feeding area for Azure

Hawker, as well as Northern Emerald, White-faced Darter and the very common Four-spotted Chaser. All of these species breed locally in the very exposed peat-bog pools 300m to the north. Generally, the lochans do not hold the rarer species, but have lots of Common Blue, Emerald, Blue-tailed and Large Red Damselflies. Common Hawker, Highland and Black Darters, and Golden-ringed Dragonfly are widespread.

In such a vast area of open country with its endless valleys and hills, its lochans and its bogs, it would be invidious to single out other particular areas. Better to explore and make one's own discoveries. Is it really the case that the northern distribution of the White-faced Darter and the Northern Emerald ends at the latitude of the north of Skye?

This is wilderness country maintained as such by the prevailing Atlantic winds, so be prepared for bad weather. Take a colander or sieve to search for larvae, and look out, too, for that rarest of exuviae, that of the Azure Hawker. When the sky clears and the sun shines, the bog pools become alive with dragonflies. Against a background of hill and loch, the observer is treated to an unforgettable experience.
Betty & Bob Smith

Ireland

There are 24 species of resident dragonfly in Ireland, so the Irish dragonfly fauna is considerably poorer than that of Great Britain. Some of the absences can be explained by the lack of suitable habitat but a number cannot be so easily accounted for. The proportion of larger dragonfly species amongst the Irish species is lower than in

Great Britain, with heathland and riverine species and also, strangely in view of the apparently suitable habitat, some bogland species being poorly represented. One species, the Irish Damselfly, is not present in Great Britain. There are, however, a number of features about the Irish fauna which set it apart. Amongst the common Irish species, those typical of lowland lakes dominate, and some species which are uncommon in Britain are widespread in Ireland, most notably the Variable Damselfly and the Hairy Dragonfly. The dragonfly fauna in Ireland has seen some dramatic and exciting events in recent years in common with much of north-west Europe. There have been several large influxes of darters, mainly Red-veined Darters. The Lesser Emperor was seen for the first time in 2000 and two species, the Migrant Hawker and the Emperor, have colonised and spread rapidly along the south and east coast.

Raised bogs

Raised bogs once covered large areas of the central lowland plain. Few of these now remain untouched, as they have nearly all been exploited for fuel. Intact raised bogs are, however, actually rather poor in dragonflies as most do not have large areas of open water. Where peat has been extracted from the bogs by traditional hand-cutting, the remnant bogs often have a complex mosaic of pools of different ages and depths. In addition, many of the cutover bogs have areas of birch woodland on the drier margins which give shelter and provide rich feeding grounds for dragonflies. It is these sites that support the richest and most diverse popula-

tions. The Variable Damselfly is often the dominant species on cut-over bogs, and some of the largest have colonies of the Irish Damselfly. Black Darters and Common Hawkers are frequently very common. Cutover bogs support all the common Irish anisopteran dragonflies and scarcer species, including the Hairy Dragonfly. Good examples of cut-over bogs can be seen in the **Lough Neagh** area of N. Ireland at **Brackagh Bog NNR** (J0251) and **Peatlands Park** (H8960) both in Co. Armagh, and at the **Lough Boora Parklands** in Co. Offaly (N1818).

South-west Ireland

In the south-west of Ireland, the countryside around Killarney, Co. Kerry, is a mosaic of native oak woodlands, lakes and bogs. More species of dragonfly have been recorded in this region than in any other part of Ireland. The Killarney area is the only region where there are colonies of both Northern and Downy Emeralds. Both species can be seen within the **Killarney National Park** particularly along the south shore of the **Upper Lake** (V8981, V9081). Other common species in Kerry include the Beautiful Demoiselle and the Keeled Skimmer. The Keeled Skimmer is found widely in all the mountain areas of Ireland in wet flushed heaths, a habitat in which the Scarce Blue-tailed Damselfly is also found, but records of this species are fewer and more localised.

The Burren

In the north of Co. Clare lies the Burren, a huge area of limestone pavement. The area is not often thought of as having water, but in the large depressions within the limestone there are temporary lakes known as

Brackagh Bog, County Armagh, 1989.

turloughs. These lakes, which are flooded in winter but which hold little or no water in summer, are unique to Ireland. The turloughs are the principal habitat for the Scarce Emerald Damselfly. Ruddy Darters are another characteristic species. Excellent examples can be seen at **Knockaunroe** (R3098) and **Lough Gealain** (R3194) within the Burren National Park, to the north of **Corofin** and at **Dromore Nature Reserve** (R3586). The turlough at **Burren village** (M2711) supports one of the largest colonies of the Scarce Emerald. Along the eastern side of the Burren between Corofin and Gort are a series of permanent clear limestone lakes, including **Lough Bunny** (R3897) and **Ballyeighter Loughs** (R3595). These lakes are the centre of the Irish distribution of the Black-tailed Skimmer, a scarce species in Ireland.

Northern Counties

In Northern Ireland, especially Co. Fermanagh, and the northern counties of the Republic there is a vast belt of low hills, called drumlins, dotted with small lakes and bogs in the poorly drained hollows. Many of these sites are open for fishing so have public access. All the common Irish lake species are found here, including Brown and Hairy Hawkers, Four-spotted Chasers and most of the damselfly species. This is also the centre of the distribution of the Irish Damselfly. Colonies of this species are scattered and most are small, but it can be seen at the **Montiaghs Nature Reserve** (J0965), in Co. Antrim. Around the margins of many of the lakes there are small areas of bog adjacent to them, and at these sites Black Darters and Common Hawkers can frequently be seen. Between eight and ten species can be seen in a whole season at many of these lakes, with the total for the best sites, such as **Mill Lough** (H2438) and the lakes on the National Trust's **Crom** (H32) and **Castle Coole** estates (H2542) Co. Fermanagh, reaching 13 species.

South coast

For migrant dragonflies the coast of Co. Wexford in the south-east is the first point they reach. This is also where both the recent additions to the resident Irish fauna were seen first. Wetlands are scarcer in this region than elsewhere and so dragonflies tend to be concentrated at a few localities. Two of the largest wetlands, **Lady's Island Lake** (T1004) and **Tacumshin** (T0305), despite being brackish, have attracted Lesser Emperor and Red-veined and Yellow-winged Darters. A full range of common species, as well as Migrant Hawker and Emperor, can be seen at the **Raven Nature Reserve** (T1126). Further west in Co. Cork, **Ballyvergan**, near Youghal (X0775), is a productive site where Hairy Dragonfly, Migrant Hawker and Emperor can be seen.

This brief account has highlighted some of the more interesting Irish dragonfly sites and habitats. Much remains to be learnt and many areas deserve more attention.

Brian Nelson

Identification

Keys and descriptions

Dichotomous keys are provided on the following pages of the guide which can be used to identify larvae to species, and adult dragonflies to family level. Dichotomous keys are a useful identification tool when dealing with many species that differ primarily in fine details of morphological structure, as in dragonfly larvae. To use the key you should start at the first pair of statements and follow the statement that most closely matches the specimen you wish to identify, then by working through the key using the numbers and statements indicated you should reach a description that leads to a species name.

Adult dragonflies are best distinguished by comparing their colour patterns and, in some cases, the shapes of the genitalia. Such differences are often difficult to describe succinctly, but are easily appreciated when comparing illustrations. For this reason, keys are not provided for the identification of adults to genus and species level. Instead, you are encouraged to leaf through the book until you find an illustration that most closely matches the specimen you have seen or photographed. Annotations next to the illustrations highlight the most important features that characterise each species. You should also compare your specimen with the text description. Technical terms have been kept to a mimimum, but the following definitions and illustrations should help to explain the most commonly used terms.

Glossary

Anal appendages These are appendages at the end of the abdomen, sometimes referred to as 'claspers'. There are superior (upper) and inferior (lower) appendages. In male dragonflies they are used to clasp the female around the head (anisopteran dragonflies) or the pronotum (damselflies) during mating and when in tandem.

Antehumeral stripes Stripes along the antehumeral region of the thorax.

Diapause A state of suspended development that may occur at some stage or stages in the life-cycle and that typically constitutes an anticipatory response to conditions unfavourable for uninterrupted development.

Exuvia The shed larval skin.

Maturation period The immature period before the adult dragonfly is sexually mature, also the time when some dragonflies disperse to new breeding grounds.

Oviposition Egg-laying.

Ovipositor This is used to lay the eggs and is located beneath abdominal segments 8-10 in females. It is blade-like and is used to oviposit into plant tissue.

Prolarva The stage immediately after hatching when the larva is still enclosed in a membrane.

Pronotum A shield-like plate covering the top of the prothorax; the shape of the rear edge is diagnostic in some damselflies.

Pruinescence A bluish bloom that develops on various parts of the body as the dragonfly matures, this is especially noticeable on some chaser dragonflies.

Stadium Formerly known as instar. Each time a larva moults its skin it enters another stadium; a larva may go through 8-18 stadia, depending on the species. The prolarva is the first stadium.

Teneral A newly emerged adult dragonfly, sometimes shiny and without the full coloration of the mature adult.

Vulvar scale A flap below abdominal segment 8 in females which can be prominent in some species. It is present in those that do not oviposit into plant tissue.

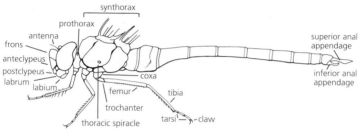

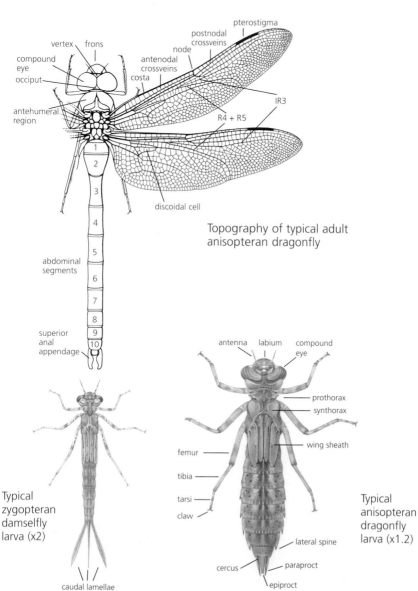

Topography of typical adult
anisopteran dragonfly

Typical
zygopteran
damselfly
larva (x2)

caudal lamellae

Typical
anisopteran
dragonfly
larva (x1.2)

Key to dragonfly larvae

The identification of dragonfly larvae is much more difficult than the identification of adults. Species can often be distinguished only by subtle differences in shape, including the length of spines, and even the presence or absence of spines can be difficult to ascertain in the field when the larvae are covered in debris. At family level, Libellulidae and Corduliidae can be difficult to distinguish, and many of the Coenagrionidae species appear rather similar. Species-level identification should be confirmed by examination under 10 x magnification using a hand lens or binocular microscope. Exuviae should be collected for examination at home to confirm field determinations and to provide voucher material. Early-stadium larvae may not have developed some of the characters used in this key, which is most reliable for final-stadium larvae and exuviae.

1 Larva with three (NB any or all may be absent) leaf-like caudal appendages at tip of abdomen (*1a*)   DAMSELFLIES (ZYGOPTERA) **2**

   Larva with no caudal lamellae, but instead with five short spines at tip of abdomen (*1b*)   DRAGONFLIES (ANISOPTERA) **17**

2 Antennae long, first antennal segment as long as combined length of other segments (*2d*); larvae stick-like with long legs (*2a*)
                    DEMOISELLES (CALOPTERYGIDAE) **5**

   Antennae short, first antennal segment considerably shorter than combined length of other segments (*2c*); legs relatively short (*2b*) **3**

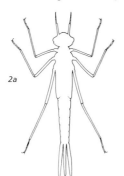
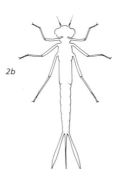

2a   *2b*   *2c*   *2d*

3 Caudal lamellae with long narrow filament at apex (*3a*); setae on labium in one field   **White-legged Damselfly** *Platycnemis pennipes*

   Caudal lamellae without long apical filament (*3b*); setae on labium in two fields   **4**

4 Caudal lamellae with prominent black transverse bands
                    EMERALD DAMSELFLIES (LESTIDAE) **6**

   Caudal lamellae without prominent banding, and if bands present then restricted just to apical half of lamellae   COENAGRIONIDAE **7**

5 Head with prominent vertical occipital tooth behind eyes (*5a*); caudal lamellae usually with single pale vertical band (*5c*)
                    Beautiful Demoiselle *Calopteryx virgo*

   Occipital tooth inconspicuous (*5b*); caudal lamellae usually with two vertical pale bands (*5d*)
                    Banded Demoiselle *Calopteryx splendens*

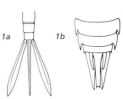

3a

3b

5c

5d

5a   *5b*

6 Lateral caudal lamellae tapering in apical half (*6a*); labial palp with 3 setae (*6c*)   **Scarce Emerald Damselfly** *Lestes dryas*

Lateral caudal lamellae parallel-sided for entire length, not tapering apically (*6b*); labial palp with 2 setae (*6d*)
    Emerald Damselfly *Lestes sponsa*

 *6a*    *6b*

6c   *6d*

7 Abdominal segments with rows of bristles. Caudal lamellae with 3 broad black bands in apical half (*7a*)
    Red-eyed Damselfly *Erythromma najas*

Abdominal segments with rows of bristles. Caudal lamellae blunt, nodate, banding absent   **Small Red-eyed Damselfly** *E. viridulum*

Caudal lamellae unmarked, or with narrow dark stripes or irregular blotching. Abdominal segments without rows of bristles   **8**

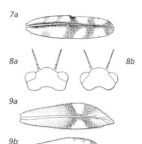
7a

8a   *8b*

8 Head broad, hardly tapering posteriorly (*8a*)   **9**

Head narrow, tapering behind eyes (*8b*)   **10**

9 Caudal lamellae broad, tapering abruptly at tip, with prominent blotches in apical half, often forming the shape of an 'x'; fine setae present on margin in apical half (*9a*)
    Large Red Damselfly *Pyrrhosoma nymphula*

Caudal lamellae marked with obscure irregular blotches; no setae present on apical margin of caudal lamellae (*9b*)
    Small Red Damselfly *Ceriagrion tenellum*

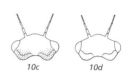
9a

9b

10 Caudal lamellae nodate, having a distinct junction between thickened basal half and thinner outer half (*10a*); dorsum of head in posterior region distinctly spotted (*10c*)   **11**

Caudal lamellae not distinctly nodate (*10b*); spots at rear of head absent or indistinct (*10d*)   **14**

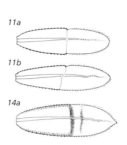
10c   *10d*

10a    *10b*

11 Antennae with 6 segments; nodal line perpendicular to margins of caudal lamellae (*11a*)   **12**

Antennae with 7 segments; nodal line oblique (*11b*)   **13**

12 Labial palp with 4 setae; spots on rear dorsum of head regular, evenly distributed   **Northern Damselfly** *Coenagrion hastulatum*

Labial palp with 5 setae; spots on rear dorsum of head irregular, becoming sparser towards margin   **Irish Damselfly** *C. lunulatum*

13 Apex of caudal lamellae usually rounded; larvae usually brownish
    Variable Damselfly *Coenagrion pulchellum*

Apex of caudal lamellae usually pointed; larvae usually green, with brownish wing buds and caudal lamellae
    Azure Damselfly *Coenagrion puella*

14 Caudal lamellae narrow (about four times as long as broad), pointed apically; stout setae on margin of lamellae extending to mid-point on one margin only (*10b*)   **15**

Caudal lamellae broader (about three times as long as broad); stout marginal setae reaching to mid-point on both margins (*14a*)   **16**

15 Prementum with 4-5 setae in lateral field; labial palp with 6-7 setae (*15b*); distinct dark bands on femora (*15a*)
    Blue-tailed Damselfly *Ischnura elegans*

Prementum with 6 setae in lateral field; labial palp with 5 setae (*15c*); dark bands on femora at most indistinct
    Scarce Blue-tailed Damselfly *Ischnura pumilio*

16 Antennae with 6 segments (*16a*); 1-3 narrow transverse stripes usually present on lamellae (*14a*), lamellae more than 3mm long
    Common Blue Damselfly *Enallagma cyathigerum*

Antennae 7-segmented (*16b*); lamellae unmarked, less than 3mm long   **Southern Damselfly** *Coenagrion mercuriale*

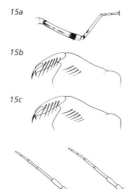
11a

11b

14a

15a

15b

15c

16a   *16b*

17 Labium flat, not covering front of face (*17a*)   **18**

    Labium spoon-shaped, covering front of face like a mask (*17b*)   **19**

17a   *17b*

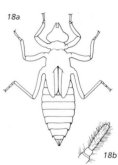

18 Body squat, spider-like (*18a*); antennae with 4 segments, third segment longer than combined length of previous two segments (*18b*)
    Club-tailed Dragonfly *Gomphus vulgatissimus*

    Body slender, torpedo-shaped (*18c*); antennae with 6-7 segments, filiform, segments subequal in length (*18d*)
    HAWKER DRAGONFLIES (AESHNIDAE) **20**

19 Apical margin of labial palps intermeshing with broad, deep-cut, irregular teeth (*19a*)
    Golden-ringed Dragonfly *Cordulegaster boltonii*

    Apical margin of labial palps not deeply serrated (*19b*)
    DARTER AND EMERALD DRAGONFLIES
    (CORDULIIDAE and LIBELLULIDAE) **27**

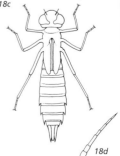

19a   *19b*

20 Eyes small, less than half the length of the lateral margin of head; head tapering strongly (*20a*); dorsal spine present on abdominal segment 9   **Hairy Dragonfly *Brachytron pratense***

    Eyes large, greater than half length of lateral margin; head not tapering posteriorly (*20b*); abdomen without dorsal spines   **21**

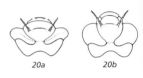

20a   *20b*

21 Head, when viewed from above, rounded; hind margin of eyes parallel with hind margin of head (*21a*); lateral spines present on abdominal segments 7-9
    Emperor Dragonfly *Anax imperator*

    Head, when viewed from above, pentagonal; hind margin of eyes at 45° to hind margin of head (*20b*); lateral spines present on abdominal segments 6-9   **22**

21a

22 Cerci long, about 2/3 length of paraprocts (*22a*)
    Norfolk Hawker *Aeshna isosceles*

    Cerci shorter, less than 1/2 length of paraprocts (*22b*)   **23**

23 Labium narrow, Four times as long as broad (at narrowest section) (*23a*)   **24**

    Labium broad, 2.5 times as long as broad (*23b*)   **26**

22a   *22b*

23a   *23b*

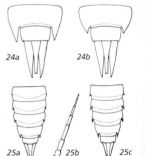

24a   *24b*

24 Lateral spine on abdominal segment 9 reaching apex of segment 10 (*24a*)   **Migrant Hawker *Aeshna mixta***

    Lateral spine on segment 9 less than half as long as segment 10 (*24b*)   **25**

25 Lateral spine on segment 6 vestigial (*25a*); antennae with 6 segments (*25b*)   **Azure Hawker *Aeshna caerulea***

    Lateral spine on segment 6 prominent (*25c*); antennae with 7 segments   **Southern Hawker *Aeshna cyanea***

25a   *25b*   *25c*

26 Legs with distinct banding. Lateral spine present on abdominal segment 6; lateral spine on segment 9 reaching at least to middle of segment 10 (*26a*)   **Brown Hawker** *Aeshna grandis*

Legs without distinct banding. Lateral spine vestigial or absent from segment 6; lateral spine on segment 9 short, not reaching middle of segment 10 (*26b*)   **Common Hawker** *Aeshna juncea*

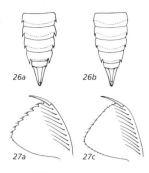

26a   *26b*

27 Apex of labial palp with deep serrations (*27a*) (NB Larvae of the Broad-bodied Chaser also have deeply serrated labial palps, but can be distinguished from emerald dragonfly larvae, with which they frequently occur, by the pale yellowish fleck on the side of the labial palp); cerci more than half the length of paraprocts (*27b*)   **28**

Apex of labial palp with only shallow serrations (*27c*); cerci less than half length of paraprocts (*27d*)   **31**

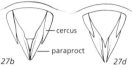

27a   *27c*

28 Prominent mid-dorsal spines present on abdomen (*28a*)   **29**

Mid-dorsal spines absent from abdomen (*28b*)   **30**

28a   *28b*

— cercus

— paraproct

27b   *27d*

29 Thorax marked with prominent dark lateral stripes. Each abdominal segment with pale yellowish dorso-lateral spot; abdominal segment 9 with dorsal spine absent or minute (*28a*)
     Downy Emerald *Cordulia aenea*

Thorax without dark lateral bands. Each abdominal segment with dark dorso-lateral spot; segment 9 with large dorsal spine (*29a*)
     Brilliant Emerald *Somatochlora metallica*

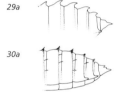

29a

30a

30 Small mid-dorsal tubercle present on each abdominal segment. Abdominal segments 8 and 9 with short lateral spine; setae on dorsum of abdomen pectinate (fringed at apex) (*30a*)
     Orange-spotted Emerald *Oxygastra curtisii*

Abdomen without mid-dorsal tubercles. Lateral spines absent from abdominal segments 8 and 9; dorsal abdominal setae filiform (not fringed at apex) (*30b*)   **Northern Emerald** *Somatochlora arctica*

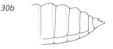

30b

31 Legs long, when stretched apex of tibia extending well beyond tip of abdomen. Head tapering behind eyes when viewed dorsally (*31a*). Larvae usually living amongst submerged aquatic plants   **32**

Legs short, when stretched apex of tibia not extending beyond tip of abdomen. When viewed dorsally, head appears rectangular, and not tapering behind eyes (*31b*). Labium sometimes marked with yellowish fleck. Larvae living amongst bottom debris   **38**

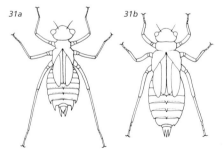

31a   *31b*

32a

32 Underside of abdomen marked with prominent dark longitudinal bands (*32a*)   **White-faced Darter** *Leucorrhinia dubia*

Underside of abdomen unicolorous   **33**

33a

33 Abdomen without mid-dorsal spines (*33a*); abdomen marked with prominent dark dorso-lateral bands
     Red-veined Darter *Sympetrum fonscolombii*

33b

Mid-dorsal spines present on abdomen (*33b*); dark dorso-lateral bands absent   **34**

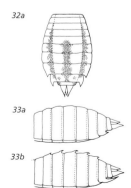

34 Lateral spine on segment 9 short, about half length of segment 9 (*34a*)   **35**

Lateral spine on segment 9 long, more than half length of segment 9 (*34b*)   **36**

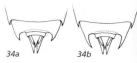

34a   *34b*

35 Mid-dorsal spine absent from abdominal segment 8 (*35a*) (a vestigial spine may sometimes be present); basal one or two setae on labial palp considerably shorter than remaining setae (*35c*).
     Black Darter *Sympetrum danae*

Mid-dorsal spine present on abdominal segment 8 (*35b*); all setae on labial palp long (*35d*)   **Yellow-winged Darter *S. flaveolum***

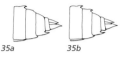 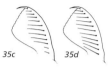

35a   *35b*   *35c*   *35d*

36 Short mid-dorsal spine present on abdominal segment 3 (*36a*)
     Vagrant Darter *Sympetrum vulgatum*

Mid-dorsal spine absent from segment 3   **37**

37 Lateral spine on segment 9 shorter (0.25-0.40mm) than length of this segment (*34b*); prementum with 12-14 setae in lateral field, of which 8-9 are long (*37b*)   **Ruddy Darter *Sympetrum sanguineum***

Lateral spine on abdominal segment 9 longer (0.45-0.80mm) than length of this segment (*37a*); prementum with 14-16 setae in lateral field, of which 10-11 are long (*37c*).
     Common Darter *Sympetrum striolatum*

38 Abdominal segment 8 with mid-dorsal spine (*38a*)   **39**

Abdominal segment 8 without mid-dorsal spine   **41**

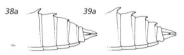

38a   *39a*

39 Mid-dorsal spines long, prominent, with spine present on segment 9 (*39a*)   **Scarce Chaser *Libellula fulva***

Mid-dorsal spines short, not so prominent, and spine absent from segment 9 (*38a*)   **40**

40 Dorsum of abdomen alternately marked with pale and dark longitudinal bands. Prementum with 9-11 long setae and 3-5 short setae in each lateral field (*40b*); labial palps with deep apical serrations (*40a*)   **Broad-bodied Chaser *Libellula depressa***

Dorsum of abdomen unicolorous. Prementum with 6-9 long setae and 4-7 short setae in each lateral field (*40d*); labial palp with shallow apical serrations (*40c*)
     Four-spotted Chaser *Libellula quadrimaculata*

41 Abdominal segments 7-9 unicolorous. Labial palp with 3-5 setae (*41a*)   **Keeled Skimmer *Orthetrum coerulescens***

Abdominal segments 7-9 with paired dorso-lateral dark spots. Labial palp with 6-8 setae (*41b*)
     Black-tailed Skimmer *Orthetrum cancellatum*

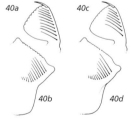

36a

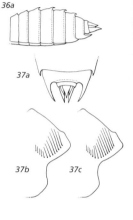

37a   *37b*   *37c*

40a   *40c*   *40b*   *40d*

41a   *41b*

Damselfly and dragonfly larvae

Zygopterans **1** White-legged Damselfly *Platycnemis pennipes* (photographed in May); **2** Beautiful Demoiselle *Calopteryx virgo* (July); **3** Emerald Damselfly *Lestes sponsa* (June); **4** Large Red Damselfly *Pyrrhosoma nymphula* (March); **5** Irish Damselfly *Coenagrion lunulatum* (May); **6** Blue-tailed Damselfly *Ischnura elegans* (May).
Anisopterans **7** Club-tailed Dragonfly *Gomphus vulgatissimus* (May); **8** Golden-ringed Dragonfly *Cordulegaster boltonii* (April).

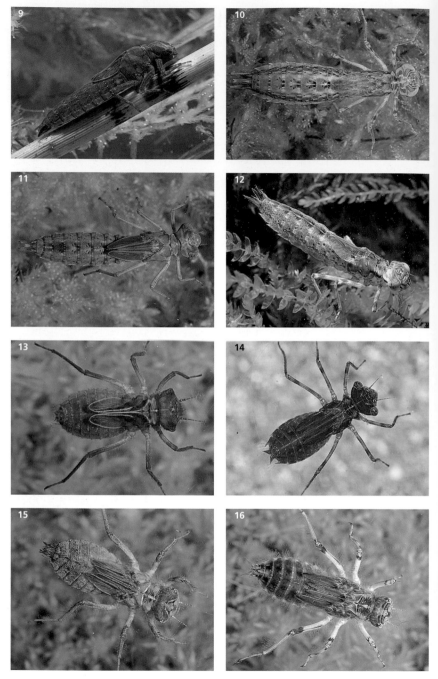

Anisopterans (continued) **9** Hairy Dragonfly *Brachytron pratense* (October); **10** Emperor Dragonfly *Anax imperator* (November); **11** Azure Hawker *Aeshna caerulea* (July); **12** Southern Hawker *Aeshna cyanea* (May); **13** Northern Emerald *Somatochlora arctica* (May); **14** Black Darter *Sympetrum danae* (June); **15** Scarce Chaser *Libellula fulva* (May); **16** Black-tailed Skimmer *Orthetrum cancellatum* (May).

Family key to adult dragonflies

1   Small, slender, with weak fluttering flight. Most
     species hold wings closed over top of abdomen
     when at rest; fore and hind wings of similar
     shape. Head rectangular with eyes at outer ends.
                  DAMSELFLIES ZYGOPTERA (page 59) **2**

     Medium to large with strong, powerful flight. All
     species hold wings open when at rest; fore wings
     narrower than hind wings. Head globular with
     eyes wrapping round top, front and sides of
     head.   **DRAGONFLIES ANISOPTERA** (page 97) **5**

2   Large damselflies with metallic green or blue
     bodies. Males with broad, dark blue markings on
     wings that expand gradually from the base
     rather than having a narrow stalk (not
     petiolate); numerous antenodal crossveins.
     Mainly restricted to flowing water.
                               DEMOISELLES
                        CALOPTERYGIDAE (page 59)

     Small damselflies, with or without metallic
     coloration. Wings uncoloured; petiolate, with
     narrow stalk at base; only two antenodal
     crossveins present. Found at standing or flowing
     water.   **3**

3   Medium-sized metallic green damselflies. When
     resting wings held half open. Mainly restricted to
     shallow, standing water with dense emergent
     vegetation. Veins IR3 and R4+5 meet radial
     sector (Rs) basal of node.
                        EMERALD DAMSELFLIES
                              LESTIDAE (page 64)

     Bodies without metallic green coloration. When
     resting wings held closed over top of abdomen.
     Veins IR3 and R4+5 meet radial sector at node.
                                                   4

4   Medium-sized damselflies with broadened white
     legs. Usually restricted to slow-flowing rivers.
     Discoidal cell almost rectangular; vein on leading
     edge of cell slightly shorter than vein on
     posterior margin.
                    WHITE-LEGGED DAMSELFLIES
                       PLATYCNEMIDIDAE (page 68)

     Small to medium-sized, blue-and-black or red-
     and-black damselflies. Occur in full range of
     aquatic habitats. Discoidal cell strongly angled
     apically; vein on leading edge of cell
     considerably shorter than vein on posterior
     margin
     RED DAMSELFLIES and BLUE DAMSELFLIES
                       COENAGRIONIDAE (page70)

5   Medium-sized dragonflies with greenish-yellow
     and black markings. Eyes widely separated; not
     meeting over top of head. Restricted to slow-
     flowing rivers.
                     CLUB-TAILED DRAGONFLIES
                          GOMPHIDAE (page 118)

     Medium to large dragonflies. Eyes meeting on
     top of head.   **6**

Photographs: **1** Female Beautiful Demoiselle
(Calopterygidae); **2** Male Emerald Damselfly (Lestidae);
3 Male Azure Damselfly (Coenagrionidae); **4** Female Club-
tailed Dragonfly (Gomphidae)

6　Large dragonflies striped yellow and black.
　　Green eyes meet at a point on top of head.
　　Usually seen patrolling upland streams.
　　　　　　　　　　GOLDEN-RINGED DRAGONFLIES
　　　　　　　　　　CORDULEGASTRIDAE (page 120)

　　Medium to large dragonflies. Eyes meeting
　　broadly over top of head.　　　　　　　　**7**

7　Medium-sized metallic green dragonflies. Rarely
　　settling, but hanging down from vegetation
　　when at rest. Usually breed in standing water
　　close to woodland.　　**EMERALD DRAGONFLIES**
　　　　　　　　　　　CORDULIIDAE (page 123)

　　Medium to large dragonflies without metallic
　　coloration.　　　　　　　　　　　　　　**8**

8　Large dragonflies with restless, hawking flight.
　　Rarely settling, but hanging down from branches
　　when at rest.　　　　　**HAWKER DRAGONFLIES**
　　　　　　　　　　　　AESHNIDAE (page 97)

　　Small to medium-sized blue, red or yellow
　　dragonflies. Darting flight, frequently perched
　　(not hanging downwards) among marginal
　　plants.
　　　　DARTER, CHASER & SKIMMER DRAGONFLIES
　　　　　　　　　　　LIBELLULIDAE (page 132)

Photographs: **5** Male Emperor Dragonfly (Aeshnidae);
6 Female Scarce Chaser (Libellulidae)

Introduction to species descriptions

Systematic order　The species in this account are placed largely in systematic order. Species belonging to the same family and genus are placed together and closely related species are placed next to each other. The sequence begins with the most primitive species, which are damselflies belonging to the genus *Calopteryx*. The sequence ends with libellulids. These advanced dragonflies share many characters that probably appeared late in the evolutionary history of the Odonata. We can deduce that these characters represent an advanced state because they are shared by just a few closely related species and are not widespread in the Odonata.

　　The main exception in the guide to this systematic sequence is that the Small Red Damselfly is placed next to the Large Red Damselfly as the two species superficially resemble each other, although they are actually distant relatives.

Artworks　The colour artworks are drawn to scale. The damselflies are depicted at 1.8 times life-size and the anisopteran dragonflies are illustrated at 1.4 times life-size. The measurements in the descriptions refer to range of length of the abdomen (ab) and hind wing (hw). The colour artworks of damselflies that show details of particular body parts, such as abdominal segments and anal appendages are enlarged by 8 times life-size, unless otherwise marked. Annotations accompanying the illustrations are meant to highlight various diagnostic features and should be used in conjunction with the descriptive part of the text.

Maps　The maps provide a general impression of the regional distribution of the species in Great Britain and Ireland. (For a more detailed guide to distribution the reader is referred to Merrit *et al.* 1996 – see page 158). Dark green denotes the main range of the species, pale green indicates where the species has a scattered population or is rare. Underneath each map is a calendar indicating the main flight season of the species.

ZYGOPTERA Damselflies

These insects are small and slender, with a weak fluttering flight. Most species characteristically hold their wings closed over the top of the abdomen when at rest. The fore and hind wings are similar in shape. The head is rectangular, with eyes at the outer ends. There are 17 resident species, two vagrants and a further two that are now extinct in Great Britain.

CALOPTERYGIDAE Demoiselles

These are large damselflies with a metallic green or blue body. The males have characteristic dark blue wings. They are mainly restricted to flowing water. In Great Britain and Ireland there are two resident species in the genus *Calopteryx*.

Beautiful Demoiselle
Calopteryx virgo (Linnaeus)

Description

Jizz This large damselfly has a characteristic, graceful, butterfly-like flitting flight over emergent vegetation in fast-flowing clean streams. The species rarely shows interest in other species, unless it co-occurs with the Banded Demoiselle, when interactions between males are common. **Field characters** Ab 33-40mm; hw 27-36mm. The males are unmistakable. They have a metallic blue-green body with broad, dark brown-black wings and iridescent wing-veins. The wing pigment covers the whole wing, but is often lighter towards the tip and base. Although the metallic green females are spectacular in the hand, they are very cryptic against bankside vegetation. They are generally difficult to spot unless in tandem with a male or ovipositing into emergent vegetation. They have a distinct white pseudo-pterostigma near the tip of the leading edge of each wing. **Similar species** This species is very similar to the Banded Demoiselle. The males can easily be distinguished because the pigment in the wings of the male Beautiful Demoiselle extends to the base of the wing. Females are harder to distinguish, but Beautiful Demoiselle females tend to have broader wings with a brownish tint. They also have a narrow brownish stripe on the dorsal midline of their last three abdominal segments, which is darker than in the Banded Demoiselle.

Status and conservation

Locally abundant and more or less restricted to the west of a line drawn between Liverpool and Folkestone, with isolated populations in the Lake District, western Scotland and the North York Moors; in Ireland it is restricted to the southern part. It is common throughout western Europe. This species is very sensitive to pollution.

Ecology and behaviour

Habitat This is a damselfly of fast-flowing, clean, pebble- or sandy-bottomed streams, often in heathland and moorland districts. It is more tolerant of shade than the Banded Demoiselle.

The **larvae** are found among roots or submerged vegetation and are most active at night. They overwinter buried in the gravel and usually emerge as temperatures rise in the late spring. Larval development takes two years. The stiff-bodied larvae are unmistakable: they have long, spidery legs and are much more stick-like than the larvae of other damselfly families. The larvae can sometimes be distinguished from those of Banded Demoiselle by the presence on each caudal lamella of a single, vertical, light band: unfortunately, however, there is considerable variation in this trait, so it best serves as a rule of thumb.

Adults begin to **emerge** towards the end of May and continue to emerge until late August. The process of emergence takes about two hours. Newly emerged adults have a distinctive 'glassy' appearance, with opaque eyes. They are commonly found at dawn on bankside vegetation. Exuviae can be found on vegetation up to 50cm above water level anywhere from the water's edge to several metres away.

The duration of the teneral period is undocumented but, depending on weather conditions, lasts 4-10 days in similar species. During this period the adults stay away from reproductive sites and spend their time feeding. Only when they are fully mature do they venture over streams. The **flight season** lasts until September.

Reproductively active males will attempt to defend the emergent vegetation into which females lay their eggs. As soon as a female enters a male's territory, he flies towards her in a charac-

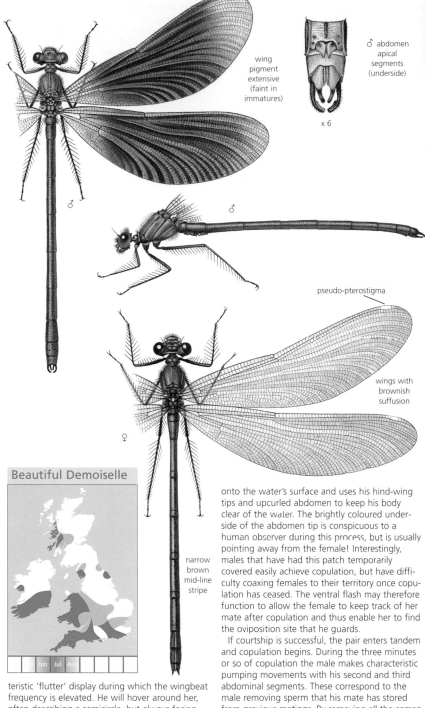

wing pigment extensive (faint in immatures)

♂ abdomen apical segments (underside)

x 6

♂

pseudo-pterostigma

wings with brownish suffusion

♀

Beautiful Demoiselle

narrow brown mid-line stripe

Jun Jul Aug

teristic 'flutter' display during which the wingbeat frequency is elevated. He will hover around her, often describing a semicircle, but always facing his potential mate. Occasionally he throws himself onto the water's surface and uses his hind-wing tips and upcurled abdomen to keep his body clear of the water. The brightly coloured underside of the abdomen tip is conspicuous to a human observer during this process, but is usually pointing away from the female! Interestingly, males that have had this patch temporarily covered easily achieve copulation, but have difficulty coaxing females to their territory once copulation has ceased. The ventral flash may therefore function to allow the female to keep track of her mate after copulation and thus enable her to find the oviposition site that he guards.

If courtship is successful, the pair enters tandem and copulation begins. During the three minutes or so of copulation the male makes characteristic pumping movements with his second and third abdominal segments. These correspond to the male removing sperm that his mate has stored from previous matings. By removing all the semen of rivals before he inseminates the female, the copulating male ensures that he fertilises all the eggs his mate lays. Because all males remove stored sperm from their mates, males guard their mates during the period of egg-laying that follows copulation. Territorial males can remain in residence at the same territory for up to ten days.

Females are usually seen only at the bankside, or over water, if they are gravid and ready to lay eggs. They are most active over, and near, territories between 11.00am and 2.00pm on warm sunny days. The female will begin laying eggs almost immediately after copulation, with her mate nearby. This species prefers to oviposit into bur-reeds (*Sparganium*), water-crowfoots (*Ranunculus*), Water Mint (*Mentha aquatica*) and water-speedwells (*Veronica*), and will rarely submerge during oviposition. If undisturbed, the female will oviposit for up to 30 minutes, during which time she will insert 250-300 eggs into her chosen substrate. The eggs take about 14 days to develop and hatch.

Mike Siva-Jothy

Banded Demoiselle
Calopteryx splendens (Harris)

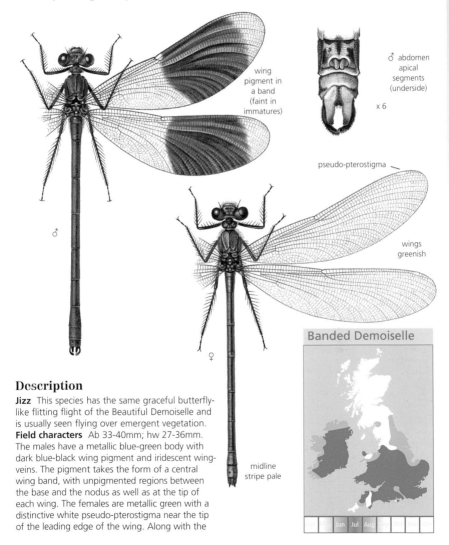

wing pigment in a band (faint in immatures)

♂ abdomen apical segments (underside)

x 6

pseudo-pterostigma

wings greenish

♂

♀

midline stripe pale

Banded Demoiselle

Jun Jul Aug

Description

Jizz This species has the same graceful butterfly-like flitting flight of the Beautiful Demoiselle and is usually seen flying over emergent vegetation.
Field characters Ab 33-40mm; hw 27-36mm. The males have a metallic blue-green body with dark blue-black wing pigment and iridescent wing-veins. The pigment takes the form of a central wing band, with unpigmented regions between the base and the nodus as well as at the tip of each wing. The females are metallic green with a distinctive white pseudo-pterostigma near the tip of the leading edge of the wing. Along with the

Beautiful Demoiselle, this is the largest damselfly species in the area.

Similar species It is very similar to the Beautiful Demoiselle, but can be distinguished because it tends to be found on slower-flowing rivers and canals, in contrast to the faster-flowing streams favoured by the Beautiful Demoiselle. Moreover, the pigment in the males' wings does not extend below the nodus and there is a distinctive unpigmented strip at the apex of the wing. Females are difficult to distinguish, but Banded Demoiselle females tend to have a greenish tint to their narrower wings. They possess a distinctive sandy-coloured stripe on the dorsal midline of the abdomen, which is often paler than the stripe in female Beautiful Demoiselles.

Status and conservation

It is largely restricted to the south of a line drawn between Blackpool and Middlesbrough, with isolated populations in the north of the Lake District. Found throughout most of Ireland. It is common throughout Eurasia and has several distinctive subspecies. Like the Beautiful Demoiselle, this species is very sensitive to pollution and needs healthy emergent plants for perches and egg-laying.

Ecology and behaviour

Habitat The Banded Demoiselle prefers slow-flowing, mud-bottomed streams, rivers and canals, with open banksides and adjoining meadows, but will breed in lakes adjacent to rivers.

The **larvae** are found among roots or submerged vegetation, especially on south-facing banks. Like those of the Beautiful Demoiselle, the larvae are most active at night, but can easily be caught during daylight. They have the same stick-like appearance as Beautiful Demoiselle larvae, but tend to have two vertical light bands on the caudal lamellae. They overwinter in the muddy bottom. Larval development usually requires two years, including two overwintering periods.

Adults begin to **emerge** in mid May and continue emerging until September. Larvae travel relatively long distances to emerge and can be found 100m away from the nearest water, usually in shrubs and trees. The teneral period lasts about 7-10 days. Only when males are fully mature do they venture over streams. The **flight season** lasts into September.

Reproductively active males arrive at suitable oviposition sites and will attempt to defend the emergent vegetation into which females lay their eggs. Because males often outnumber the available oviposition sites, many adopt an alternative mate-securing tactic: rather than defend a territory, they perch on bankside vegetation and attempt to enter tandem with females making their way to oviposition sites, or attempt to mate with already mated and ovipositing females. In years of high population density these males can be very conspicuous, and often cover small bankside shrubs, chasing after arriving females like metallic blue comets. By contrast, territorial males court newly arriving females with a characteristic fluttering courtship flight that is often interrupted by the male 'throwing' himself onto the oviposition site. If the female responds to this display, the male lands on the female's wings and climbs down towards her head. The pair then enters tandem and copulation begins. During the 90-second copulation the male shows similar movements to those described for the Beautiful Demoiselle. Copulation serves the dual purpose of sperm removal and insemination. Consequently, the male guards his mate whilst she lays her eggs. Territorial males can remain in residence at the same territory for up to ten days. Territory turnover occurs in one of several ways, but by far the most spectacular is an escalated fight. Two males will engage in a series of stereotyped flight patterns, including see-saws and spirals, sometimes for hours. These fights are contests of stamina and the male with the most fat reserves wins.

Females are seen only at the bankside, or over water, if they are gravid and ready to lay eggs. They are most active over, and near, territories from 10.00am to 2.00pm on warm sunny days. The female begins laying eggs almost immediately after copulation, with her mate in close attendance. This species is relatively unfussy regarding oviposition substrates, and will lay into bur-reeds (*Sparganium*), water-crowfoots (*Ranunculus*), water-milfoils (*Myriophyllum*), Arrowhead (*Sagittaria sagittifolia*), Lesser Water-parsnip (*Berula erecta*), Reed Canary-grass (*Phalaris arundinacea*) and Flowering-rush (*Butomus umbellatus*). Females frequently submerge completely during oviposition: they are able to respire whilst submerged because they trap a layer of air between their wings which is continuous with their tracheal system. Females can insert an egg into the plant substrate every two seconds, but because they often spend a lot of time searching and probing for suitable sites in the plant this averages out to an egg every six seconds or so. They can oviposit for 45 minutes if undisturbed. The eggs take about 14 days to develop and hatch.

Mike Siva-Jothy

LESTIDAE Emerald damselflies

These are medium-sized metallic green damselflies. They rest with their wings half open and are mainly restricted to shallow, standing water with dense emergent vegetation. There are two resident and two vagrants in the genus *Lestes*.

Emerald Damselfly
Lestes sponsa (Hansemann)

Description

Jizz The Emerald Damselfly, in keeping with other lestids, perches with its wings half open. The Emerald has a relatively weak, fluttery flight, though it looks more robust than most other damselflies. It is often encountered perched among dense emergent vegetation by shallow ponds.

Field characters Ab 25-33mm; hw 19-24mm. Males are a metallic green. Females are duller green, going into pale brown on the sides of the thorax and abdomen.

Similar species The species with which the Emerald Damselfly is most likely to be confused is the Scarce Emerald Damselfly, but see also Southern and Willow Emerald. Males of both Emerald and Scarce Emerald are emerald-green and, as they mature, both develop a powdery

bluish-white pruinescence on the thorax between the wings, on the first two abdominal segments, and on the apex of the abdomen. The pruinescence can obscure the metallic spots on the first abdominal segment, which are triangular (or teardrop-shaped) in the Emerald, but rectangular in the Scarce Emerald. The inferior anal appendages of the male Emerald are straight, whereas those of the Scarce Emerald are club-shaped when viewed from above. The Emerald is a much more slender species.

Female demoiselles also have a metallic green body, but are much larger than the emerald damselflies, their large wings are suffused green or brown, and they are usually encountered over flowing water, whereas the emerald damselflies are mostly restricted to standing-water sites.

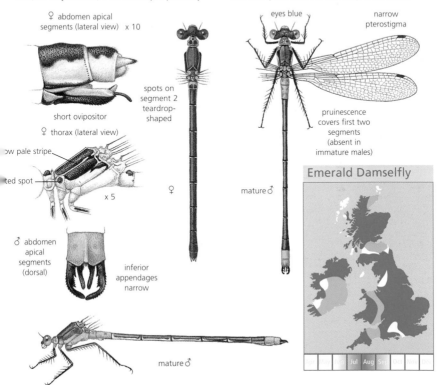

♀ abdomen apical segments (lateral view) x 10

short ovipositor

♀ thorax (lateral view)

ow pale stripe

ted spot

x 5

spots on segment 2 teardrop-shaped

♂ abdomen apical segments (dorsal)

inferior appendages narrow

♀

eyes blue

narrow pterostigma

pruinescence covers first two segments (absent in immature males)

mature ♂

Emerald Damselfly

mature ♂

Jul Aug

Status and conservation

The Emerald Damselfly has a wide Palaearctic distribution extending to Japan in the east. In central and northern Europe, it is the commonest lestid. It occurs throughout the British Isles and can be locally common if there are suitable habitats. Populations may be adversely affected by excessive clearance of emergent plants, although the species is not currently threatened nationally.

Ecology and behaviour

Habitat The species is often associated with acid bog pools and with fairly brackish water, but it also occurs in ponds, ditches, canals and lake margins with luxuriant emergent vegetation. Unlike coenagrionids, adults often roost next to water.

The **larvae** are most successful in shallow waters which lack fish or which have sufficiently dense marginal vegetation where they can avoid fish.

The Emerald Damselfly has a one-year life history. There is an obligate diapause in the egg stage, the consequence of which is that there is synchronised hatching of the eggs in April and the larvae grow rapidly. Full-grown larvae are larger than those of most other damselflies and have characteristic banding on the caudal lamellae. From laboratory feeding studies, it seems that the larvae are able to feed at roughly twice the rate of coenagrionids of a comparable size. Field estimates of the length of larval life in England range from 68 days (in Cheshire) to 83 days (in Durham). There are typically nine larval stadia (excluding the prolarva). The larvae live among aquatic vegetation. Unlike coenagrionids, which are predominantly sit-and-wait predators, lestid larvae devote more of their time to hunting prey. Their method of avoiding predators also differs from that of coenagrionids: they swim vigorously when disturbed. The larval diet is mainly small crustaceans, particularly copepods and chydorids, and mayfly and midge larvae. However, they consume significantly higher proportions of crustaceans than do coenagrionids and this is reflected in their higher position among vegetation.

Emergence begins in late June and is earlier in the south, reflecting the effect of temperature on larval growth. The sex ratio at emergence is roughly equal. Occasionally some late-developing larvae overwinter in the final instar. The immature period of the Emerald Damselfly varies with latitude, but it is usually around 16 days in Britain, contrasting with a period of around 30 days in northern Japan. The adults are long-lived and there is a record of a marked individual surviving for 69 days. The **flight season** lasts until the end of September.

Copulation usually takes place close to the breeding site, though tandem pairs can be seen elsewhere. Where tandems are formed depends largely upon the density of the vegetation surrounding the breeding site, but Emerald females often arrive already in tandem. Copulation is long, lasting from around 30 minutes to more than one hour. Oviposition takes place into the stems of emergent macrophytes such as rushes, sedges or horsetails, usually in tandem. The female begins ovipositing at the water surface and works her way downwards, sometimes ending up completely submerged. The male remains with the female and he, too, may completely submerge. Females have been recorded to stay underwater for up to 30 minutes. The Emerald Damselfly is able to use temporary waterbodies because of its egg diapause, and may oviposit in vegetation above the water-line, relying on the pond to fill before the eggs hatch the following spring.

Dave Thompson

Scarce Emerald Damselfly
Lestes dryas Kirby

Description

Jizz A metallic green damselfly that perches with wings half open on stems within dense vegetation surrounding shallow pools and ditches.

Field characters Ab 25-33mm; hw 20-25mm. This is a rare species, very similar in appearance to the Emerald Damselfly but of more robust appearance. Close examination of the anal appendages or ovipositor is required to confirm identification.

Similar species Apart from other emerald damselflies, the only damselflies with a metallic green coloration are the female demoiselles, which are much larger, have tinted wings and breed almost exclusively on rivers. The Scarce Emerald is very similar to the Emerald, but is on average larger. Males are distinguishable by the shape of the inferior anal appendages, which are curved inwards at the apex in the Scarce Emerald rather than being straight as in the Emerald. In the female, the length of the ovipositor valve on the underside of the end of the abdomen is longer in the Scarce Emerald than in the Emerald. There are more subtle differences between males in some other characters including, in the Scarce Emerald, the squarer shape of the pterostigma, the less extensive pruinescence on abdominal segment two and the brighter blue colour of the eyes. In female Scarce Emeralds the green spots on segment two of the abdomen are rectangular, rather than teardrop-shaped as in the Emerald.

Status and conservation

The Scarce Emerald is one of the most widespread species in the northern hemisphere, extending across Europe, Asia and North America. In Britain and Ireland it has never been common, but it has

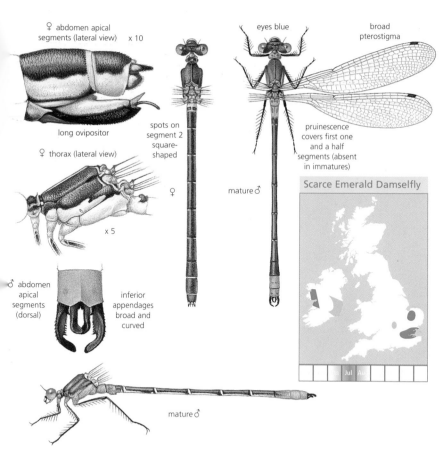

♀ abdomen apical
segments (lateral view)   x 10

long ovipositor

♀ thorax (lateral view)

x 5

spots on
segment 2
square-
shaped

♀

♂ abdomen
apical
segments
(dorsal)

inferior
appendages
broad and
curved

eyes blue

broad
pterostigma

mature ♂

pruinescence
covers first one
and a half
segments (absent
in immatures)

Scarce Emerald Damselfly

Jul   Au

mature ♂

also been under-recorded. It once occurred in fens in eastern England from Sussex to south Yorkshire, but it is now extinct at many of these sites. There was a period in the 1970s when it was presumed extinct in Britain, but this was never substantiated. Following its rediscovery in Essex, it has been found widely on the Thames estuary and again inland in Norfolk and the south Midlands. In Ireland, it is found in the midland counties, but principally occurs in the western counties of Clare and Galway. At some of these sites it has apparently become extinct, but others, particularly in the west, have very large colonies.

Its shallow, marshy breeding sites are threatened by habitat change, over-abstraction, pollution, nutrient enrichment and reclamation, with a long-term threat at coastal sites of sea-level change. Heavy grazing by cattle may reduce the extent of tall emergent vegetation and also result in eutrophication. Because the species' breeding sites are typically transient in nature, it is essential that a mosaic of habitats in different stages of succession is available for colonisation.

Ecology and behaviour

Habitat The Scarce Emerald is well adapted to

the seasonal nature of the pools and ditches in which it breeds. The coastal sites used in south-east England are typically freshwater or brackish ditches with dense emergent vegetation in areas of grazing marsh. Inland, the species is found in small, sometimes shaded, pools with thick vegetation, which in Norfolk include pingos and in Ireland, turloughs. These last two lake types have naturally fluctuating water levels and are areas where the species has undoubtedly survived for a long time. A common characteristic of these sites is that they may dry out in summer. The Scarce Emerald is able to survive in these pools and ditches as a result of its rapid larval development. The species can tolerate brackish waters but is not restricted to these conditions on coastal sites. Lakes or ponds that are near the end of their natural cycle and are infilling with vegetation also provide suitable conditions for the Scarce Emerald, but these sites will become unsuitable unless managed. A number of the British sites are protected within reserves. The apparent preference by the species for sites that are generally suboptimal for other dragonfly species may be due to the fact that larvae can survive only in habitats in which predation pressures are reduced.

Like other emerald damselflies, but unlike all other British damselflies, the eggs overwinter and hatch in the late winter or spring. The **larvae** develop quickly and can mature into adults within eight weeks. The large larvae have banded caudal lamellae and are distinguishable from those of the Emerald Damselfly only by close examination of the mouthparts. The larvae live among dense vegetation, and in the final instar often occur in large concentrations in the decreasing area of water which is available to them. Although the eggs will tolerate drought, the larvae are unable to survive if the waterbody dries up.

Adults **emerge** towards the end of June, slightly earlier than the usual emergence time of the Emerald Damselfly. Adults have a marked tendency to stay within dense vegetation close to the breeding sites. The **flight season** lasts until the end of August.

It is unknown whether the males are territorial. Mating is protracted, taking up to two hours, and pairs perch amongst dense emergent vegetation close to breeding sites. The pair usually stays in tandem during egg-laying. The eggs are laid into plant stems in marginal vegetation. Egg-laying sites are usually above water level in pools and ditches that are frequently dry from mid-summer, but become covered as water levels rise in winter.

Brian Nelson

Southern Emerald Damselfly
Lestes barbarus (Fabricius)

Description
Field characters Ab 26-35mm; hw 20-25mm. Metallic green with broad yellow stripes on top of the thorax. Bicoloured pterostigma is diagnostic, with the outer third whitish to pale yellow and the inner part brown. Rear of head yellow. Pale blue pruinescence absent or reduced to a small patch at the tip of the abdomen on segment 10. Male anal appendages yellowish with dark tips; inferior appendages pale, finger-like and diverging at tips.
Similar species The Southern Emerald Damselfly is superficially similar to the other metallic-green emerald damselflies. The species can be distinguished by its bicoloured pterostigma; in all other British damselflies the pterostigma is uniform brown or black. The diverging inferior appendages will distinguish males of the Southern Emerald Damselfly from the other *Lestes* species, in which the inferiors are straight or converge at the tips. The lower rear of the head is entirely yellow in the Southern Emerald Damselfly, whereas in the other emerald damselflies recorded from Great Britain and Ireland the metallic green extends down the back of the head.

Status and conservation
The Southern Emerald Damselfly is distributed throughout southern and central Europe, although is absent from alpine regions. The species is more common in the southern part of its range, although in the last decade it has been expanding northwards. In Britain it was first recorded in July and August 2002 on a nature reserve on the Norfolk coast. Only a few males were seen. In 2003, a single female was seen near the Norfolk site and also another male in Kent.

Ecology and behaviour
The species was discovered by Geoff Nobes at a shallow, stagnant, muddy dune pool in an area of marsh. No submerged vegetation was present but there was a stand of Bulrush (*Typha latifolia*) in the pool, with a fringe of Jointed Rush (*Juncus articulatus*) and Marsh Pennywort (*Hydrocotyle vulgaris*). This is typical of habitats used by the species in Europe, where it has also been recorded from brackish water.

Eggs are laid by solitary females or by tandem pairs into emergent aquatic plants or into the branches of bankside trees and shrubs. The egg is the over-wintering stage and the larvae hatch the following spring to complete development within two months. Adults are on the wing in southern Europe by mid-May, and in northern Europe are still present until the end of October.

Steve Brooks

Willow Emerald Damselfly
Lestes viridis (Vander Linden)

Description
Field characters Ab 30-40mm; hw 23-28mm. Large, metallic dark green. Pterostigma pale brown, with black borders. Rear of head bronze green or green-blue. Pruinescence undeveloped. Male anal appendages conspicuously pale with dark tips; inferiors dark, parallel, upturned at tip, broad and short, less than half the length of superiors.
Similar species The Willow Emerald Damselfly is

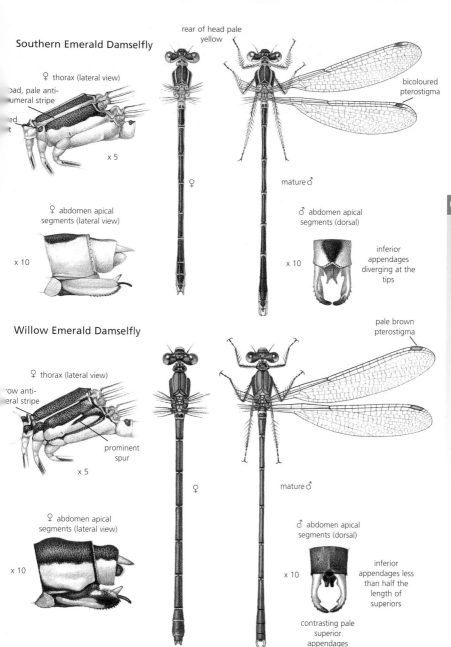

Southern Emerald Damselfly

rear of head pale yellow

bicoloured pterostigma

♀ thorax (lateral view)

broad, pale anti-humeral stripe

x 5

♀

mature ♂

♀ abdomen apical segments (lateral view)

x 10

♂ abdomen apical segments (dorsal)

x 10

inferior appendages diverging at the tips

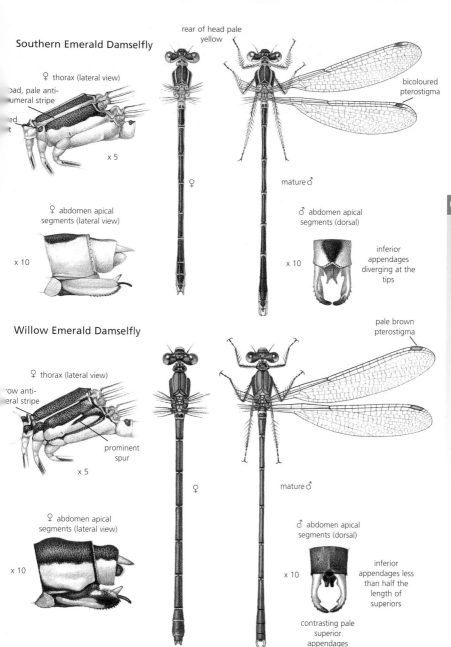

Willow Emerald Damselfly

pale brown pterostigma

♀ thorax (lateral view)

narrow anti-humeral stripe

prominent spur

x 5

♀

mature ♂

♀ abdomen apical segments (lateral view)

x 10

♂ abdomen apical segments (dorsal)

x 10

inferior appendages less than half the length of superiors

contrasting pale superior appendages

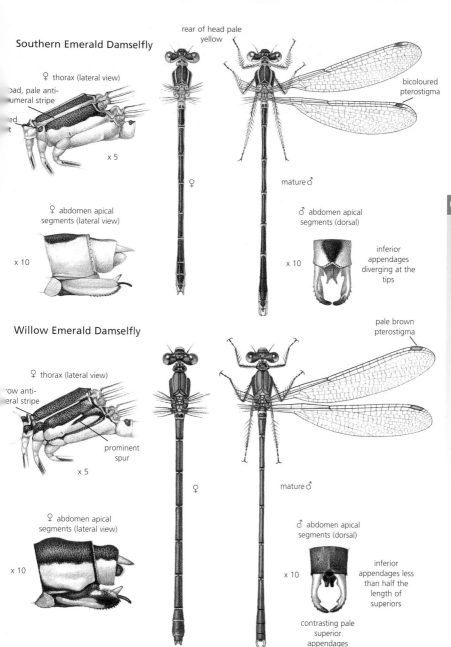

larger and darker green than other emerald damselflies. The pale brown, black-bordered pterostigma is also distinctive since in other lestids the pterostigma is bicoloured or black-brown. The inferior appendages, at less than half the length of the superiors, will distinguish male Willow Emerald Damselflies from other emerald damselflies, in which the inferiors are longer than half the length of the superiors.

The structure of the lower lip (the labium) of the larva distinguishes the Willow Emerald Damselfly from all other European species of *Lestes* and this has led some authors to place the Willow Emerald Damselfly in the genus *Chalcolestes*. In larvae of *Chalcolestes* the labium is broad and tapers gradually towards the base. In species of *Lestes* the labium is abruptly narrowed, giving it a stalked or racket-shaped appearance.

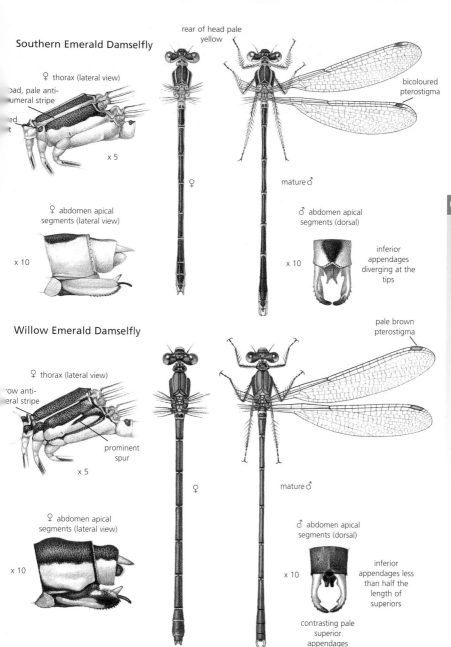

Lestidae

Status and conservation

The Willow Emerald Damselfly is distributed throughout southern and central Europe, where it is common and can be locally abundant. A single larval exuvia of the species was collected by John and Gill Brook in 1992 in the North Kent marshes. No adults were found and the species has not been seen subsequently. However, the correct identity of the specimen only came to light in 2003, so it is possible that the species has been overlooked and it has obviously bred successfully at least once in southern England.

Ecology and behaviour

In Europe the species breeds in a wide variety of ponds, lakes and slow-flowing rivers, but has a requirement for bankside shrubs or trees, especially willows, into the branches of which the females lay their eggs. Where the eggs are laid, the trees often develop galls (small swellings) which may be visible for several years afterwards. The eggs overwinter and larvae hatch in early spring to complete development within three months. The optimum flight period is August and September, but adults may be on the wing from June until November.

Steve Brooks

PLATYCNEMIDIDAE
White-legged damselflies

These are medium-sized damselflies with broadened white legs and a narrow head. They are usually restricted to slow-flowing rivers. There is one resident species in the genus *Platycnemis*.

White-legged Damselfly
Platycnemis pennipes (Pallas)

Description

Jizz Adults are most often encountered at the breeding sites in dense bankside vegetation along rivers and streams. During the maturation period they can often be found in lush meadows close to breeding sites. This species has the appearance of being lighter in coloration than other damselflies. The pale blue males fly with a bouncy, jerking flight and conspicuously dangling legs, especially in the presence of females.

Field characters Ab 27-31mm; hw 19-23mm. The distinctive legs are creamy white and have a broad, feather-like appearance, especially in males. Adults of both sexes undergo age-related changes which lead to progressively bolder black markings on the abdomen. These markings, however, are much reduced compared with other similar-sized damselflies. During maturation, females are especially light in colour and develop from the creamy-white '*lactea*' phase into light green mature individuals with more pronounced markings. Tenerals are very pale with an orangey-pink tinge, which can be quite conspicuous.

Similar species Immature forms of the Common Blue Damselfly have a pale body and legs and might be confused with the White-legged Damselfly. If the legs and abdominal markings can be closely examined the White-legged is readily distinguishable.

Status and conservation

The White-legged Damselfly occurs throughout most of western and central Europe. It has a very marked southern distribution in England and Wales and is largely dependent on lowland rivers and canals. Along some rivers it has a disjunct distribution, influenced by differences in vegetation.

It is vulnerable to pollution and especially physical disturbance to bankside habitats. On some rivers it has made a dramatic comeback as vegetation has recovered following large-scale bank clearance. It occurs on a number of lowland river systems and, on some, sizeable colonies have been recorded even along stretches subject to frequent boat traffic. Whilst the White-legged has been recorded from a number of still-water sites, it has been confirmed breeding at only a few. The factors determining the use of these sites are not understood, although this species will regularly breed in such sites in France.

Ecology and behaviour

Habitat The White-legged Damselfly favours unshaded slow-flowing stretches of rivers and canals with luxuriant floating and emergent vegetation, such as Reed Sweet-grass (*Glyceria maxima*), although certain vegetation, such as bur-reeds (*Sparganium*) and Common Club-rush

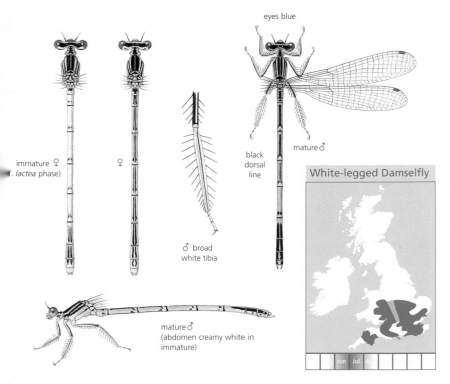

eyes blue

immature ♀
(f. *lactea* phase)

♀

black
dorsal
line

mature ♂

♂ broad
white tibia

mature ♂
(abdomen creamy white in
immature)

White-legged Damselfly

Jun Jul Au

(*Schoenoplectus lacustris*), appear to be avoided. Where vegetation conditions are favourable it can often be the most numerous species present.

The **larvae** live on bottom substrates among leaves and detritus, and in some situations the fine hairs on the body can become coated in small particles. The larvae are quite distinctive, appearing squat, with the caudal lamellae having dark blotches and a pale, markedly pointed apical thread. Prior to emergence they move up through the submerged vegetation, assisted by the caudal lamellae.

Adults **emerge** on bankside vegetation from late May with the **flight season** lasting through to mid August. Emergence occurs throughout the morning and into the afternoon. During maturation, adults move away from the breeding site and are often encountered in nearby lush meadows. In favourable years, colonies can reach high numbers.

Males will fly over aquatic and bankside vegetation where females are most likely to be encountered. This is the only non-demoiselle species of damselfly to exhibit a courtship display. A series of stimuli is necessary to initiate pre-copulatory behaviour in males. The bouncy, jerking flight of females, which occurs at a particular frequency, combined with the specific patterns on their body, appears to attract males. Males display their conspicuous white legs prominently in front of a female before taking her in tandem. The legs are also sometimes used in flight as a threat display to other males. Females are grasped by males in flight and taken to surrounding vegetation. The legs of the males, with their expanded tibia, also function in the tactile stimulation of females prior to copulation. The White-legged Damselfly is one species in which males are sometimes observed transferring sperm to their secondary genitalia whilst still in tandem. Tactile stimulation of the female continues throughout copulation, which can last for over 30 minutes. Copulation is usually terminated when the male pushes the female away from his secondary genitalia, resulting in the tandem pair flying off to commence oviposition.

On returning to the water, pairs remain in tandem during oviposition, alighting on floating or emergent vegetation. During periods of egg-laying, the male remains quite passive. The eggs are laid into the underside of floating vegetation in a zigzag or helical pattern. In high-density colonies, tandem pairs congregate at prime oviposition sites, such as flower heads of the Yellow Water-lily (*Nuphar lutea*). The female probes both inside and outside the flower heads and often oviposits below the water surface, climbing down the stem until her thorax is partially submerged.

Steve Cham

COENAGRIONIDAE
Red damselflies and blue damselflies

These are small to medium-sized, blue-and-black or red-and-black damselflies. They occur in the full range of aquatic habitats. In Great Britain and Ireland there are 12 resident species in the genera *Pyrrhosoma*, *Ceriagrion*, *Coenagrion*, *Enallagma*, *Ischnura* and *Erythromma*, plus two extinct species.

Large Red Damselfly
Pyrrhosoma nymphula (Sulzer)

Description

Jizz This is a distinctive red-and-black damselfly that is often the first to be seen in spring. Males are usually encountered perched on waterside vegetation or flying out to investigate potential competitors or mates.
Field characters Ab 25-29mm; hw 19-24mm. This large red damselfly with extensive black markings is unlikely to be mistaken for anything else. There are three female colour forms, which vary in the amount of black on the abdomen.
Similar species The Small Red Damselfly is the only other predominantly red-and-black damselfly in the region. As its name suggests, however, the Large Red is a bigger and more robust insect. It can be distinguished easily from the Small Red by its black legs and the broad red or yellow antehumeral stripes. In the Small Red, the legs are red and the antehumeral stripes are absent or very narrow.

Status and conservation

The Large Red is a widespread and common breeding species in Britain and Ireland. It reaches as far north as the Orkneys. It is common across much of northern Europe, but in southern Europe it is more local. It is not threatened in the British Isles, though it has declined in the last 30 years in intensively cultivated areas, notably eastern England.

Ecology and behaviour

Habitat Occurs at ponds, canals, ditches and acid bogs. Away from breeding sites, it can be found feeding in patches of sunlight in woodlands or along hedge margins, sometimes in large numbers.

The Large Red has a two-year life cycle throughout the British Isles. It may, under circumstances of low food availability and/or low temperatures, even take up to three years, though this is thought to be unusual. The eggs are transparent when laid, but turn brown after a few days. They hatch 2-3 weeks after laying. There are typically 11 larval stadia, excluding the prolarva.

The **larvae** are dark and stout, with a distinctive X-shape on the outer half of the broad lamellae. They are found on the bottom – more often than other coenagrionids – among both living and dead vegetation. Second-stadium larvae eat mainly large protozoans, such as *Paramecium*, and small rotifers. In the third stadium they move on to more solid prey and eat small crustaceans. The diet of later stadia varies with size and season, but consists of midge larvae, mayfly larvae, copepods and other small crustaceans. Midge larvae are particularly well represented in the diets of later-stadium larvae, reflecting their preference for bottom-dwelling.

Unusually for dragonflies, the larvae display vigorous territorial behaviour and use the X-shape on their caudal lamellae to signal occupancy of a perch to rivals. The Large Red spends its first winter in a range of early stadia and enters the penultimate stadium in the following summer. Towards the end of summer it enters the final stadium and remains there in diapause until the following spring. This allows the majority of a year-class to respond synchronously to rising

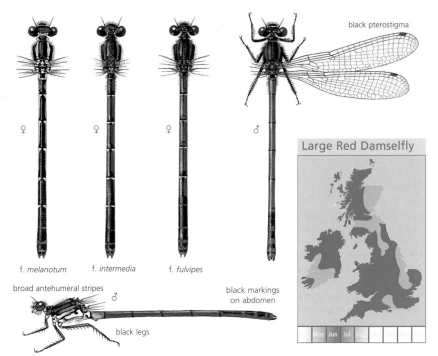

f. *melanotum*   f. *intermedia*   f. *fulvipes*

broad antehumeral stripes ♂

black legs

black pterostigma

black markings
on abdomen

Coenagrionidae

Large Red Damselfly

May Jun Jul

temperatures and increased daylength, and means that adult **emergence** occurs over a relatively short period of around three weeks in spring. A few larvae emerge asynchronously, without entering diapause, in late summer.

Studies of emergence from adjacent ponds have shown that there is variation in emergence dates, presumably a result of differing prey availability within the ponds. Males emerge slightly earlier than females, and there is usually a male-biased sex ratio at emergence (around 1.1-1.2 males for each female). Males are smaller than females (mean weights around 37mg and 40mg respectively). Mortality at emergence can be high, with birds, ants, spiders and inclement weather all taking their toll.

The main **flight season** varies with latitude and lasts from the second half of May (occasionally late April) to the first half of July in southern England, but June and all of July in northern Scotland, although late-emerging adults may be present into early September.

The body size of emerging adults declines through the season, because late-hatching larvae are excluded from the best feeding sites; females later in the season lay smaller clutches of smaller eggs, though this effect can be masked by weather conditions.

The immature period lasts longer for females than for males (typically 16 days and 12 days respectively). Immatures are seldom seen at the breeding site and this period represents the main time for dispersal. Both sexes change colour and gain weight in the immature period, with males putting on up to 14% of their emergence weight. Females increase in weight by around 66%, and this is predominantly due to the abdomen becoming full of eggs. On each visit to the pond, provided she is not disturbed too seriously, the female will lay all of the eggs which she has matured. The mean clutch size is around 350 eggs, though the number can reach as high as 750 if the female has not visited the breeding site for a few days.

Males neither defend oviposition sites nor display any type of courtship behaviour, but they are territorial. From their perch, resident males have a vantage point from which they make sallies out to patrolling males, pairs in tandem and potential mates. Territorial disputes are almost invariably won by the resident, irrespective of the relative sizes of the combatants, and males that win fights secure more matings. Mating occurs on warm sunny days, with copulation lasting around 15-20 minutes. Oviposition takes place in tandem. Eggs are laid into submerged vegetation or on the undersides of floating leaves. The mean mature-adult lifespan is 7 days for males and 5.5 days for females. There are records of both sexes living up to six weeks as adults.

Dave Thompson

Small Red Damselfly
Ceriagrion tenellum (Villers)

Description

Jizz A small, red, weak-flying damselfly restricted to mires, heathland and bogs in southern England and Wales. The species is usually seen hovering a few centimetres above small heathland bog pools and seepages, or flying or perched among marginal vegetation. Its red coloration and small size render it surprisingly cryptic as it flits and settles among the grasses and rushes across the bog surface.

Field characters Ab 22-27mm; hw 15-21mm. Both sexes have red eyes, with the head and thorax predominantly bronzy black. In males, and females of the *erythrogastrum* colour form, the abdomen is entirely blood-red. In other female forms the abdomen is entirely bronze-black or is marked red on the basal segments. The legs of both sexes are red or yellowish. The pterostigmata are also red.

Similar species The species is likely to be confused only with the much larger Large Red Damselfly, with which it may share a locality. In the Large Red, however, the male abdomen has extensive black markings on the last four segments, whereas Small Red males lack black abdominal markings. Females of the Large Red are best distinguished by the broad red or yellow antehumeral stripes; in the Small Red the upper thorax is marked with very narrow yellow stripes. The legs and pterostigmata are black in the Large Red.

Status and conservation

Restricted to southern England and Wales, where it may be locally abundant. The species is widespread in south-west Europe, but in Britain is at the extreme north-western limits of its range. Its absence from apparently suitable habitat in northern Britain and Ireland suggests that climatic factors restrict its distribution in these islands.

The species requires sunny sites with shallow, oligotrophic waters and may be eliminated by afforestation, lowering of the water table, eutrophication and industrial-scale peat-mining. Over-deepening of seepages and shading by trees and shrubs are also detrimental. Suitable breeding sites can be created by tree removal and the digging of small hollows. The species has not proved to be amenable to reintroduction attempts by translocation of adults and larvae.

Ecology and behaviour

Habitat The species is typically associated with shallow, unshaded acidic bog pools, seepages and small, slow-flowing streams with conditions that are suitable for dense growths of Marsh St John's-wort (*Hypericum elodes*), although this plant is not always present at breeding sites. Small Reds also occur, however, in base-rich sites, such as calcareous valley mires, fens or clay or marl pits, where there are suitable unshaded shallow-water conditions. It is less common in shaded waters or narrow, deeply cut streams with overhanging vegetation or a gravelly bed. It will breed in the margins of large well-vegetated ponds with neutral or slightly acidic water, especially where these are close to heathlands. Nevertheless, these sites seldom support large populations, possibly because of competition with other dragonfly species or because the larvae are prone to fish predation. The species does particularly well where it can exploit tiny bog pools, with very shallow water overlying *Sphagnum* mats.

The Small Red Damselfly is a Mediterranean species at the edge of its range in Britain and requires warm water for egg and larval

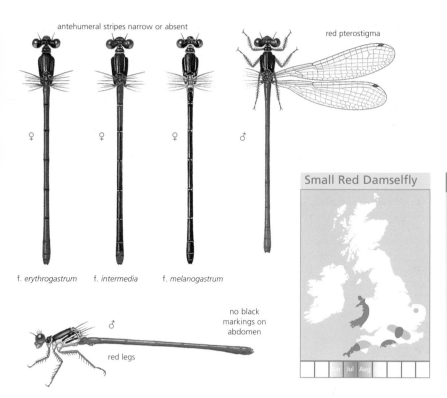

antehumeral stripes narrow or absent

red pterostigma

♀   ♀   ♀   ♂

f. *erythrogastrum*   f. *intermedia*   f. *melanogastrum*

♂

no black markings on abdomen

red legs

Small Red Damselfly

Jun Jul Aug

development. Similarly, adults are strongly affected by weather conditions and will fly only in conditions of sunshine, high temperature and low wind speed.

The **larvae** live among *Sphagnum* mats, detritus and bottom sediments. They are compact, with a distinctive broad, angular head and narrow lamellae marked with faint marginal blotches. Despite the small size of fully grown larvae and the relatively warm water in which they live, they take two years to complete development. This is probably a reflection of the paucity of prey available in the nutrient-poor bog pools and seepages. During the second autumn of development, larvae in the penultimate stadium enter diapause, induced by decreasing daylength.

Emergence is unsynchronised, leading to a prolonged **flight season** from early June to early September.

Adults seldom move far from the breeding sites and so are slow to colonise new sites or recolonise sites from which they have become extinct.

Males are territorial but are unable to defend large territories. They will perch within 0.5m of each other, and may therefore be abundant at some sites. They will clash aggressively with other males, including males of the Large Red Damselfly. Except in dense populations, they do not usually drive their opponents away from the water, but rather cause a shift in distribution around the site. In warm sunny weather, males rendezvous with females close to the breeding sites between 10.00am and 5.00pm. Pairs perch in tandem low down among emergent vegetation at the water's edge. Copulation can be prolonged, lasting 40-90 minutes. Intruding males are discouraged by wing-flicking.

Females oviposit with the male in tandem into the stems of submerged and emergent plants, such as Marsh St John's-wort, or into *Sphagnum* moss. The pair will sometimes fully submerge during oviposition. The eggs hatch after about one month.

Steve Brooks

Southern Damselfly
Coenagrion mercuriale (Charpentier)

Description

Jizz Males are usually found meandering slowly along short stretches of small, unshaded streams or runnels, with abundant aquatic vegetation, in bogs or larger base-enriched streams, flying within 25cm of the surface.

Field characters Ab 22-26mm; hw 15-20mm. The male Southern Damselfly appears smaller and darker than male Common Blue or Azure Damselflies, and the blue looks slightly deeper. This is because there is more black on the abdomen, which also makes the insect appear smaller than it really is. The combination of small size and proximity of suitable habitat is a useful guide to identification. The species is seldom found cohabiting with other blue damselflies. Male Southern Damselflies can be positively identified only by examination of the anal appendages. The 'mercury' sign on abdominal segment 2 is a useful guide, but can be variable. In females, the shape of the posterior margin of the pronotum is diagnostic, as the female blue form of the Azure can carry a similar mark on abdominal segment 2. In both sexes of the Southern, the pterostigma is taller than it is long and is distinctly shorter than other *Coenagrion* species.

Similar species The Southern Damselfly overlaps in range with only two other blue damselflies: the Azure and the Common Blue. Both of these are larger and appear paler blue. The Azure may inhabit the same streams but seldom the same areas. Azure males are distinguishable by the black U-shaped marking on abdominal segment 2; females by the absence of a pale bar between the post-ocular lobes. The Common Blue usually occurs in different habitats, but it may occasionally be found in pooled areas of streams, although its typical low flight over open water will help to distinguish it. Common Blue males have a black mushroom-shaped spot on abdominal segment 2; females have one short stripe on the side of the thorax (two in *Coenagrion* species) and a short spine below abdominal segment 8.

Status and conservation

This is a rare species and in Britain is living on the extreme north-western fringe of its European range, where it is confined to the south and west. It is currently protected under the Wildlife & Countryside Act.

Its two main strongholds are in the New Forest, Hampshire, and the Prescelli mountains, Pembrokeshire. Smaller colonies exist in Dorset, Devon, Gower, Anglesey, and on the Test and Itchen Rivers in Hampshire. Where it does occur, it may be abundant under ideal conditions. The main threat to its survival is the removal of grazing animals, which are necessary to maintain the open character of the damselflies' breeding sites. This has led to the reduction or loss of some colonies in Dorset, Devon and west Wales, but elsewhere populations are stable. Over-abstraction, dredging and nutrient enrichment also pose a threat.

Ecology and behaviour

Habitat This is primarily a species of slow-flowing, base-rich streams within acid heathland, but additional colonies occur on chalk streams in Hampshire. Although apparently dissimilar, these habitats have a common attribute in maintaining a relatively constant water temperature, which at source seldom drops below 10°C. This is most important in winter, when minimum temperatures may well be a determining factor in habitat suitability. The species avoids shaded stretches, preferring more open situations where water temperatures are likely to be highest.

Larval development usually takes two years. The larvae are distinctive in having unusually short, unmarked lamellae. During their first year, larvae live in detritus among plant roots and avoid areas of high current flow. In the second year, they move on to the surface of the substrate and up into the foliage of aquatic plants. This spatial distinction is often not clear in the field because, in some cases, the total depth of water may be only about 1cm. In such conditions colonies may be at risk in particularly cold winters.

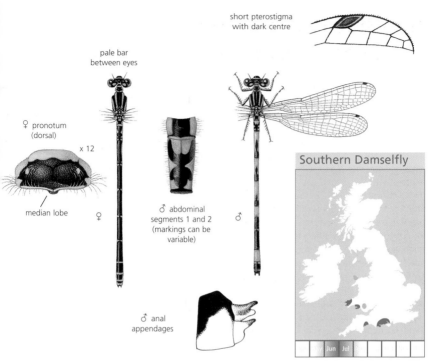

short pterostigma with dark centre

pale bar between eyes

♀ pronotum (dorsal)

x 12

median lobe ♀

♂ abdominal segments 1 and 2 (markings can be variable)

♂

♂ anal appendages

Southern Damselfly

May Jun Jul

However, larvae also occur in water over 50cm deep.

Adults emerge during the morning, sometimes quite early, using any suitable support, including the stems of grasses or rushes, and seldom climb above 12cm. **Emergence** begins in mid to late May and continues through to mid July, the peak being towards the end of June. The emerging adults do not fly far from water, and maturation takes only a few days. The **flight season** lasts until the beginning of August.

In high summer adults may begin to fly earlier in the day than other species, before the dew has left the grass, or in overcast conditions that deter other species. They are good competitors and may drive off the Azure Damselfly from patrol areas, which are typically located in stretches where there is a change in stream flow-rate. They fly slowly, erratically and low over riffles, runnels and rills, pausing frequently to perch for short periods on the vegetation. In most localities they seem to prefer some protective vegetation, although they seem disinclined to fly among it. They will not tolerate areas which are wholly overgrown or shaded and prefer the water to be reasonably clear of emergent grasses, sedges and rushes. In heathland localities, their usual flying companions are Small Red Damselflies and there is seldom any conflict. The maximum life expectancy of an adult is about six weeks, although half of the population does not survive beyond five days. Little is known about their natural enemies, but the remains of adults are often seen in spiders' webs, and crab spiders will prey on them. Insectivorous plants are another frequent cause of mortality.

Breeding areas attract maximum numbers at or shortly after midday, with females seldom comprising more than 20% of the total. Copulation is lengthy, taking an hour or more, with the pair frequently moving from perch to perch. Egg-laying takes place with the pair in tandem, the female inserting the eggs into soft plant tissue. The underside of the leaves of Bog Pondweed (*Potamogeton polygonifolius*) is a favourite site, but plants such as Marsh St John's-wort (*Hypericum elodes*) or Lesser Marshwort (*Apium inundatum*) will suffice. In the absence of aquatic vegetation, the submerged bases of rushes and sedges provide an alternative. The eggs hatch within 3-4 weeks.

Dave Winsland

Northern Damselfly
Coenagrion hastulatum (Charpentier)

Description

Jizz The blue-and-black males fly slowly and weakly among widely spaced stems of emergent sedges, adjoining open patches of water in Scottish lochans. Flight is well below the top of the vegetation, perhaps 20-60cm above water.

Field characters Ab 22-26mm; hw16-22mm. The male anal appendages, which are easily seen with a hand-lens, are absolutely diagnostic. Abdominal markings on segments 2 and 3 can vary considerably and are not reliable for identification purposes. In both sexes, the undersides of the eyes and face are bright green. In side view, the pale parts of the females are pea-green, unlike females of related species. This colour may darken with age.

Similar species The Common Blue Damselfly is usually the only blue-and-black species inhabiting the same waterbodies as the Northern Damselfly in Britain (although there is a report of a single male Azure Damselfly at one Perthshire site). The Common Blue is generally more active, flying off more quickly and strongly when disturbed. It has a brighter blue abdomen rather than the greenish-blue tint of the Northern Damselfly. The Northern Damselfly tends to be less conspicuous and does not fly over large expanses of open water. When seen in the hand, the Northern has two short black lines on each side of the thorax, distinguishing it from the Common Blue, which has only one short black line. Compare also the shape of the male anal appendages and the hind margin of the pronotum in females.

Status and conservation

A northern European species, with outlying southerly populations in montane regions (Pyrenees, Massif Central, Alps). It is currently known from 26 Scottish sites, and it seems unlikely that many more will be discovered. At most sites adults are not abundant, and there are few at which over 100 adults have been seen at one time. The sites tend to be small and shallow, and many are overgrown with sedges and in danger of eventually silting up. This species is one of our rarest damselflies and regular monitoring and conservation measures are necessary. At one very shallow bog, recent afforestation too close to the breeding site has lowered the water table and the Northern Damselfly is suffering badly. Pools 60cm deep have been dug in the bog and may yet save the species here. Damming at one Old Caledonian Pine Forest reserve has shown that the Northern Damselfly, if present in an area, will quickly colonise a new site provided that the rather precise micro-habitat is present.

Ecology and behaviour

Habitat Breeding waters tend to be shallow, with an optimum depth of 30-60cm, and sheltered by dense stands of tall sedges. The larvae cling to underwater vegetation, such as Water Horsetail (*Equisetum fluviatile*), sedges or the leaf-stalks of pondweeds (*Potamogeton*) in fairly open water. Small larvae may be more frequent in the latter. The structure of the vegetation is important, with dense clumps of sedges being entirely avoided. The open nature of their preferred habitat, and the observation in Scandinavian populations that larvae are equally active in hunting for prey during the day and at night, must make them vulnerable to fish predation, and in most, but not all, sites fish are completely absent.

The **larvae** closely resemble other *Coenagrion* species but the distinctive lamellae have rounded tips and are edged with black at the oppositely positioned node. They take two years to develop. Between 30% and 50% of the second-year larvae overwinter in the final stadium, most of the remainder being in the penultimate stadium.

In this little-known species there is no record of **emergence** ever having been observed in Scotland. Exuviae have been found in sheltered corners of ponds 4-8cm above water on sedges and Water Horsetail, apparently avoiding the denser vegetation. At one site in 1995, most emergences took

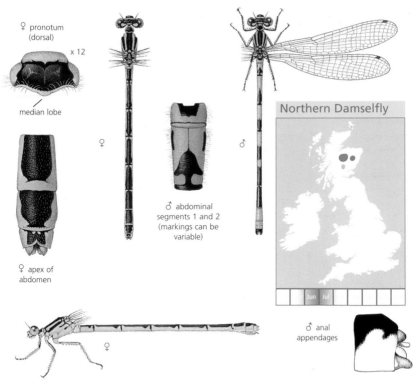

♀ pronotum (dorsal)

x 12

median lobe

♀

♂

♀ apex of abdomen

♂ abdominal segments 1 and 2 (markings can be variable)

Northern Damselfly

Jun Jul

♀

♂ anal appendages

place before 21 May. The **flight season** is over by the first week of August.

After emergence, the immatures disperse several hundred metres and can be found in sheltered heathery glades among pines and birches. One teneral female was pink, with no trace of green. Return of mature adults to the breeding site has been noted by the beginning of June.

In calm, sunny weather the males perch on low vegetation at or near water level, occasionally moving around, but always keeping a short distance from other males. Several have been noted flying around a restricted area of open water (about 2 x 3m) with 50% cover of White Water-lily (*Nymphaea alba*), edged by denser sedges. They weaved their way, some 20cm above the water, through sparse sedges and over open water for perhaps 2m, then circled back as though occupying a territory. They would confront other males they met and one would give way, slowly flying off, suggesting that, at times, there may be territorial activity.

Little is known of this species' reproductive behaviour in Scotland, although pairs have been noted to spend 40 minutes in copulation. Mating pairs perch on dead stems some 15cm above water and also on nearby heather. At one pond, after an overcast morning, the sun came out, bringing instant warmth. Soon, pairs of Northern Damselflies appeared in tandem from the surrounding vegetation and began prospecting for oviposition sites among Water Horsetails in the centre of the pond, in an area sheltered from the wind. Oviposition is completed in tandem, and one female was noted to lay into the petiole of a pondweed leaf, moving backwards until underwater. The male, settled flat on the leaf, was also pulled backwards until his abdomen was completely underwater, whereupon he pulled his mate out again and the two flew off elsewhere. Another pair completely submerged to 5cm under water for 25 minutes. Males occasionally adopt a half-sentinel position when egg-laying starts but soon lie flat on the leaf, so becoming much less conspicuous. The eggs hatch within a few weeks, and tiny 1.5mm larvae start to appear by mid July.

Betty and Bob Smith

Irish Damselfly
Coenagrion lunulatum (Charpentier)

Description

Jizz A typical damselfly in general behaviour. Not seen in flight for long, perching frequently on plants. Males characteristically perch on floating leaves of aquatic plants on breeding pools and lakes.

Field characters Ab 22-26mm; hw 16-20mm. In general appearance both sexes are darker and shorter-bodied than the Azure and Variable Damselflies, with which this species coexists. Males can be distinguished from these species by the large proportion of black on the abdomen, the all-blue abdominal segments 8-9, and the bright green coloration on the underside of the thorax, head and eyes. This is often a striking feature even in flight. The blue is of a darker shade compared with similar species. Females are a rather undistinguished dull green with black markings with a brassy sheen. Specimens of either sex should be examined in the hand to confirm identification.

Similar species The male Irish Damselfly can easily be distinguished from the other blue-and-black damselflies by the combination of size, colour pattern and the characteristic 'crescent' shape of the marking on abdominal segment 2. The Northern Damselfly is the most similar British species, but it is not so dark and males can be distinguished by the shape of the abdominal segment 2 markings and anal appendages. The female Irish Damselfly is identified most easily by the shape of the hind margin of the pronotum, which has a distinct raised lobe; this is more prominent than in the female Variable Damselfly.

Status and conservation

The Irish Damselfly is rare throughout much of its range and occurs in scattered populations in northern and eastern Europe. It was first discovered in Ireland in 1981 but has yet to be found in Britain, although suitable habitat does exist in North Wales, north-west England and south-west Scotland. In Ireland, it is confined to the southern part of Northern Ireland and northern counties of the Irish Republic. Within this area it is found in widely scattered colonies.

Some sites in Northern Ireland and at least one in the Republic are covered by a conservation designation. The majority of the lake sites are probably not directly threatened, as many are in marginal hilly areas. A long-term threat may be declining water quality due to agricultural change within the lake catchments. The few colonies on cut-over bogs may be affected by long-term habitat change, resulting in the loss of the open water. A recent survey of the species in Northern Ireland showed that most colonies were small, and that as many as 25% of the recorded colonies have died out in the last ten years. The only substantial colonies are found in relatively isolated small lakes and bogland sites which have not been affected by agricultural intensification or drainage. The losses at individual sites are attributable to the effects of nutrient enrichment and lowering of lake levels.

Ecology and behaviour

Habitat The Irish Damselfly is found mostly in small mesotrophic sheltered lakes. These typically have clear water and are relatively shallow, with beds of floating aquatics and sparse fringing beds of emergent plants, usually sedges. A few colonies are found on cut-over bogs, where the species breeds on shallow pools created by peat extraction.

The life history of this species is still poorly known, especially in the larval stage. **Larvae** have been caught fully grown in early summer in shallow peaty pools. They closely resemble other *Coenagrion* species and can be difficult to identify conclusively.

Adults have been seen to **emerge** from a lake during the day on dead reed stems 60-90cm above the water. The adults generally stay close to water in sheltered vegetation. The distribution on the individual sites is often highly localised, though this is perhaps related to factors such as shelter. There have been a number of records, including the first Irish record, of males well away from

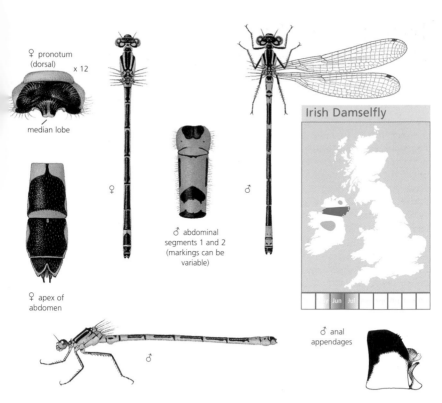

♀ pronotum (dorsal) x 12

median lobe

♀

♀ apex of abdomen

♂ abdominal segments 1 and 2 (markings can be variable)

♂

♂

Irish Damselfly

Jun Jul

♂ anal appendages

breeding sites. The recorded **flight season** lasts from mid May to the end of July, with most records between mid June and mid July.

Mating has been observed in the vegetation beside breeding sites. Males, however, do rest characteristically on floating leaves of aquatic plants on ponds and lakes, though whether this is territorial behaviour is not known as yet. Oviposition occurs in tandem, with females climbing down flower stalks of pondweeds (*Potamogeton*) until half-submerged.

Brian Nelson

Azure Damselfly
Coenagrion puella (Linnaeus)

Description

Jizz Mature males are variegated blue and black and are usually seen perched on, or patrolling around, vegetation at the edges of ponds, lakes, ditches, slow-moving canals and rivers. Away from the breeding sites, mature and immature adults may be seen feeding by sunlit hedge banks, field margins and woodland glades.

Field characters Ab 23-30mm; hw 16-23mm. Adult male Azure Damselflies superfi-cially resemble other coenagrionid damselflies in that their head, thorax and abdomen are coloured black and blue. Females are predominantly black, with green or blue sides to the thorax. Positive identification should be confirmed by examination in the hand.

Similar species The male Azure Damselfly can best be distinguished from the Common Blue Damselfly by the much narrower blue antehumeral stripes on the thorax and the characteristic black U-shaped mark isolated from the black ring at the posterior end of abdominal segment 2. The Common Blue has a club-shaped marking on this segment. In the hand (or net) in Britain, it is likely to be confused only with the Variable Damselfly, in which the U-shaped mark is (almost) invariably attached to the black ring and the pale antehumeral stripes are discontinuous.

Female Azures can be distinguished from female Common Blues by the absence of a spine below abdominal segment 8 and also by the presence of two black stripes on the side of the thorax. They are also similar to females of other *Coenagrion* species and are best distinguished by examination of the posterior lobe of the pronotum.

There are two colour forms in the female, the blue form (homochromic type) and the green form (heterochromic type). The blue form closely resembles the female Variable Damselfly and may sometimes have a similar marking on abdominal segment 2.

Status and conservation

The Azure Damselfly is a very common British damselfly. It occurs in England, Wales and the lowlands of south and central Scotland. It is one of the commonest damselflies in Europe, with a distribution that stretches from southern Scandinavia to North Africa. Populations may be reduced by excessive clearance of aquatic plants, but it is not nationally threatened.

Ecology and behaviour

Habitat Found in a wide range of waterbodies, but prefers smaller, sheltered ponds, including garden ponds, where there is plenty of emergent vegetation. It will tolerate eutrophic sites but is sensitive to pollution.

The Azure Damselfly usually has a one-year life cycle. However, at the northern edge of its range, or when food is scarce or its density is very high, a proportion of the population takes two years. There are 10 or 11 larval stadia (excluding the prolarva). The **larvae** closely resemble other *Coenagrion* species with nodate lamellae, and the species are difficult to separate reliably. They live among both living and dead aquatic vegetation. They are 'sit-and-wait' predators, equally adept at catching food by day or by night. The exact composition of their diet varies with their size and with the season, but consists of midge larvae, mayfly larvae, copepods and other small crustaceans. The most important prey items numerically are small crustaceans and, in terms of biomass, midge larvae.

Emergence is reasonably well synchronised and occurs from mid May to mid June, with typically 95% of the population emerging in just under three weeks. Females emerge on average about a day or two earlier than males, though there is, of course, considerable overlap in their emergence distributions. The sex ratio at emergence is 1:1. Larvae use emergent vegetation on which to complete their metamorphosis. Peak emergence occurs in mid-morning. Emergence is greatly affected by the weather. Few Azure Damselflies emerge on cool, rainy days, presumably because there is greater risk from predators during the longer time taken to emerge and harden the wings. The maiden flight is usually near-vertical until the insects are carried in the direction of the prevailing wind. The **flight season** lasts until late August.

The immature period lasts longer for females than for males (typically 16 and 13 days respectively). Immature adults are seldom seen at the breeding site. In one study, 23% of males and 12% of females returned to breed at their natal pond. The main dispersal period for the Azure Damselfly is in the immature stage. Once mature, adults tend to remain in the same locality unless moved by extremes of weather. Males change colour during the maturation period, but do not put on weight (remaining at around 35mg), whereas females may increase from 40 to 55mg.

The Azure Damselfly is not territorial. Patrolling males generally fly close to the water surface, but they perch close to the top of vegetation, looking for females. Females are seen at breeding sites when they come to oviposit. Tandem pairs are seen away from the breeding site only if they have been disturbed. Males spend their time waiting for new females to come to the breeding site, or try to secure matings by attacking tandem pairs, at which they have some small degree of success.

Copulation lasts for about 30 minutes and oviposition for 90 minutes. Mating takes

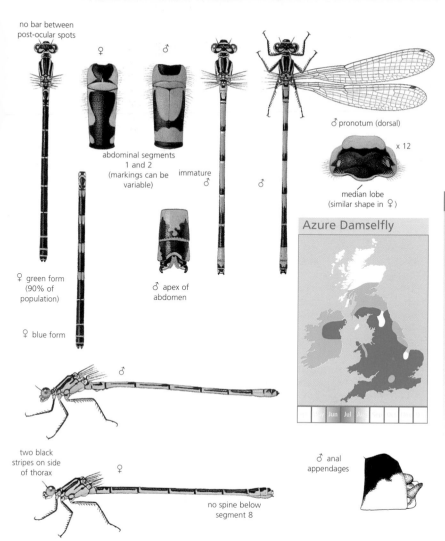

no bar between post-ocular spots

♀   ♂

abdominal segments 1 and 2 (markings can be variable)

immature ♂

♂

♂ pronotum (dorsal)

x 12

median lobe (similar shape in ♀)

Azure Damselfly

♀ green form (90% of population)

♂ apex of abdomen

♀ blue form

Jun Jul Aug

♂

two black stripes on side of thorax

♀

no spine below segment 8

♂ anal appendages

place only on warm, sunny days, usually between 10am and 4pm. Oviposition takes place in tandem except at the end of the breeding season, when there may be a female-biased sex ratio. Eggs are laid into floating or submerged plants. Males often hold themselves erect during oviposition, presumably keeping watch for predators. Oviposition is a risky time for both sexes, but particularly for females, which can be taken by water beetles, newts and even dragonfly larvae. The mean mature-adult lifespan is 5.5 days. In one study, the most successful male recorded took ten days to reach maturity, lived a further 26 days and obtained 18 matings. If weather conditions are suitable,

mature females come to the breeding site to lay a clutch of eggs on almost all days of their life. The most successful female in the same study lived for 26 days as a mature insect and produced 15 clutches of eggs (an estimated total of 4,200 eggs). Female clutch size depends on the time since the previous clutch was laid, and bigger females lay larger clutches of eggs only if bad weather has prevented oviposition for more than two days. Both female colour forms have similar reproductive success. Eggs hatch without diapause, with the exact time being temperature-dependent: 2-5 weeks would be typical for British waters.

Dave Thompson

Variable Damselfly
Coenagrion pulchellum (Vander Linden)

Description

Jizz This damselfly is one of several blue or bluish species and it can resemble two of the commonest species, the Azure and Common Blue Damselflies.

Field characters Ab 23-30mm; hw 16-23mm. When males are seen in company with Azure and Common Blue Damselflies, careful observation will reveal that the Variable appears to be a more slender and distinctly darker insect because of the more extensive black markings. Most individuals of the Variable may be identified by the black thoracic and abdominal markings and the strongly trilobate margins of the pronotum, but the markings can vary. In males the antehumeral stripes are normally broken, resembling exclamation marks, but in females they are usually complete. The U-shaped black marking on segment 2 of males is normally joined to the black ring below, so that it resembles a wine glass. Females are dimorphic, having a green and a blue form. The black pattern on segment 2 is like a thistlehead or mercury sign, but some Azure females also have this pattern, so the distinctive shape of the pronotum should be used to distinguish them.

Similar species Careful examination in the hand is needed to confirm the differences between the Variable, Azure and Common Blue Damselflies. Other blue damselflies (Northern, Southern and Dainty) are similar to the Variable, but are unlikely to occur in the same habitat. The Variable and Azure are unequivocally separated by comparing the very different abdominal appendages in the male. The antehumeral stripes are complete in male Azure and Common Blue Damselflies. The mark on segment 2 is U-shaped in the Azure and club-shaped in the Common Blue. Females of the Common Blue have a short spine on the underside of segment 8, this being absent in *Coenagrion* species. The prominent, narrow central lobe on the posterior margin of the pronotum (more pronounced in the female) in the Variable differs markedly from the broader, flatter central lobe of the Azure.

Status and conservation

The Variable Damselfly is an enigmatic species in that its distribution is scattered over many parts of England and Wales, extending into Scotland, but the colonies are often restricted to small areas which appear no different from much of the surrounding countryside. Populations may be faithful to long-time colony sites or may sometimes shift their concentrations to neighbouring areas from year to year. In contrast, in Ireland the species is common and widespread. It has a central European distribution and is absent from much of southern and northern regions.

On the Somerset Levels, where the Variable breeds in drainage ditches and slow rivers, mechanical ditch clearance can eliminate a local population, but usually, in these favoured areas, the species soon re-establishes itself or a new colony appears nearby. In recent years the species has been unaccountably absent from some apparently suitable sites which are surrounded by existing Variable Damselfly colonies, and this emphasises that we do not understand the key environmental requirements of this damselfly. Active conservation of the Variable is therefore not easy to achieve, but habitats suitable for the Azure may also attract it, especially if luxuriant waterside vegetation and protective bushes are present.

Ecology and behaviour

Habitat Occurs close to stagnant or slow-flowing water, such as ponds and ditches, flying among fringing vegetation or sheltering in adjacent hedgerows.

The **larvae** vary from light to dark brown and the caudal lamellae usually have a rounded apex. The epicranium (post-ocular lobes and occiput) is finely covered with small dark spots. Distinguishing larvae of the Variable from other coenagrionids, however, is difficult because of variability in these characters.

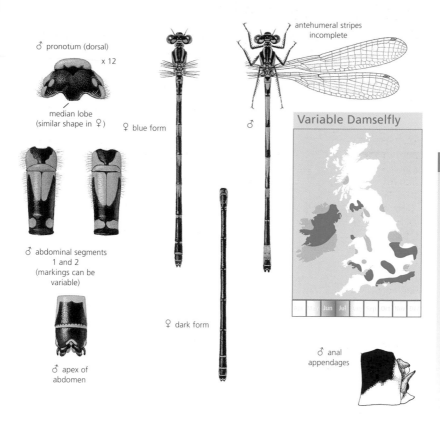

♂ pronotum (dorsal)

x 12

median lobe
(similar shape in ♀)

♀ blue form

♂ abdominal segments
1 and 2
(markings can be
variable)

♂ apex of
abdomen

♀ dark form

antehumeral stripes
incomplete

♂

Variable Damselfly

♂ anal
appendages

Emergence commences in mid May or early June but continues for much of the **flight season**, which extends into August. The maturation period is spent away from water, and immature individuals may be seen in meadows, close to hedgerows and in tall herbaceous vegetation.

Sexually mature males spend much time by the waterside, feeding among fringing vegetation. Females appear at water only to mate and to oviposit, spending most of their time away from water in tall herbage and near hedgerows which provide shelter. Copulation occurs at or near water and is completed within 10-15 minutes, to be followed by oviposition in various living or decomposing plant tissues such as Canadian pondweeds (*Elodea*), pondweeds (*Potamogeton*), Water Mint (*Mentha aquatica*), and water-lilies (*Nymphaea* and *Nuphar*). When water-lilies are used, the eggs are preferentially laid in old, decaying and torn leaves. The female will oviposit only if she can reach the underside, especially through holes in the water-lily leaf. Tandems are attracted to oviposition sites by the presence of other pairs that are already ovipositing. The male and female remain in tandem during egg-laying, and the female often descends partially below the water surface to reach suitable plant material for oviposition. After a batch of eggs has been laid, the male assists his mate to fly clear of the water before the pair finds a new oviposition site or they separate. When the tandem is broken, the female normally leaves the waterside to allow further eggs to mature before returning and mating again. The eggs hatch in about one month, and in France larval development is completed in just under one year. The life history is probably similar in Britain, except that it is to be expected that a proportion of the population will have a two-year life cycle in the north of its range.

Mike Parr

Norfolk Damselfly
Coenagrion armatum (Charpentier)

Description

Jizz This is a delicate, slender damselfly with a low, strong flight among dense emergent vegetation.

Field characters Ab 22-26mm; hw 16-20mm. Both males and females are predominantly bronze-black. Males have strikingly long, curved inferior appendages at the tip of the abdomen which are about twice as long as abdominal segment 10 and can be clearly visible in flight. The greenish-blue abdominal markings are restricted to the base of the abdomen and segments 8 and 9, while the top of the thorax is almost entirely black. The female has broad emerald-green antehumeral stripes and prominent greenish-blue patches at the base of the abdomen and towards the tip on segment 8. The very narrow, elongate posterior margin of the pronotum is diagnostic in females.

Similar species Resembles other blue-and-black damselflies, but males are most likely to be confused with Blue-tailed or Red-eyed Damselflies, which have a similar distribution of blue markings.

Status and conservation

The species is apparently extinct in Britain. It was first discovered in 1902 at Stalham, Norfolk, and subsequently found at Sutton and Hickling Broads. It was last recorded in 1957. The loss of the species can be attributed to the encroachment of reed, sallow and alder carr and the drying-out of the habitat. In Europe the species has a boreal distribution, with its stronghold in Scandinavia and the Baltic regions, eastwards to Siberia and Mongolia.

Ecology and behaviour

Habitat The species typically breeds in ponds, ditches and slow-flowing rivers of moderate nutrient enrichment with dense aquatic vegetation and extensive beds of reeds and sedges.

The **larvae** live among submerged aquatic plants. The life cycle is probably completed in one year. The **flight season** in eastern England was from late May to mid July. Mature males fly among dense emergent vegetation and frequently settle on the leaves of floating vegetation. Males are thought to display to females with a courtship dance prior to mating. Females oviposit directly into the stems and leaves of aquatic plants, in particular Frogbit (*Hydrocharis morsus-ranae*).

Steve Brooks

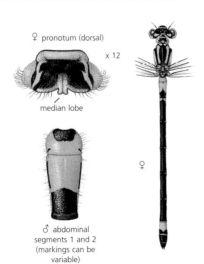

♀ pronotum (dorsal)

x 12

median lobe

♀

♂ abdominal segments 1 and 2 (markings can be variable)

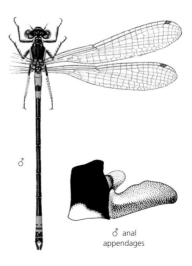

♂

♂ anal appendages

Dainty Damselfly
Coenagrion scitulum (Rambur)

Description

Jizz The Dainty Damselfly has similar behaviour and style of flight to other blue damselflies found in the British Isles. In flight, the small size and dark appearance of the male can offer a useful clue.

Field characters Ab 22-26mm; hw 15-20mm. The lemon-yellow on the underside of the head, thorax and abdomen is striking in perched specimens. Because the Dainty Damselfly is now extinct in Britain, accurate identification of claimed British specimens is very important. This calls for close, detailed examination in the hand. The Dainty Damselfly could be confused with any of the other blue damselfly species but is characterised by the shape of the pterostigma, which is almost twice as long as it is wide. In contrast, all other blue-and-black damselflies have pterostigmata that are almost as wide as they are long.

In male Dainty Damselflies, the black marking on top of abdominal segment 2 is typically U-shaped and is generally connected by a narrow stalk to the black ring at the apex of segment 3. This marking can be subject to much variation and is an unreliable character. Occasionally it may be so reduced that it can resemble the marking seen on the male Common Blue Damselfly. Similarly, the marking can resemble that of the Azure and Variable Damselflies. The female Dainty Damselfly most closely resembles the female Common Blue (but lacks the spine on the underside of the eighth abdominal segment of that species) and Southern Blue. The shape of the pronotum, however, is diagnostic.

Similar species Compared with the Azure and Variable Damselflies, with which it may occur, the male Dainty appears slightly smaller and has slightly more extensive dorsal black markings on segments 5, 6 and 7. It most closely resembles the Southern Damselfly in stature and markings and is best separated from it by the shape of the anal appendages. In the Dainty, when viewed laterally, the superior appendages are longer than the inferiors, quite unlike any of the similar species mentioned.

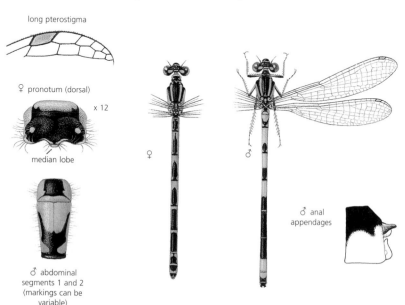

long pterostigma

♀ pronotum (dorsal)

x 12

median lobe

♂ abdominal segments 1 and 2 (markings can be variable)

♀

♂

♂ anal appendages

Status and conservation

The Dainty Damselfly is now considered to be extinct in the British Isles. Previously confined to Essex, it was known there only between 1946 and 1953. The first specimens (one male and two females) were caught on the coastal marshes of south-east Essex near Benfleet. Some time later, a pond near Hadleigh was shown to be a major breeding site. Sadly, it was not to be long before catastrophe struck. In early 1953, sea defences were breached, leading to severe floods. All known breeding sites were affected. Despite diligent searches, the insect was not seen again.

Various theories have been suggested as to how this insect came to colonise the Essex marshes. It was, perhaps, a chance colonisation from wind-borne or ship-borne migrants, but we shall never know for certain. The Dainty Damselfly is largely confined to Mediterranean regions of Europe, but it is not uncommon, locally, in parts of western, southern and north-central France and has also been known to breed in the Channel Islands. In France, it appears to have been much overlooked until recent years.

Ecology and behaviour

Habitat In continental Europe, the Dainty Damselfly appears to be very tolerant of a wide range of conditions, occupying habitats from large lakes to small seepages and streams. Breeding sites may be mesotrophic to eutrophic and are usually well vegetated, with an abundance of emergent and submerged vegetation such as water-milfoils (*Myriophyllum*) and hornworts (*Cerato-phyllum*). The species is frequently found on the ditches and dykes of coastal marshes, becoming less frequent in the highly saline waters close to the sea. However, it would appear that the larva is capable of tolerating a moderate degree of salinity. Open sunny locations appear to be preferred.

The eggs take about six weeks to hatch and larval development takes just under one year. The **larvae** are generally found clinging to submerged vegetation in shallow water. In Essex, the Dainty Damselfly occupied ditches and drains on the Thames marshes near Benfleet and Hadleigh. At the time of its original discovery, the ditches were described as stagnant and full of Spiked Water-milfoil (*Myriophyllum spicatum*) and Sea Club-rush (*Bolboschoenus maritimus*). The main breeding site had abundant Common Water-crowfoot (*Ranunculus aquatilis*).

Adults begin to **emerge** towards the last week of May and the **flight season** lasts until the end of July. Emergence generally takes place in the morning, even on cool, cloudy days. Dispersal by tenerals is directed away from water, but it would appear that the bulk of the population rarely moves more than a few hundred metres from the breeding site. On open coastal marshes close to the Loire estuary in France, tenerals were seen to confine themselves to the relative shelter of long grass on adjacent grazing land.

Mating behaviour appears to be of the manner typical of the genus. During oviposition the male and female remain in tandem, the female probing and inserting eggs within floating vegetation. During this process, the male is said to adopt an unusual, characteristic, forward-slanting attitude rather than the more typical vertical posture. But perhaps it is the strength of the prevailing wind that influences the male posture. Single mature males are often seen settled upon exposed floating plant material well away from the margin of the waterbody, and interact quickly with other males that fly or settle nearby. Detailed studies on the behaviour of this species are lacking.

Bob Kemp

Common Blue Damselfly
Enallagma cyathigerum (Charpentier)

Description

Jizz Males are bright blue and often numerous near still or slow-flowing water-bodies. Pairs in tandem and single males fly fast and low over water, sometimes up to several hundred metres from the bank. Often observed in tandem flying towards, or as single males perched at, the water's edge, they sometimes occur in clusters of many hundreds of individuals. Males are often encountered 100m or more away from the pond, flying among tall grass. In dull, cool weather they perch among grass or bushes inland.

Field characters Ab 24-28mm; hw 18-21mm. Males can be distinguished from other blue damselflies by the club-shaped black mark on top of segment 2 and by the all-blue upper surface of segments 8 and 9, which often appear to be brighter blue than other segments. Females can be distin-guished from all species except the blue-tailed damselflies (*Ischnura*) by the medial spine on the underside of segment 8.

Similar species This species often flies with the Azure Damselfly, but the Azure prefers less open sites and seldom ventures as far out over the water, and its flight is less powerful. Common Blues also occur with any of the

Larva of Common Blue Damselfly. Note the narrow bands on the caudal lamellae.

other *Coenagrion* species from which they can be distinguished by the presence of a single short stripe on the side of the thorax, the marking on segment 2 of the abdomen or the shape of the pronotum.

Status and conservation

This is one of the commonest dragonflies in all parts of Great Britain and Ireland and is often abundant. It occurs across a wide range of altitudes and latitudes and is the only breeding dragonfly in the Shetlands. In Europe the species is widespread, but absent from much of the Mediterranean.

It is not threatened, but it may become less common as sites develop dense stands of emergent vegetation which begin to encroach on the open-water habitats that it favours.

Ecology and behaviour

Habitat The Common Blue Damselfly occurs in a great variety of habitats, including gravel pits, lakes, ponds, slow rivers and canals, as well as Scottish lochs, alkaline and acid waters and habitats varying greatly in size.

The **larvae** closely resemble other coenagri-onids, but late-stadium specimens may be distinguished by the presence of 1-3 narrow, transverse bands near the middle of the

lamellae. They are ambush predators occurring at high densities in gravel pits among submerged water plants such as Canadian pondweeds (*Elodea*) and pondweeds (*Potamogeton*). They rarely interact with other larvae or defend feeding sites. Since they occur in habitats often with abundant fish populations, their relative passivity may protect them from predation. Development takes about a year in the south, but 2-4 years in the north.

Emergence occurs at any time during warm days from May onwards, with tenerals still being found in August or September. This is a typical 'summer species' with no diapause. Since the larvae may inhabit dense patches of vegetation far from shores, they may have to make long migrations underwater to find suitable plants for emergence. Having reached the shore, they sometimes travel many metres inland prior to emergence. After emergence, tenerals typically fly upwards and inland to perch on bushes or trees. Maturation, which lasts for 10-14 days depending on the weather, may occur several hundred metres from the water. The **flight season** lasts until early September.

When feeding, the damselflies take up prominent perches on low vegetation and fly off in pursuit of passing prey. They also actively search for prey among vegetation, hovering over settled insects such as aphids, then pouncing and capturing them with their legs. They commonly attack dark spots on leaves, apparently mistaking them for small insects.

Individuals often clump at certain points around lake or gravel-pit margins, usually where they are sheltered from wind but in the sun. It is not known if they are congregating at an optimal site or are responding to each other gregariously.

In sunny weather, tandems are commonly formed in the morning, often 100-200m from the water where feeding occurs. Copulation takes place either well away from water or after a pair has flown towards the water. It lasts about 20-30 minutes and has three well-marked stages. The first and longest is concerned with sperm removal from the female, and the second with sperm transfer. The third passive stage may allow sperm to reach the spermathecae. Copulation is often interrupted by brief flights, sometimes with the genitalia uncoupling.

After copulation, pairs make their way in tandem to water, passing high over any surrounding bushes or trees, and then seek oviposition sites. They may oviposit close to the shore or fly out several hundred metres low over the open water surface. The female oviposits either in tandem on vegetation at the surface or alone after climbing down on submerged vegetation, the latter occurring particularly when population densities are high. The male normally releases the female as soon as she is below the surface unless there is strong harassment from other males, when he may retain the tandem grip until after he is completely submerged. The female may spend up to 60 minutes submerged, placing eggs individually into the stems of plants such as Canadian pondweeds, water-milfoils (*Myriophyllum*) and bur-reeds (*Sparganium*) and also into the roots of willows and other plants. The male may guard the female's point of descent, but at high densities he soon abandons her.

When oviposition is complete, and sometimes before, a female releases her grip and floats to the surface, flexing her abdomen as she does so. The presence of a struggling female trapped in the surface meniscus excites males to attempt rescue. A successful male drags, or more usually lifts, a female in tandem and flies with her to the water margin, where he invites copulation. A female still containing some ripe eggs may accept copulation and afterwards resume egg-laying. Females sometimes surface spontaneously and then climb down again to continue oviposition, perhaps thereby renewing the air attached to the outside of their body on which they depend for respiration. After a brief submergence a female may be capable of taking off from the water surface without assistance, but after more than about 5-10 minutes most females become so waterlogged that they become trapped in the meniscus. However, they may be able to propel themselves along the water surface by beating their fore wings, which remain dry between the hind wings during a dive.

The species is active only on warm days, usually when the sun shines. At temperatures below about 5°C blue males turn grey, and this may be of thermoregulatory significance.

Peter Miller

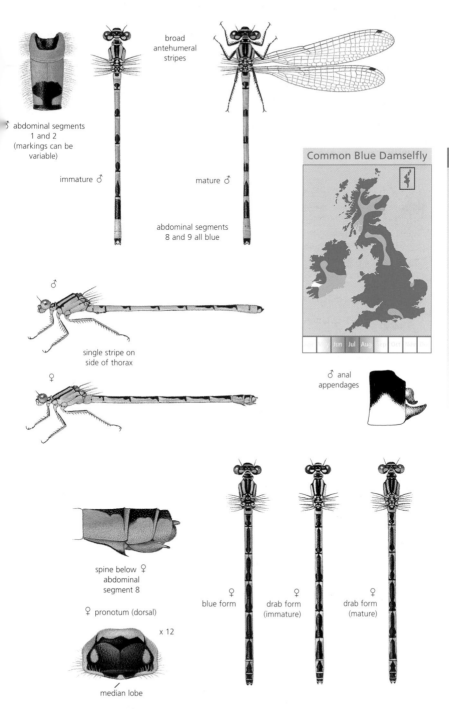

abdominal segments
1 and 2
(markings can be
variable)

broad
antehumeral
stripes

immature ♂

mature ♂

abdominal segments
8 and 9 all blue

Common Blue Damselfly

♂

single stripe on
side of thorax

♀

♂ anal
appendages

Jun Jul Aug

spine below ♀
abdominal
segment 8

♀ pronotum (dorsal)

x 12

median lobe

♀
blue form

♀
drab form
(immature)

♀
drab form
(mature)

Scarce Blue-tailed Damselfly
Ischnura pumilio (Charpentier)

Description

Jizz Adults of both sexes are most often encountered either flying or settled in low vegetation at shallow flushes and breeding pools. First impressions are of a small, weak-flying damselfly with a somewhat jerky flight.
Field characters Ab 21-25mm; hw 14-18mm. Males typically are black, with a blue tip to the abdomen, and with green or blue sides to the thorax. The black abdomen has segment 9 predominantly blue, with two small black spots, and a small portion of the posterior dorsal surface of segment 8 also blue. Markings on the thorax of males develop from a pale drab straw coloration in newly emerged specimens, through green and turquoise to deep blue in mature individuals.

Females are unlike males but also undergo age-related colour changes, which develop from bright orange of the *aurantiaca* phase through to greeny-brown in more mature individuals.
Similar species Males can easily be confused with the more common Blue-tailed Damselfly and should be netted and carefully examined. Males of the Blue-tail have segment 8 all blue and segment 9 black. Mature females are less likely to be mistaken for other species. However, the female Small Red Damselfly var. *melanogastrum* appears similar and occasionally occurs at the same bog sites. Male Scarce Blue-tails have been recorded mating with this form.

Status and conservation

The Scarce Blue-tail occurs at scattered sites across southern Britain and Ireland. In Europe it has a southerly distribution.

Although showing some range expansion in recent years, the species has very specific habitat requirements. The insect remains threatened in many areas owing to the limited availability of habitat for colonisation. Colonies appear to undergo considerable fluctuations as habitat conditions change, and the species may be eliminated from sites in which seral successional development is allowed to proceed and open habitats develop dense vegetation.

Ecology and behaviour

Habitat The Scarce Blue-tail has a strong preference for shallow-water conditions with little vegetation, such as occur in valley mires and some earth-extraction sites. At man-made sites, the Scarce Blue-tail occurs at spring-fed seepages and shallow pools in areas of active workings. Water-filled vehicle tracks also provide suitable micro-habitat at such sites.

A common feature of most sites is a degree of habitat disturbance which perpetuates bare substrates and openness of vegetation. Grazing and trampling by livestock maintain favourable conditions at some sites.

The **larvae** live in or on silty substrates in shallow water which support lower plants or are in the early stages of colonisation by higher plants. Such conditions offer little shade, maintaining relatively high water temperatures which enable rapid larval development within one year. The larvae are very similar to the Common Blue-tail but tend to lack the dark banding on the femora. They often take on the colour of the background by becoming coated with small particles of substrate. Larvae occasionally fall prey to surface-dwelling spiders which are attracted to movements below the water's surface.

The **emergence** period begins in late May and continues through to July, with a peak in mid June. Emergence takes place throughout the morning under favourable conditions but, when delayed by cool, overcast conditions, a sudden warm spell will trigger emergence at other times of the day. Larvae climb 2-3cm above the water surface, using stems emerging directly from the water. Freshly emerged teneral adults are dull brown but develop brighter colours by the following day. During the maturation period, adults remain in vegetation close to the emergence site. The **flight season** lasts until early September.

Mature adult males perch low down on vegetation at the breeding areas, awaiting females. They are quick to investigate any passing damselfly and will vigorously pursue a likely-looking female. Colour appears not

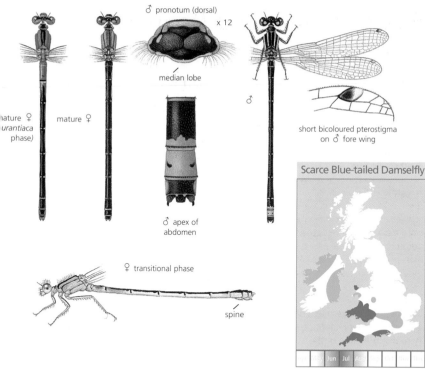

♂ pronotum (dorsal)

x 12

median lobe

immature ♀
(aurantiaca
phase)

mature ♀

♂

♂ apex of
abdomen

short bicoloured pterostigma
on ♂ fore wing

♀ transitional phase

spine

Jun Jul Au

to be the main attraction stimulus as males will readily form tandem not only with green or brown mature females, but also with the bright orange immature *aurantiaca* females which do not contain mature eggs. At present, it is not known whether immature females are able to store sperm until the eggs mature.

Females are pursued in flight, and tandem linkage is often completed on the ground or in vegetation after an initial struggle. Copulation is initiated while the pair is perched, but mating pairs are frequently seen in flight. Mating may take in excess of 90 minutes. After copulation, the pair perches briefly in post-copulatory tandem, before parting. However, males occasionally remain near the female to repel other males. Females oviposit unaccompanied and settle on suitable stems just above the water surface. They are usually seen laying eggs into emergent aquatic plants in shallow water. Most favoured are grasses, such as sweet-grasses (*Glyceria*) or foxtails (*Alopecurus*), rushes, especially Hard Rush (*Juncus inflexus*) and Jointed Rush (*J. articulatus*), and spike-rushes, such as Common Spike-rush

(*Eleocharis palustris*). The abdomen is curved strongly, enabling the ovipositor to be thrust into the plant tissue. Egg-laying commences just above water level, and as each egg is laid the female descends into the water until the effects of surface tension on the thorax prevent it from entering any further. At this point, the female either moves around the stem to repeat the procedure or flies off to find another stem. Females sometimes continue to oviposit to the base of a plant stem and into the substrate. Under these circumstances the wings and abdomen become stained with mud. Eggs are laid vertically above each other under the surface layers of the stem. Synchronised hatching of eggs has been observed after 17 days.

Rapid larval development and high adult mobility are essential attributes of a species that colonises temporary sites. On warm sunny days, with little or no cloud cover, adults fly vertically upwards in a positive and direct manner. They are assisted by rising thermals which enable them to reach high altitudes, where they are carried away by prevailing wind currents.

Steve Cham

Blue-tailed Damselfly

Ischnura elegans (Vander Linden)

Description

Jizz Both sexes fly low down among rushes, reeds and other waterside vegetation. Breeding in ponds, lakes and slow-flowing water, the species may be seen almost anywhere, even at long distances from water.

Field characters Ab 22-29mm; hw 14-20mm. Because of the range of colour forms, which are genetically and age-determined, individuals vary widely in appearance. Males appear dark, having a metallic black abdomen, but with a bright blue segment 8 and a green or blue thorax. Females may have the same colour pattern as males, or be predominantly various combinations of black, green, orange and violet. Immature males have a predominantly green thorax, which changes to blue-green after 5-6 days and then to blue within two weeks of emerging. Females commence life either as *rufescens* (reddish-pink thorax with a mid-dorsal black stripe and with segment 8 blue) or *violacea* (violet thorax with mid-dorsal black stripe, black humeral stripes and segment 8 blue). After about eight days the thorax and blue abdominal segment of *rufescens* become yellowish-brown, giving the mature form known as *rufescens-obsoleta* previously called *infuscans-obsoleta*. The *violacea* form can mature either into the *andromorph* with a male-like colour pattern, or into *infuscans* with brownish thorax, black thoracic stripes and brown segment 8.

Similar species The Blue-tailed Damselfly closely resembles the much rarer Scarce Blue-tailed Damselfly. The former is larger than its rarer relative, and the blue at the end of the male abdomen covers the whole of segment 8. In the Scarce Blue-tailed only a part of segment 8 is blue, but segment 9 is completely blue. The shapes of the pterostigma and pronotum are also different between the two species.

The Blue-tailed could also be confused with the male Red-eyed Damselfly, which is also predominantly black with a blue pruinose tip to the abdomen. However, the Red-eyed Damselfly is much more bulky than the Blue-tailed, and males of the former species are characterised by their reddish-brown eyes.

Status and conservation

The Blue-tailed is one of the commonest damselflies in Britain, occurring at all latitudes up to the north coast of Scotland. It is found throughout central Europe, but is absent from much of Scandinavia and has a restricted distribution in Spain.

Ecology and behaviour

Habitat This damselfly is an early coloniser of new ponds and tolerates a degree of pollution and brackish water. It is a ubiquitous species, although not always abundant at sites, and is extremely adaptable.

The **larvae** have narrow, pointed lamellae and prominent dark banding on the femora. They may be found among aquatic plants in the shallow water of ponds, lakes, ditches, canals and slow-flowing rivers. In southern England the life cycle is completed in one year (univoltine), but in Lancashire about 6% of the population require about 21 months to complete development (semi-voltine). Probably over much of Scotland, most individuals take two years to develop. The most common prey for large larvae are small crustaceans and midge and mayfly larvae.

At **emergence**, many larvae climb only a short distance out of the water on low-growing emergent plants. Inverted (upside-down) emergence is common, the reason for this being unknown. In northern England, the numbers emerging peak in mid June and again in July/August. The first peak consists of a mixture of semivoltine individuals and the most rapidly developing univoltine insects, emerging in that order. Second emergence peak is derived from univoltine larvae still in the penultimate and antepenultimate stages in May, which have hatched from eggs laid the previous July.

Unlike most dragonflies, the immature newly emerged Blue-tails show a strong tendency to remain close to the waterside while undergoing sexual maturation. However, some individuals are wanderers, as the species is a classic pioneer, colonising new habitats quickly. The **flight season** extends from May to September and, although some individuals may live for 7-8 weeks, the average survival time for the adult insect is about ten days.

Weather conditions are far less limiting for the Blue-tail than for many other species of dragonfly. A full range of activities may be observed in dull, windy and cool weather.

Sexual maturation of the Blue-tail is faster than for many other species: it is capable of copulation only 3-4 days after emergence. Occasionally, mating may be observed in apparently immature green males and *violacea* or *rufescens* females. Copulation commonly lasts 3-6 hours. It is probable that the long mating period acts as a form of guarding of the female, preventing her from mating again. Unlike many damselflies, the female oviposits alone and often late in the day when most male activity has ceased. The eggs are placed in slits cut in aquatic vegetation. In contrast to other damselflies, the females are often seen at water. Feeding methods include both aerial capture and picking small settled insects off vegetation. They will also feed on spiders, and have been seen to glean small flies from a spider's web while the owner was in residence!

Mike Parr

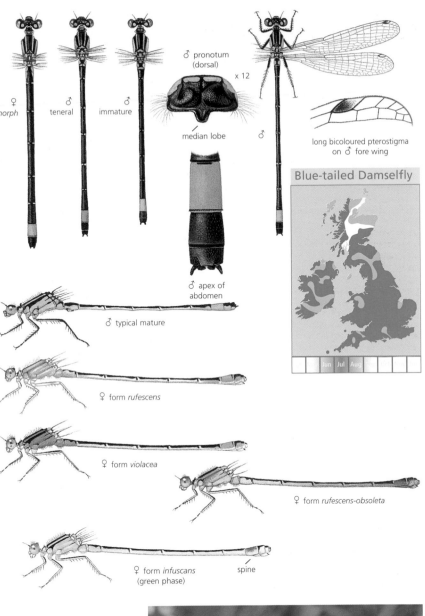

♀ *morph*

♂ teneral

♂ immature

♂ pronotum (dorsal) × 12

median lobe

♂

long bicoloured pterostigma on ♂ fore wing

♂ apex of abdomen

Blue-tailed Damselfly

Jun Jul Aug

♂ typical mature

♀ form *rufescens*

♀ form *violacea*

♀ form *rufescens-obsoleta*

♀ form *infuscans* (green phase)

spine

Female Blue-tailed Damselfly form *violacea*.

Red-eyed Damselfly
Erythromma najas (Hansemann)

Description

Jizz Adult males are most often encountered over water, away from the bank, where they are best observed through binoculars. They typically spend long periods of time perched on the floating leaves of waterplants and mats of algae. The powerful, hovering flight is low over the water's surface as they make sorties to capture prey or to see off rival males.

Field characters Ab 25-30mm; hw 19-24mm. As the name suggests, males can be readily identified by the blood-red eyes but also by the blue pruinose tip to the abdomen, which are conspicuous even at a distance through binoculars. In females, the brown-red eyes are less distinctive and the blue tail is lacking. Adults appear more robust and have a stronger and more purposeful flight than other damselflies, especially when other species are present for comparison.

Similar species The males of the Red-eyed Damselfly can resemble blue-tailed damselflies, but the latter are much more slender, lack the distinctive red eyes and have abdominal segment 8 blue rather than segments 9 and 10. Female Red-eyes undergo age-related colour changes from yellow to green and could be confused with females of other coenagrionids. The metallic black-green body can also lead to confusion with emerald damselflies, although these are generally brighter green. Close examination of the eyes and the unmarked all-black abdomen (except for narrow blue rings between the rear segments) will separate females of this species from other common damselflies. See also Small Red Damselfly.

Status and conservation

The Red-eyed Damselfly has a southern distribution in England and the Welsh borders, where it is locally common. It becomes less frequent in south-west England. Over the last two decades there appears to have been a westward and northward range expansion. In Europe the species has a central distribution and is absent from the far north and Mediterranean regions.

Excessive clearance or increased water velocity, which reduces the amount of floating vegetation, will have a negative impact on this species.

Ecology and behaviour

Habitat The Red-eyed Damselfly favours still-water habitats with large expanses of floating vegetation. Especially favoured are the leaves of Yellow (*Nuphar lutea*) and White Water-lilies (*Nymphaea alba*), Fringed Water-lily (*Nymphoides peltata*), Broad-leaved Pondweed (*Potamogeton natans*) and Amphibious Bistort (*Polygonum amphibium*). It is also found on slow-moving rivers and canals where waterflow is sufficiently sluggish to encourage water-lilies and plants with similar floating leaves. The presence of large floating mats of algae has led to colonisation of some sites which would otherwise be unattractive to this species.

The **larvae** can be found among submerged vegetation of various types at breeding sites, and can take up to two years to develop. They are distinctive, appearing larger and more robust than other coenagrionid species. The abdomen often has a banded appearance, and the characteristic caudal lamellae have dark banding in the apical half with rounded tips. There is a very clear median node before the banding. The ground colour of larvae is variable, ranging from brown to green depending on the type of aquatic plants on which they are living. They are highly active and will readily use the caudal lamellae to propel themselves through the water.

Emergence begins in mid May in warm springs, with adult numbers reaching a peak in June and early July. Emergent vegetation of various types is used for emergence, which can take place throughout the day. To avoid competition at breeding sites, immature adults and females move into surrounding areas, where they are usually encountered among low bushes and tall grasses. The **flight season** lasts until mid August.

On returning to the water, mature males will adopt floating vegetation as territorial platforms, which they will defend from rivals. In the presence of the more aggressive male Common Blues, however, they are often forced to move well away from the lake margins to avoid competition.

Mating can take place either over the water or in bankside vegetation. Pairs remain in tandem during egg-laying, this serving as an efficient mechanism for fending off other males when competition is high. The eggs are usually laid into the undersides of floating vegetation, especially lily pads, although emergent plants are also used. Where Red-eyes occur at waters devoid of floating vegetation, they will use the flowering stems of submerged pondweeds. Oviposition has also been recorded into the tissue of dead bulrush (*Typha*). Tandem pairs will often descend more than 0.5m below the water's surface and in some cases have been recorded to stay submerged for more than 30 minutes during oviposition. The female retains a large bubble of air around her thoracic spiracles, providing oxygen for respiration during periods of prolonged submergence. The male sometimes releases the female, leaving her to continue to oviposit underwater alone. On completion of her task, she releases her grip of the plant stem and rises to the surface, aided by the bubble of air trapped between the wings and body.

Steve Cham

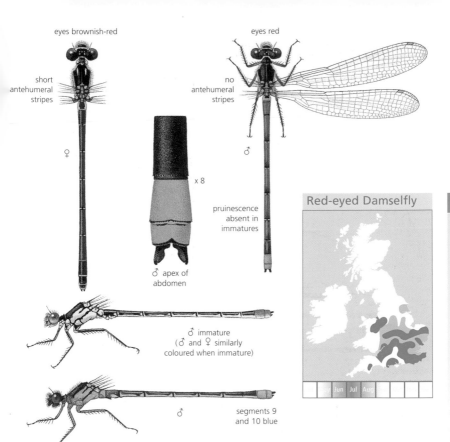

eyes brownish-red

short antehumeral stripes

♀

eyes red

no antehumeral stripes

♂

× 8

pruinescence absent in immatures

♂ apex of abdomen

Red-eyed Damselfly

Jun Jul Aug

♂ immature
(♂ and ♀ similarly coloured when immature)

♂

segments 9 and 10 blue

Final stadium larva of Red-eyed Damselfly.

Small Red-eyed Damselfly
Erythromma viridulum (Charpentier)

Description

Jizz Like the larger Red-eyed Damselfly, adults are most often seen away from banks where they spend long periods perched on floating vegetation, as well as algal mats. Unlike the Red-eyed Damselfly, they often curve their abdomen upwards when at rest. It has a low, hovering flight. **Field characters** Ab 22-25mm; hw 16-20mm. The red eyes and blue tip to the abdomen of the male should separate this species, except from male Red-eyed. The extent of the blue markings on the abdomen of the male is the most distinctive characteristic. In lateral view the sides of abdominal segments 2 and 8 are entirely blue, whereas in Red-eyed they are almost totally black. The abdomen often appears to have a metallic reflection under bright conditions, but the Red-eyed Damselfly develops varying amounts of blue pruinescence along the abdomen, making it less reflective. When viewed from above, abdominal segment 10 shows reduced blue markings on the dorsal surface compared with Red-eyed. This has the effect of creating a black 'X' mark, which is diagnostic. In Red-eyed, segment 10 is blue all over. The eyes of Red-eyed are a deep burgundy-red, whereas those of Small Red-eyed can appear a brighter tomato-red, but this feature can vary according to the light. When at rest the wings of Small Red-eyed Damselfly extend just past the join between segments 6 and 7 giving the impression of shorter wings. In the Red-eyed Damselfly the wings extend over segment 8.

Female red-eyed damselflies are less distinct. They lack the post-ocular spots that are present in *Coenagrion* species. The female Small Red-eyed has a bold antehumeral stripe that forms a complete line, whereas the female Red-eyed has a reduced line, often breaking up to form an exclamation mark. The colour of the thorax can vary with age, changing from yellow to green and to blue. The blue form of female is distinctive. **Similar species** Apart from Red-eyed Damselfly, could be confused at a distance with the Blue-tailed Damselfly, but males of this species lack the distinctive red eyes.

Status and conservation

This species was first discovered in Essex in July 1999. In 2000 it was recorded at more sites in Essex as well as a number of sites on the Isle of Wight. A large influx from the Continent in 2001 led to its discovery at numerous sites along the coast of south-east England from the Isle of Wight to north Norfolk. This influx also led to dispersal inland with the furthest sites to date in Bedfordshire and Buckinghamshire. Breeding was confirmed at several sites in 2002 and it seems to be consolidating its population. On the Continent it has been extending its range in recent years.

Ecology and behaviour

Habitat It favours eutrophic waters, such as lakes, gravel pits and ponds with floating vegetation, including hornwort (*Ceratophyllum*), water-milfoil (*Myriophyllum*) and waterweed (*Elodea*). The **larvae** lack the distinctive dark banding on the caudal lamellae found in Red-eyed larvae. **Emergence** of this species on the Continent is usually 2-3 weeks later than in Red-eyed, reaching a peak between the end of July and the middle of August.

Steve Cham

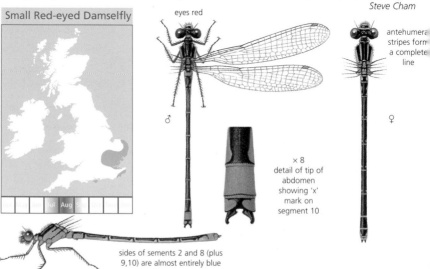

Small Red-eyed Damselfly

eyes red

antehumeral stripes form a complete line

♂

♀

×8 detail of tip of abdomen showing 'x' mark on segment 10

Jul Aug

sides of sements 2 and 8 (plus 9,10) are almost entirely blue

ANISOPTERA
Dragonflies

This sub-order of the Odonata comprises small to large dragonflies with strong, powerful flight. All the species characteristically hold their wings open when at rest. The fore wings are narrower than the hind wings. The heads are globular with the eyes wrapping round the top, front and sides. In Great Britain and Ireland there are 23 resident species, a further one is now extinct, and another 11 species occur as non-breeding migrants or occasional breeders.

Male Brilliant Emerald, Scotland, July.

AESHNIDAE
Hawker dragonflies

These are medium to large dragonflies with restless, hawking flight. The eyes occupy most of the head. When at rest they hang down from branches. They are mainly restricted to standing-water habitats. There are eight resident species among the genera *Aeshna*, *Anax* and *Brachytron*.

Hairy Dragonfly
Brachytron pratense (Müller)

Description

Jizz This is the first hawker dragonfly of the year on the wing. Males are usually seen patrolling still waterbodies during May and early June. They have a typical low-level zig-zagging flight in and out of clearings among fringing reeds and other vegetation. Clashes are frequent between rival males with adjacent territories. Males quickly disappear into cover once clouds obscure the sun. If disturbed from their resting places, the dragonflies make short flights, quickly seeking shelter again. Females are more secretive and are usually found away from water, unless pairing or ovipositing. They are fond of resting in the sun among tall vegetation or on leaves of trees.

Field characters Ab 37-46mm; hw 34-37mm. The Hairy Dragonfly has a noticeably downy thorax, unlike other hawkers, and a long thin pterostigma. The abdomen may appear to be rather dark, as the paired, blue pear-shaped spots (in male) along the body are not easily visible unless the observer is relatively close. Females have paired pale yellow spots on the abdomen.

Similar species The early appearance of this species makes confusion with other hawker dragonflies unlikely. The Emperor may be on the wing at the same time, but it is larger, and has an entirely green thorax and a black dorsal stripe on a bright blue (male) or green (female) abdomen. The flight season of the Norfolk Hawker may also overlap, but that species is pale brown with green eyes and is confined to East Anglia.

Status and conservation

Until recently, the Hairy Dragonfly was considered a rather scarce species, but it appears to be extending its range in the British Isles. A decline over the post-war period (possibly due to changes in land use and pollution), followed by an increase in numbers, which has partly coincided with a series of recent warm summers, has resulted in the species now being recorded in new areas. However, it is a rather localised insect and is not found in large numbers at any

site. Its current distribution is still predominantly confined to the southern half of Britain, although it is known from several sites in Scotland and is fairly widely distributed in central Ireland. It is widespread across western and central Europe.

It is never recorded in isolation, and is found in the presence of other dragonfly species at clean waters with lush surrounding vegetation and nearby shelter. Maintenance of such habitats is essential to conserve the species, although it appears to survive periodic ditch clearance at sites in the Somerset Levels.

Ecology and behaviour

Habitat Larvae are found in many types of clean, still waterbodies on all soils, although well-vegetated linear sites such as ditches, lodes, dykes and canals are favoured. Sites with a high diversity of plant species, such as coastal grazing marshes, are most likely to support populations.

The **larvae** are extremely difficult to find and tend to be associated with submerged plant debris, such as broken stems, roots, peat and dead vegetation. When handled, they fold their legs alongside the body and lie quiet for some minutes. They have small eyes, with prominent post-ocular lobes sloping inwards. The labium is conspicuously long and waisted, and the abdomen has a small dorsal spine on segment 9. Larval development usually takes at least two years, but there are records of development being completed in one season.

Emergence begins in early May and usually takes place in the early morning. The range of emergence sites and substrates is very wide. Height of emergence varies from a few centimetres above water to a metre or more. At some sites, emergence is confined to short stretches of bank and occasionally exuviae are found near to one another. Exuviae may be well hidden and difficult to find, particularly since they occur at a low density.

Teneral dragonflies may use long grass in adjacent fields while their wings harden after emergence. Once mature, adult males

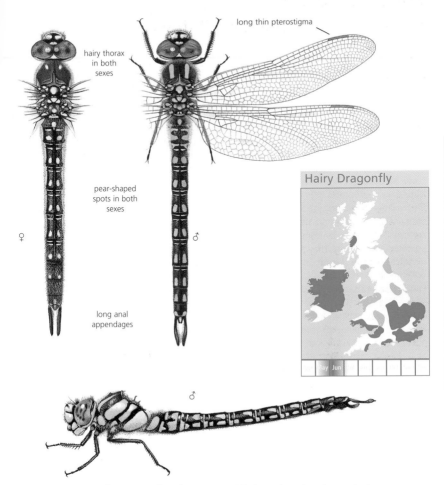

long thin pterostigma

hairy thorax in both sexes

pear-shaped spots in both sexes

♀

♂

long anal appendages

Hairy Dragonfly

May Jun

♂

appear at their patrolling sites a few days later. The **flight season** of the Hairy Dragonfly is relatively short compared with other species, generally extending from early to mid May through to late June or possibly early July.

The length of territory patrolled typically covers 25-100m, but this may vary depending on the number of males present at a site and the shape and size of the waterbody. Male Hairy Dragonflies patrolling territories also clash with other dragonfly species, such as Four-spotted Chasers and Emperors, and will readily see off the latter. When feeding, observed prey items have included insects as large as damselflies, sawflies and mayflies.

Mating takes place in nearby trees or vegetation and pairs are often disturbed from long grass. Duration of copulation is variable, but it has been observed to last over 40 minutes under cloudy skies.

Ovipositing is not often observed, but is usually into submerged plant material. Females lay eggs alone or with a nearby accompanying male. They generally insert eggs into semi-decomposing floating detritus, such as rushes, sedges or reeds and other dead or living plant stems and organic material, usually close to the water's edge. As the Hairy Dragonfly is a spring species, it lays non-diapause eggs, which hatch after 3-4 weeks.

Val Perrin

Azure Hawker
Aeshna caerulea (Ström)

Description

Jizz A medium-sized early flying hawker occurring mainly in the Scottish Highlands. It seems especially responsive to the changeable northern weather conditions. In calm, sunny conditions males are active and wary, flying low and fast as they investigate the edges of bog pools. In less settled or cooler conditions, they often bask on sunlit rocks, hummocks of *Rhacomitrium* moss or tree trunks, sometimes two or more together. In such circumstances they can be approached and may even settle on light-coloured clothing. Females also bask.

Field characters Ab 42-48mm; hw 38-41mm. The mature males show more blue than other hawkers. The short contact of the eyes (equal to length of occipital triangle), the narrow blue bands on the side of the thorax and the reduced antehumeral stripes (absent in females) are further confirmatory characters. Females have two main colour forms, in which the abdominal markings are either yellow/beige or blue. These forms are not age-dependent and are equally abundant. The blue form can sometimes be as brightly coloured as the male, though showing less blue and lacking the antehumeral stripes. In both sexes, colour intensity is lower in reduced sunlight or temperature, which can make the species quite inconspicuous on lichen- and moss-covered rocks.

Similar species The Common Hawker is the only hawker likely to be seen in the same habitats as this species, but the size and colour differences are not always easy to appreciate, especially in fast flight. The basking and settling habits are usually indicative of the Azure Hawker, and the absence of yellow on the male's abdomen is distinctive. Also, neither sex has the bright yellow costa of the Common Hawker.

Status and conservation

There are no British records outside Scotland. The species seems fairly widespread, though rarely abundant, in the western, central and northern Highlands, where fresh discoveries are still being made. There is also a stable outpost population in south-west Scotland. On the Continent, the species occurs in northern Scandinavia and the higher mountains of central Europe.

The Azure Hawker seems not to be in any obvious danger at present, but afforestation, and associated drainage of its boggy moorland breeding habitats, are by far the greatest threats and must have reduced or eliminated the species at some sites.

Ecology and behaviour

Habitat Larvae are found to some extent with the more widespread Common Hawker in shallow *Sphagnum*-rich bog pools on ill-drained plateaux, saddles and peaty valley bottoms. Suitable terrain may also occur within ancient woodlands, although woodland as such does not seem essential. Sheltered streamsides and woodlands in, or close to, the breeding habitat are used by both sexes for catching insects and basking. This habitat generally offers the best opportunities for casual observers to see this species.

Breeding activity has been noted from near sea level to at least 550m. Breeding pools may be small (e.g. 2 x 2m) and, although shallow, usually have soft vegetation detritus into which larvae can retreat to survive low water levels or harsh winter conditions. The larval stage is believed normally to extend over four seasons (overwintering in three winters).

Small, early-stadium **larvae** have been found only from mid June to early July, indicating that hatching does not take place until at least the year following oviposition. In the early weeks, young larvae remain near the water surface, clinging to floating *Sphagnum* moss. Fully grown larvae can be found in most months.

Azure Hawker larvae are rather uniformly patterned, usually with a pale area on the seventh abdominal segment. By contrast, those of the Common have, from quite an early age, a broad pale longitudinal abdominal stripe on either side of a darker midline.

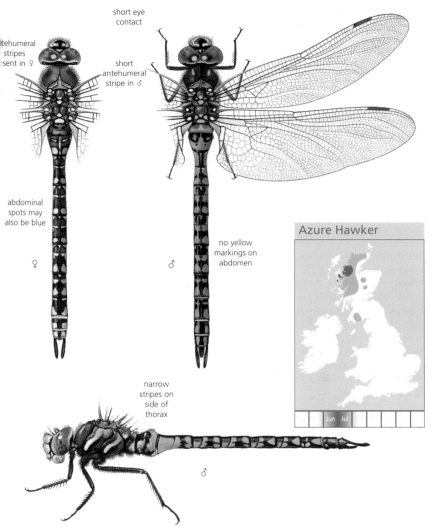

short eye
contact

antehumeral
stripes
absent in ♀

short
antehumeral
stripe in ♂

abdominal
spots may
also be blue

♀

♂

no yellow
markings on
abdomen

Azure Hawker

Jun Jul

narrow
stripes on
side of
thorax

♂

Emergence takes place close to the edges of breeding pools, where exuviae can be found on heather stems, cottongrasses (*Eriophorum*) and other supports. The Azure Hawker has a relatively early **flight season**, although emergence is not strongly synchronised. Adults can be on the wing as early as late May, but more often in mid June, and have been recorded into August.

Males seem to search for females only during sunny periods, systematically flying low around pool margins, but not remaining long at any one pool. They will sometimes seize the females of other species. An instance of a Golden-ringed Dragonfly on a

forest road becoming such a victim shows that males may be opportunistic about where they acquire females. Even when searching at pools, males may settle for short periods at or near the edge, where females might also alight: a habit not shared with the Common Hawker. Copulation lasts many minutes, and a pair in the wheel position may settle on boulders or low vegetation.

The female oviposits unaccompanied by a male. She probes with her abdomen deep into the soft, wet substrate at edges of pools or directly into moss and other vegetation in the water.

David Clarke

Common Hawker
Aeshna juncea (Linnaeus)

Description

Jizz This is a large hawker and a fast, powerful and seemingly tireless flier. Males spend long periods on the wing and rarely perch. When they do settle, in contrast to the Azure Hawker, they often use tree branches and low shrubs, rather than trunks, boulders and paths. The males show a much less positive response to people than either the Azure or the Southern Hawker, and are rarely inclined to buzz them or to settle on clothing. The species is usually alert and difficult to approach.

Field characters Ab 50-59mm; hw 40-48mm. The overall appearance of mature males is often relatively dark – at a distance the blue and yellow markings often suggest a turquoise hue. Females are usually brown with yellow markings, but the abdominal spots can be greenish; there is also a form in which the spots are blue, resembling males. The latter seems most frequent in parts of Scotland. The bright yellow costa (both sexes) is diagnostic, but not obvious in flight.

Similar species The Common Hawker can occur in some of the habitats which support the other blue-spotted species – Southern, Hairy, Migrant and Azure Hawkers – all of which are similar at first glance. The costa of all these species is brown, and not yellow as in the Common Hawker. The Southern Hawker is apple-green, and the large blotch-like antehumeral stripes of both sexes are noticeable and quite distinct from the narrow, yellow stripes of the male Common Hawker. The Hairy Hawker is distinguished by its elongate pear-shaped abdominal spots, long pterostigma, weaker flight and earlier flight season. The Migrant and Azure Hawkers are smaller, but there is potential for confusion with the Azure Hawker in Scotland, where some very blue Common Hawker males and females occur. The wings of the Common Hawker are sometimes slightly suffused with amber coloration, which can lead to momentary confusion of females with the Brown Hawker in some lights.

Status and conservation

This is a familiar species in western and northern areas of Britain, and in Ireland. It also occurs locally on some southern and eastern heathlands of England. In Europe, it is found throughout central and northern regions. Destruction of isolated sites may threaten its survival locally.

Ecology and behaviour

Habitat Breeds in a wide variety of still waters, from small moorland bog pools to large lakes. In areas where this dragonfly is common, it also occurs in garden ponds. It usually avoids alkaline waters, though it will use neutral, as well as acid, sites. Emergence has been noted from tarns above 600m on northern hills. Common Hawkers often shun the small shallow moorland pools which are used by Azure Hawkers. Solitary Common Hawkers are often seen feeding in woodland rides and other sheltered sites at considerable distances from breeding areas. Some individuals may be active until early evening.

The **larval** stage extends over at least three seasons (overwintering in two winters), and probably longer in the colder environments. The first winter is spent in the egg stage and small, early-stadium larvae appear in early summer. Young larvae are found at first near the water surface, clinging to plants or *Sphagnum* moss. Larvae are most active during the day. Larger larvae usually occur on the bottom of bog pools or clinging to low stems. They are most easily seen when pools are inspected at night by torchlight.

The larvae soon acquire their characteristic striped appearance, which persists throughout development. When dark coloration obscures the pattern, other features, such as the lateral spines on abdominal segments 7 to 9 and the relatively broad labium, assist identification. In well-grown larvae, the presence of seven antennal segments distinguishes them from the Azure Hawker, which has six.

Emergence usually occurs within about 1m of breeding pools, often in dense vegetation over water. Emerging larvae often leave the

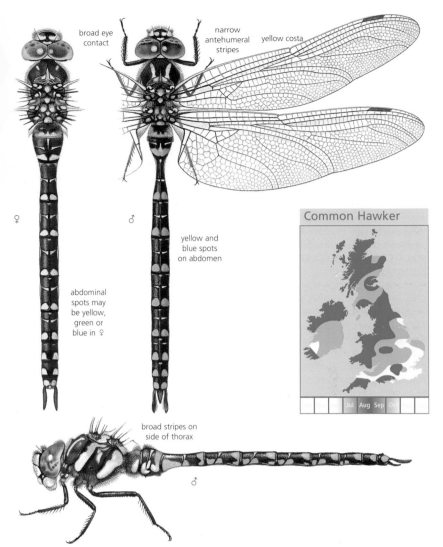

broad eye contact

narrow antehumeral stripes

yellow costa

♀

♂

yellow and blue spots on abdomen

abdominal spots may be yellow, green or blue in ♀

Common Hawker

Jul Aug Sep Oct

broad stripes on side of thorax

♂

water at night, so adults are ready for first flight in the early morning. Larval populations can be large, and exuviae close to the edges of pools are a frequent sight.

The Common Hawker is essentially a high-summer species, the main emergence commencing by early July and then continuing until at least September. Early adults can be on the wing in June and in mild seasons the **flight season** can extend into early November. Males continue to seek females in cooler, more overcast conditions than those favoured by the Azure Hawker. They systematically investigate the edges of pools, flying low over the water, where they will seize any

ovipositing female. They usually spend considerable time at a pool and interact aggressively with other large male dragonflies. Copulation is usually completed on low vegetation and lasts about one hour.

The female always oviposits alone, thrusting her abdomen below the water surface to lay the eggs into living plant tissue. She often selects the shelter of emergent vegetation, but will also stand on floating mats of *Sphagnum* moss and other plants. The rustling sound of continuous wing-whirring during such activity is often the first indication of her presence.

David Clarke

Migrant Hawker
Aeshna mixta Latrielle

Description

Jizz The Migrant Hawker is a medium-sized, late-summer and autumn dragonfly. The species is often seen flying in large numbers at treetop level in woodland glades or hedgerows. Mature males patrol low down along the edges of still and slow-moving waters, hawking and periodically hovering to look for ovipositing females.

Field characters Ab 43-49mm; hw 37-40mm. Males are predominantly blue; females appear brown and dull yellowy green. The immature Migrant Hawker has grey to pale lilac markings. On cool days the mature-male coloration may change to lilac-grey. The yellow triangle at the base of the abdomen in both sexes distinguishes the Migrant Hawker from the Common.

Similar species The Migrant Hawker is slightly smaller than the Southern and Common Hawkers. The male Southern Hawker is distinguished by the broad green antehumeral stripes and the predominantly green abdomen with the last three segments blue. The male Common Hawker has narrow, yellow antehumeral stripes; in the Migrant these stripes are much reduced in size. The male Hairy Hawker has similar sky-blue spots, but is slightly smaller, is downy, flies in early summer and has broad antehumeral stripes. The male Azure Hawker also has extensive blue markings but is confined to Scotland.

Both sexes of the Migrant Hawker have a brown costa; the Common Hawker's is diagnostically yellow. While the female Migrant Hawker is medium brown with dull yellowy green spots, the female Southern Hawker has extensive apple-green markings and the female Common Hawker has mainly lemon-coloured ones.

Status and conservation

In the 1940s this species was an uncommon migrant from southern Europe, but it has gradually extended its range from a pioneering breeding population in south-east England. Today, the majority of breeding sites are south and east of a line from Hull to south Wales, but it continues to expand north and west. The species has taken advantage of post-war gravel pits and reservoirs. In 2000, it was recorded for the first time in south-east Ireland. It is common in south-east England, with regular migrations from the Continent increasing the population in late summer. There are records of spectacular mass migrations across Europe in certain years. The species is widespread in central and southern Europe.

Ecology and behaviour

Habitat Larvae are found in ponds, lakes, gravel pits, canals and slow-moving rivers. They can also tolerate brackish water in coastal ditches, but are not found in the acidic heathland ponds in which the Common Hawker thrives.

The **larvae** hatch in early spring and grow rapidly under warm conditions throughout summer to emerge from late July to September. The rapid development of the larvae may restrict them to the warmer climate of the south, where the food supply may be more abundant earlier in the year. Larvae feed on invertebrates which they actively hunt among plants and detritus.

Emergence takes place at night in late summer and autumn. The larva crawls up a vertical plant stem of 10cm or more to emerge. The immature adult remains away from water for 7-10 days. The **flight season** lasts from late July to well into the autumn.

Large numbers of immatures can sometimes be seen feeding in open woodland, meadows, hedgerows or parks, flying high with crisscrossing flight paths and without obvious signs of aggression. They hawk back and forth along a beat, this broken occasionally by periodic soaring to a greater height after prey. Feeding occurs mainly in the afternoon and early evening. Migrant Hawkers that are seen flying high over open water are probably feeding, and not involved in territorial or sexual behaviour. Adults can be seen as late as November, hawking and sunning themselves on sheltered vegetation. Sunbathing most often occurs in the morning or after foraging. They prefer a site

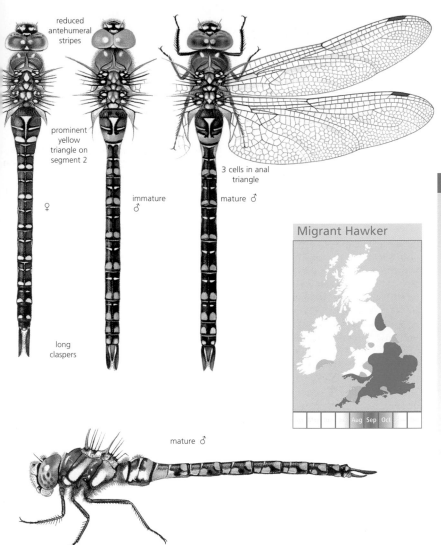

reduced antehumeral stripes

prominent yellow triangle on segment 2

♀

long claspers

immature ♂

mature ♂

3 cells in anal triangle

Migrant Hawker

Aug Sep Oct

mature ♂

low down, sheltered and facing the sun, with a clear escape flight path. When perched, the body hangs vertically, oriented to catch the most sunlight.

Mature males visit open water during the middle of the day and may remain into late afternoon. Each male will take up a shoreline territory which it patrols without showing a great deal of aggression towards other males. Flight is low over the water, with inquisitive hovering at any bays or breaks in marginal vegetation in search of females. A female will be chased vigorously and, if possible, the two insects will pair in flight

before settling in a tree or among shoreline vegetation to copulate for a lengthy period of time. The female usually oviposits alone, although tandem oviposition has been recorded. Eggs are laid in stems of plants such as bulrush (*Typha*) and Yellow Flag (*Iris pseudacorus*) by the water's edge, quite often above the water-line in anticipation of rising water levels before the next spring. With this strategy the eggs are probably safer from predators. Females have been observed ovipositing in bare mud as well. The eggs diapause in winter.

Andrew McGeeney

Southern Hawker
Aeshna cyanea (Müller)

Description

Jizz This is a large hawker dragonfly, which is usually solitary, and flies from mid to late summer. Characteristically, males will fly near an observer, hovering low to inspect the person before returning to their regular beat. In flight, the body is held horizontally and the abdomen has a slight curve.

Field characters Ab 51-60mm; hw 43-51mm. Males are marked bright green, becoming blue towards the tip of the abdomen, on a dark background. Females have a stouter abdomen and are patterned in yellow and green. Abdominal segments 9 and 10 have a dorsal stripe rather than spots. Both sexes of the Southern Hawker have two thick green or yellow antehumeral stripes. The wings are colourless when mature but acquire an amber tint with old age.

Similar species Common and Migrant Hawkers are similar, but have more blue markings. They also have thin or almost non-existent antehumeral stripes. The Hairy Dragonfly is slightly smaller, has an earlier flight period, shows a hairy thorax and lacks green abdominal markings.

Status and conservation

The Southern Hawker is very common in lowland England and Wales, becoming more local further north, with a isolated populations in Scotland and south-west Ireland. There is evidence that it is expanding its range in the north. It is widespread on the Continent.

The main threats to its survival are pollution, dredging, and infilling of ponds.

Ecology and behaviour

Habitat Commonly breeds in woodland ponds, lakes and canals. Often found in urban areas, such as park ponds and small garden pools. It may be attracted into gardens because of their resemblance to woodland clearings. Adults are frequently encountered along woodland rides.

The eggs remain dormant during winter and the larvae hatch in early spring. **Larvae** live among submerged plants and leaf-litter,

feeding on invertebrates. As they increase in size, in the second spring before emerging, they take advantage of larger prey, such as tadpoles and small fish. Large larvae can be distinguished from other hawkers by the narrow labium and characteristic arrangement of abdominal spines. Young larvae have a distinctive banded pattern which helps to camouflage them from predators, including others of their own species.

Emergence occurs any time after mid to late June. When the larva is fully mature it moves to shallow water, and finally leaves its aquatic habitat after nightfall by climbing a reed or dead twig, to transform before dawn, although emerging adults may be found at any time during the day. For the next few days the body colours are paler than those of the mature adult; most of the light markings are pale creamy-yellow.

The **flight season** lasts from July to October. Adults spend most of their time feeding in woodland rides, along hedgerows and in urban gardens, occasionally settling to bask or rest in cooler weather. After dark, their presence may sometimes be detected only by the sound of their wings.

Males are territorial; a small pond may be sufficient for a solitary individual, but larger ponds or canals may have a widely spaced population along the banks, with, on average, one male every 50m. The flight of the male is purposeful and regular at about a metre above the ground, higher when over open water, searching among the inlets and small gaps in vegetation for a receptive female. The male may fly out of sight before returning along a regular path. Occasionally it pauses to hover, before turning back on to its beat or to attack other hawker dragonflies.

Southern Hawker males will time-share a favourable site with other males, each making a visit of 10-40 minutes. The length of stay is determined in part by population density: the more males, the shorter but more frequent each visit. Males clash when they encounter each other, the outcome determined by how long an individual has been at the site. If a male is attacked early

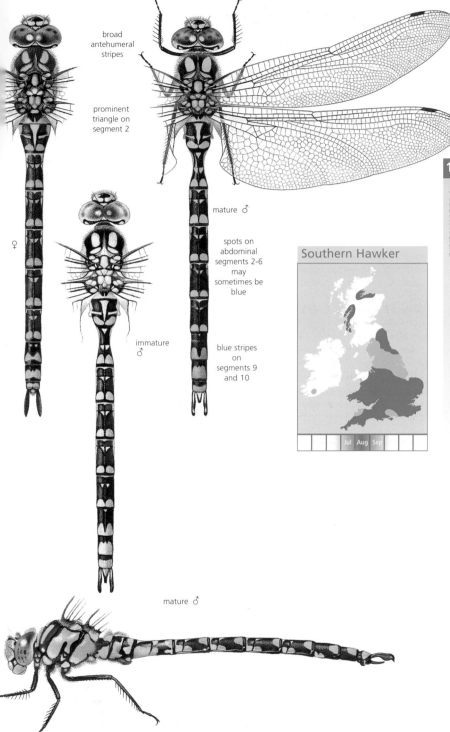

broad
antehumeral
stripes

prominent
triangle on
segment 2

mature ♂

spots on
abdominal
segments 2-6
may
sometimes be
blue

blue stripes
on
segments 9
and 10

♀

immature
♂

mature ♂

Southern Hawker

Jul Aug Sep

on in its stay, the territory is vigorously defended. At low densities, males will make long patrol flights without any territorial attachment.

Warm afternoons attract the highest number of receptive females to a rendezvous site, each female visiting once or twice every third day. Young females usually arrive in the morning to maximise their chance of meeting a territorial male. As they fly along the shore they are more noticeable than egg-laying females, who are rather secretive. After a short twisting chase, a resident male clasps the female and they fly off in the wheel position. The number of pairings peaks around midday. Copulation takes place away from water, frequently high up in trees, and can last for two hours. Non-receptive females usually come to oviposit in the early morning and evening (or even at midday on cool overcast days), when they are less likely to be disturbed. If they are chased, they will flee into surrounding vegetation and remain motionless until the male has gone.

When ovipositing, the female may betray her presence by the rustle of her wings as she seeks out suitable dead plant material near water in which to insert her eggs. Submerged logs, tree roots and live plants are also selected. Sometimes the egg-laying site is remote from water. She may settle on the ground, keeping her wings vibrating in readiness to take off, pushing eggs into damp moss or bare soil. Females have been seen attempting to lay eggs into the edge of a dry stony lane, into wooden bridges and even into shoes!

Andrew McGeeney

Brown Hawker
Aeshna grandis (Linnaeus)

Description

Jizz The Brown Hawker is a large brown, mid- to late-summer dragonfly, often seen flying over reedbeds or herbage, as well as open water. It can be encountered some distance from water. Males may hawk up and down a section of canal or slow-moving river, as well as lakes and ponds, feeding on the wing, but rarely clashing with others. The gliding flight interspersed with bursts of shallow wingbeats is characteristic, often combined with graceful turns and loops in pursuit of other insects.

Field characters Ab 49-60mm; hw 45-49mm. This large hawker has amber-tinted wings and two lemon-coloured bars on the sides of the thorax. Males have blue spots along the side of the abdomen and blue-tinted eyes, and females have pale yellow abdominal markings and yellow-tinted eyes, but neither feature may be immediately clear when the insect is in flight.

Similar species The only other brown hawker in England is the rare and localised Norfolk Hawker, which has untinted wings, green eyes, no blue markings, and an earlier flight period, and is confined to the Broads.

Status and conservation

The Brown Hawker is common and widespread in lowland areas of Britain and Ireland. It has spread northwards in recent years. It is reasonably tolerant of pollution and may be the only hawker breeding at a site. British populations may be supplemented by immigration from the Continent, where this dragonfly is widespread in western and central regions.

Ecology and behaviour

Habitat Breeds in garden ponds, dykes, lakes, canals, slow-flowing rivers, gravel pits, park ponds, and even polluted pits where the larvae do not stand a chance of survival.

The eggs, which are the largest of all the hawkers, remain in diapause during winter and hatch in spring, when the young **larvae** make their way to submerged plants, roots or rotting plant stems. Larvae living among detritus may become dark-stained, obscuring their natural coloration, and this is apparent in the exuvia. In their first year, until they are about 30mm, they are characteristically banded like many other hawker larvae. This is thought to camouflage them from preda-

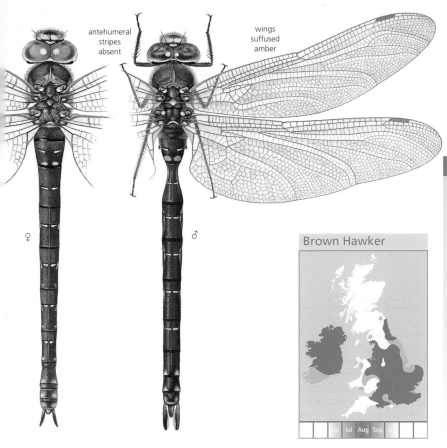

antehumeral
stripes
absent

wings
suffused
amber

♀

♂

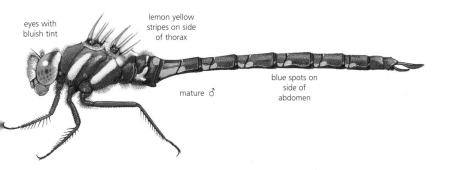

eyes with
bluish tint

lemon yellow
stripes on side
of thorax

mature ♂

blue spots on
side of
abdomen

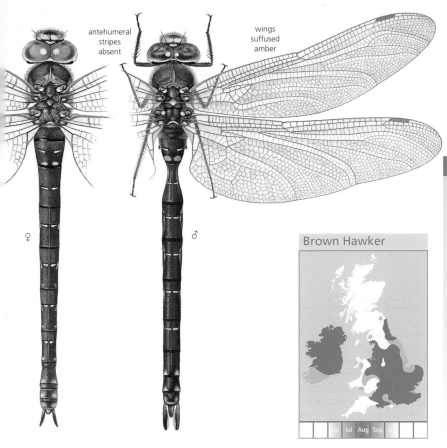

Brown Hawker

| | | Jun | Jul | Aug | Sep | Oct | | |

tors and to inhibit older larvae of their own species from eating them. The labium is broader than that of the Southern Hawker, with which it frequently occurs. Development takes 2-4 years, depending on food supply and water temperature. One study showed that over 50% of larval diet was chironomid-midge larvae; the larvae were also recorded eating a large number of adult flies from the water surface and were observed catching ovipositing damselflies.

Mature larvae **emerge** on to vegetation along the bankside at night and complete their metamorphosis 10-40cm above water. Teneral adults fly off before daybreak. The population emerges over a long period from June onwards. The **flight season** can last well into October.

Immatures are encountered flying in woodlands, sometimes crisscrossing in large numbers, feeding on insects around treetops, or lower down when the weather is cool or windy. Adults are also seen flying in the lee of hedgerows, frequently, but briefly, settling to eat an item of food. They are well camouflaged, particularly when settled on brown stems or seedheads. High densities of Brown Hawkers may be attracted to feed on swarms of flying ants, and in these situations the dragonflies do not interact aggressively. Also, some individuals use their wings to flush prey, such as midges, from nettles.

Brown Hawkers will fly quite late on warm evenings and are frequently encountered in gardens, parks and other urban sites. In these situations the Brown Hawker is less likely than other hawkers to have a regular flight path or typical height of flying.

Males are not strongly aggressive when defending a territory and tend to space themselves out, with only occasional clashes. A mature male will fly along a regular beat for long periods of time at 2m or more above the water or emergent vegetation. A cloud passing over the sun may cause it to settle for a while. Any female entering the rendezvous site will be immediately approached and pairing will be attempted. Copulation is quite lengthy and is usually completed during the morning high up in trees, but it may also occur low down among dense herbage.

The unaccompanied female flies low over the ground to oviposition sites at almost any time of day. She will investigate a likely site by hovering about 50cm above it, dropping to about 20cm before landing. Using her strong ovipositor, she inserts eggs, one at a time, into dead plant material, emergent vegetation or floating plants, just above or below the water surface. Favourite oviposition sites are partially submerged old logs that have begun to soften in the water. She begins by working her abdomen tip down the substrate, inserting parallel rows of eggs. If a female is disturbed by a male while ovipositing, she will take off and fly about 1m above the water surface with her abdomen held in a downward curl, signalling by her posture that she is not available for mating. This is usually a sufficient deterrent.

Andrew McGeeney

Norfolk Hawker
Aeshna isosceles (Müller)

Description

Jizz Male Norfolk Hawkers are usually seen patrolling ditches in East Anglian grazing marshes during early to mid summer. Like Migrant Hawkers, but unlike most other hawkers, they frequently perch on emergent vegetation. Away from water, mature males and females and immature insects frequently hunt in the shelter of trees and bushes.

Field characters Ab 47-54; hw 39-45. Male and female Norfolk Hawkers are large brown dragonflies with green eyes. At close quarters, the yellow triangle on the second abdominal segment (not found in the Brown Hawker), which gives the species its specific name, can be seen.

Similar species The only other brown-coloured hawker is the Brown Hawker, which can be identified by its pale brown wings. The Brown Hawker emerges much later than

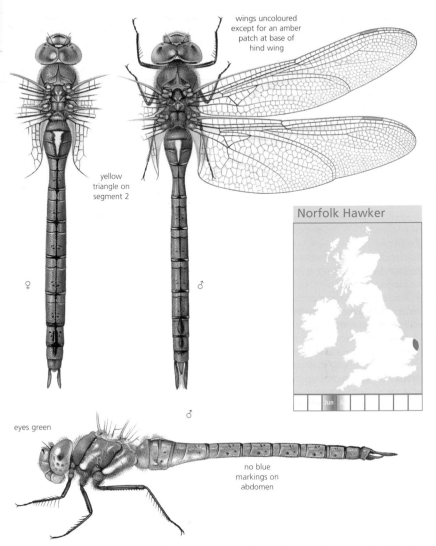

wings uncoloured except for an amber patch at base of hind wing

yellow triangle on segment 2

♀

♂

Norfolk Hawker

Jun Ju

♂

eyes green

no blue markings on abdomen

the Norfolk Hawker: the seasons of the two species normally overlap only in July. For most of June the only other hawkers on the wing are Hairy Dragonflies, which have a dark abdomen with blue spots or yellow spots. The Norfolk Hawker is therefore an easy dragonfly to identify in the field.

Status and conservation

The Norfolk Hawker has always been a scarce and local insect in Britain since records have been made. It was last seen in the Fens in 1893. Today, it is confined to the Broads district of Norfolk and Suffolk. It is cate-gorised as Endangered in Great Britain (Red Data Book Category 1) and therefore is listed in Schedule 5 of the Wildlife and Country-side Act 1981. A permit from English Nature is required before specimens of this rare species are caught. In the past, the Norfolk Hawker has been severely affected by drainage schemes undertaken when grazing marshes have been turned to arable land. Even in grazing marshes, it is vulnerable to ditch clearance when large areas are treated in one season. Locally, it is threatened by industrial and agricultural pollution and by inundation by salt water.

A male Norfolk Hawker.

In Britain, the Norfolk Hawker appears to be dependent on ditches containing Water Soldier (*Stratiotes aloides*). This strange floating plant, which moves up and down in the water, is largely confined to the Broads area, where it has a very patchy distribution. It is sensitive to eutrophication, and the largest populations of both Water Soldier and the Norfolk Hawker are in dyke systems that are isolated from polluted rivers. Both species could also be very vulnerable to the effects of a rise in sea level.

The Norfolk Hawker occurs in three National Nature Reserves, on two RSPB reserves and in several of the reserves of the Norfolk Wildlife Trust and the Suffolk Wildlife Trust. The general requirements of the species are known to the managers of these reserves, and it is being catered for sympathetically. The Broads Environmentally Sensitive Area covers all six Broadland river valleys and all the known localities of the Norfolk Hawker. The Norfolk Hawker could receive substantial support from this enlightened measure. On the Continent, it is found in central Europe and the Mediterranean region.

Ecology and behaviour

Habitat The species occurs in unpolluted ditches and dykes in grazing marshes which support Water Soldier.

The **larvae** lurk in ditches among the dense cover of Water Soldier, which provides a large surface of plant material throughout the year and supports a wide range of invertebrate animals, potential prey for the Norfolk Hawker. Little is known about the larval habits. They probably spend two years as larvae before emerging.

Emergence occurs in June. There appear to be two peaks of emergence, males predominating in the first and females in the second. The insects use a wide range of emergent plants, but in one study nearly 80% emerged on Water Soldier plants both in the middle and on the edges of ditches. Exuviae were found 10.5-21cm above the water level. More emerged on the south and east sides of ditches than on the north and west. Recently emerged insects fly to nearby wooded areas. The maturation period appears to be 2-3 weeks. The **flight season** usually lasts from early June to mid July.

Male Norfolk Hawkers patrol ditches. Territorial fighting often leads to chases over the meadows adjoining the ditches. The highest density is about nine males per 100m of ditch. This level is high for a hawker and may have something to do with the fact that males spend much of their time perching and thus remain unobserved by flying males.

Copulating pairs perch on emergent vegetation bordering the ditches. Females oviposit unaccompanied into the leaves and flower stalks of Water Soldier and occasionally in organic debris. Sometimes eggs are laid above water. Females make short flights in between laying at different sites in a ditch.

Mature males can sometimes be seen patrolling ditches which lack Water Soldier, including some which contain a rich aquatic flora of other species. To date (1996), so far as I know, no larvae or exuviae have been found in such ditches. Yet, on the Continent, the Norfolk Hawker often breeds in waterbodies which contain no Water Soldier. More research is needed to explain this intriguing paradox.

Most of the information about this species in Britain has been obtained in a study by Owen Leyshon and myself, aided by other members of the British Dragonfly Society. We have found that the Norfolk Hawker is a delight to study, because places which are good for Norfolk Hawkers are also good for other dragonflies, notably the Hairy Dragonfly, Scarce Chaser and Variable Damselfly. They are also good for birds – sometimes too good, as when a Hobby swoops along the ditches and affects the transect counts: a rare bird preying on a very rare dragonfly.

Norman Moore

Southern Migrant Hawker
Aeshna affinis
Vander Linden

This is a rare migrant from the Mediterranean region. It is similar in appearance and size to the Migrant Hawker, but has a stronger blue coloration, more spots on the abdomen and an absence of yellow markings. It is a migratory species, but there is only one definite record for Britain. This was from Kent in 1952. The flight season lasts from the end of June to late August. It breeds in shallow ponds and ditches.

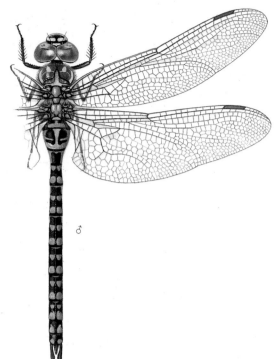

♂

Emperor Dragonfly
Anax imperator Leach

Description

Jizz On a warm, sunny summer's day, a patrolling male Emperor Dragonfly gives the unmistakable impression of being imperious and regal. It tends to survey or circumnavigate a pond from a height of several metres rather than skirting the edges close to the water, and intersperses bouts of hovering with swift lance-like flights. Its vigour, aggression and agility in flight are unequalled in Britain.

Field characters Ab 49-61mm; hw 45-51mm. The male has greenish-blue eyes, an apple-green thorax, and a sky-blue down-curved abdomen with black linear markings along the dorsal surface. The female's abdomen is predominantly green. The colour of the abdomen of the male shows reversible temperature-dependent change, being dirty greyish-green during darkness and below about 10°C, but this transformation is unlikely to occur except at night. During warm weather, the upper surface of the female's abdomen may become blue.

Similar species It can be distinguished from other hawkers by its colour combined with a lack of segmental spots on the abdomen. The marking on the frons serves to distinguish this species from the very similar Common Green Darner.

Status and conservation

The Emperor is widespread in southern Britain, though not found on the uplands of Dartmoor, in the Brecon Beacons or on the chalk downlands of Wiltshire and Hampshire. Records of the species in south-eastern Ireland during 2000 were the first for that country. In Europe, it is widespread from southern Scandinavia southwards.

Its continued existence in Britain is not

threatened, but local populations can be eliminated by destruction of its habitat, including removal of aquatic plants needed by larvae or as emergence supports.

Ecology and behaviour

Habitat The species can be locally abundant in large well-vegetated ponds, including urban garden ponds, lakes and flooded gravel pits, and sometimes ditches and canals. As a pioneer species, it may occur at high density at a site for a few years before becoming much less common or disappearing altogether.

The **larvae** live among submerged vegetation, typically close to the water surface. Until half-grown, they are strikingly patterned with black-and-white transverse bands, an arrangement that disguises their outline against a background of surface ripples, thus affording some protection from predation by larger individuals of the same species. Later, larvae are green or greenish-brown, resembling the plants among which they live. The rounded shape of the compound eyes when viewed from above is diagnostic. Larvae of different year-groups occupy different plant zones within a pond and so, to some extent, are segregated. Larvae are exceptionally active and responsive, often turning the head and body towards a moving object and sometimes swimming to pursue it. The larval diet includes a wide variety of aquatic invertebrates and sometimes tadpoles and small fish. The way in which its prey is stalked, captured, subdued and consumed depends on the kind of prey it is, the predatory sequences for snails and caddisfly larvae being especially elaborate. Sometimes the caudal appendages are used as spears to overpower prey after capture.

In Britain, a generation is usually completed in two years, but sometimes in one year. If the former, the final larval stadium, which is entered in late summer or autumn, overwinters in diapause and a synchronised emergence takes place the following spring. If the latter, the penultimate larval stadium overwinters and emergence the following spring is later and less synchronised. When both kinds of life cycle exist in the same pond, two instalments of **emergence** are usually evident. During the first synchronised instalment of annual emergence, which can comprise at least 90% of the annual population, mortality caused by incomplete moulting, incomplete wing-expansion and predation by birds can amount to 10% of the annual emergence.

During metamorphosis, the first external signs of which are detectable six weeks before emergence, larvae move among plant zones depending on the stage they have reached. Two days before emergence, individuals select a support, usually an emergent stem or tree trunk. On warm evenings emergence begins soon after sunset, the wings and body are fully extended by midnight, and the maiden flight occurs before sunrise the next morning, after a bout of wing-whirring which warms the flight muscles sufficiently to enable the teneral adult to fly. On cold evenings a day's emergence group is divided, part emerging during the night and part during the following morning.

After the maiden flight adults remain away from the water, foraging during the day and sometimes during twilight, for about two weeks before attaining sexual maturity, whereupon both sexes return to the water, the males, slightly earlier, to patrol, and the females to oviposit. When foraging, adults not infrequently catch and consume other dragonflies, including the Four-spotted Chaser. The **flight season** is long, usually lasting from early June to late August, and exceptionally into September.

The daily peak of male activity at water is centred around noon, but males show an additional crepuscular phase of activity over water, during evening twilight, and perhaps sometimes during morning twilight. Occasionally, during very warm weather, males may perch during the hottest part of the day. A patrolling male interacts promptly and vigorously with males of its own and other species, normally expelling most other species, including the Common Hawker, but not usually the Southern Hawker. When the water margin is linear, the equilibrium density seldom exceeds five patrolling Emperor males per 100m. The average longevity of males surviving the pre-reproductive period is about a month, and the maximum is at least two months.

Copulation, which lasts about ten minutes, takes place on a perch, sometimes up in a

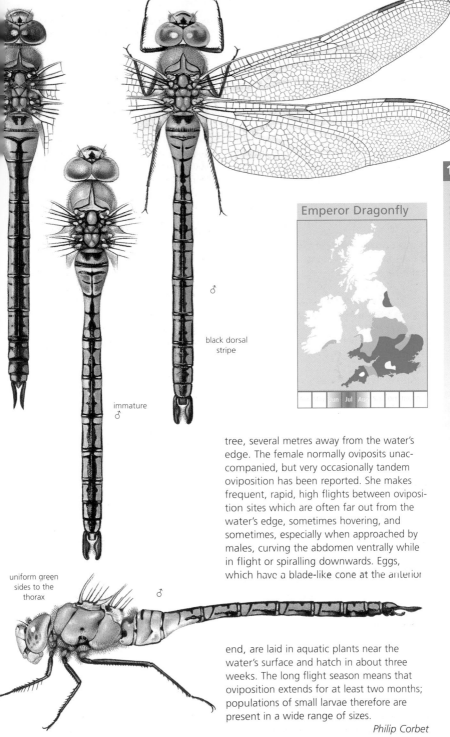

♂

black dorsal
stripe

immature
♂

Emperor Dragonfly

Jun Jul Aug

uniform green
sides to the
thorax

♂

tree, several metres away from the water's
edge. The female normally oviposits unaccompanied, but very occasionally tandem
oviposition has been reported. She makes
frequent, rapid, high flights between oviposition sites which are often far out from the
water's edge, sometimes hovering, and
sometimes, especially when approached by
males, curving the abdomen ventrally while
in flight or spiralling downwards. Eggs,
which have a blade-like cone at the anterior

end, are laid in aquatic plants near the
water's surface and hatch in about three
weeks. The long flight season means that
oviposition extends for at least two months;
populations of small larvae therefore are
present in a wide range of sizes.

Philip Corbet

Vagrant Emperor
Hemianax ephippiger (Burmeister)

Description

Field characters Ab 43-49mm; hw 43-48mm. A medium-sized yellow-brown hawker dragonfly with, in males, a bright blue band near the base of the abdomen. In females, the base is brown with a hint of violet, also the dorsal stripe continues up to segment two. It may be encountered anywhere and at any time, but generally late in the season.

Similar species The Vagrant Emperor is unlikely to be confused with any British species, except for the Lesser Emperor in which the abdomen is usually olive rather than yellow-brown and the eyes are green to blue and not brown.

Status and conservation

The Vagrant Emperor is a migrant to Britain and so far has not established itself as a breeding species. Until the mid-1980s it was rarely recorded in Britain, but since then it has been recorded almost annually. This may represent an actual increase in numbers arriving at our shores, perhaps linked with global warming. However, it may also be related to the increasing numbers of dragonfly-recorders over this period. The species' breeding range extends across sub-Saharan Africa to Pakistan. It has occasionally bred in southern Europe and Switzerland, when adults emerged in August following an invasion during the preceding spring. The species is well known for its long-distance migratory capabilities and is the only species of dragonfly recorded from Iceland.

Ecology and behaviour

Habitat This dragonfly breeds in small bodies of standing water, which are often temporary and may be saline. **Larval** development is rapid in the warm, shallow waters of desert pools. After **emergence**, adults may undergo long migratory flights to seek out new breeding sites which have recently been inundated by the arrival of the rains. The adults may fly far out to sea, and will continue to fly during the night, when they can be attracted to lights. They may be carried to the British Isles by strong south-westerlies and should be looked for at times of red desert-dust deposits. Most sightings of the species have been in the south of Britain and Ireland, but specimens have appeared further north and one was found in the Shetland Isles. Most individuals arrive during the late summer and autumn, and this coincides with the main emergence period in West Africa.

Steve Brooks

Lesser Emperor
Anax parthenope Selys

Description

Field characters Ab 46-53mm; hw 44-51mm. A medium-sized hawker dragonfly, smaller than the Emperor. The abdomen is said to be held straighter in flight than that of the latter. The thorax is green-brown and the abdomen olive with a pale blue band, sometimes with a violet tinge, near the base. Both sexes can be similar in colour, but in females the central black band on abdominal segment two is broader. There is a conspicuous yellow band at the base of segment two in both sexes. The wings may have a yellowish suffusion. The colour of the female is especially variable and the abdomen may be slate-blue to greeny-brown, with the basal band either bright blue or dull green.

Similar species The lack of black markings on the thorax should distinguish this species from other hawker dragonflies. It is smaller than the Emperor and lacks the entirely blue abdomen of males of that species. It is most similar in appearance to the Vagrant Emperor, since both species have a striking blue band near the base of the abdomen. However, the blue marking extends further down the side of the abdomen in the Lesser Emperor. The Vagrant Emperor is smaller, has brown rather than green eyes and a predominantly yellow-brown abdomen, whereas the abdomen of the Lesser Emperor is predominantly greenish-brown.

Status and conservation

The Lesser Emperor is a rare migrant to Britain and was recorded for the first time in this country in June 1996 in Gloucestershire. Further individual males have subsequently been recorded during 1997 in Cornwall and Cambridgeshire. In 1998, 11 individuals, including at least two females, were recorded between May and September from various locations along the south coast of England and also from south Wales and Nottinghamshire. The species was also recorded in 1999, including an ovipositing pair in a pool in Cornwall and an exuvia was subsequently found. Between 2000 and 2003 the species continued to appear regularly across Britain, with new records from southern Ireland and Orkney. There have also been more records of breeding activity, particularly in Cornwall. It occurs throughout southern Europe, but is seldom abundant and is rare in northern Germany and France.

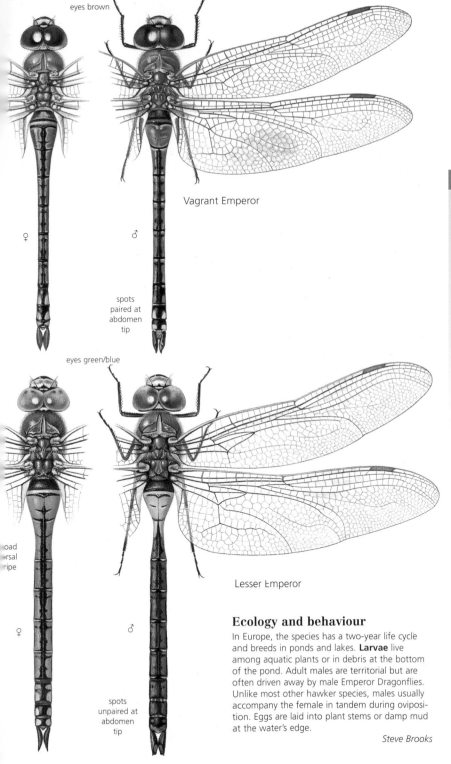

eyes brown

Vagrant Emperor

♀ ♂

spots
paired at
abdomen
tip

eyes green/blue

oad
rsal
ripe

Lesser Emperor

♀ ♂

spots
unpaired at
abdomen
tip

Ecology and behaviour

In Europe, the species has a two-year life cycle
and breeds in ponds and lakes. **Larvae** live
among aquatic plants or in debris at the bottom
of the pond. Adult males are territorial but are
often driven away by male Emperor Dragonflies.
Unlike most other hawker species, males usually
accompany the female in tandem during oviposition. Eggs are laid into plant stems or damp mud
at the water's edge.

Steve Brooks

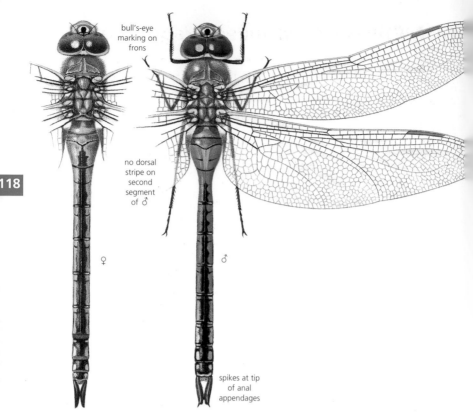

bull's-eye marking on frons

no dorsal stripe on second segment of ♂

♀

♂

spikes at tip of anal appendages

Common Green Darner *Anax junius* (Drury)

Description

Field characters Ab 47-58mm; hw 45-56mm. A large dragonfly. Males have a bright blue abdomen, becoming duller towards the tip and marked with a black dorsal stripe, and an entirely green thorax. In cool conditions the abdomen fades to a deep purple. Females are duller, with a brown dorsal stripe on a green abdomen, which is brightest at the base. In immature adults the abdomen is reddish brown or violet. Both sexes have a characteristic bull's-eye marking on top of the frons, in which the central black spot contrasts with a yellow background, surrounded by a narrow blue border. The male's anal appendages have a prominent spike at the tip.

Similar species The Green Darner is most similar to the Emperor and it is difficult to distinguish the two species on the wing. It is said that the green on the thorax of the Green Darner is slightly darker and that its flight is faster. The bright blue base of the abdomen, contrasting with the duller apical part, might also lead to initial confusion with the Lesser Emperor. However, close examination of the markings on the frons will serve to separate the species since the Emperor and Lesser Emperor both lack the characteristic bull's-eye.

Status and conservation

The Common Green Darner is a vagrant to Britain from North America. The species was recorded for the first time in Europe in September 1998 when three males and three females were seen in Cornwall and the Isles of Scilly. The species regularly migrates along the east coast of the USA and it is thought that the British specimens were carried over the Atlantic in the wake of a hurricane. At present there are no confirmed breeding records in Britain, but colonisation remains a possibility if further groups arrive here. The species is common throughout the USA, parts of Canada, Mexico and eastern Asia.

Ecology and behaviour

Habitat The Common Green Darner breeds in a wide range of standing or slow-flowing aquatic habitats including temporary and brackish waters. Males usually remain in tandem with females during oviposition, although females will sometimes oviposit unaccompanied and may submerge completely. Eggs are laid in aquatic vegetation, algae or damp mud. The males are territorial and extremely aggressive and will often inflict serious damage on rivals.

GOMPHIDAE Club-tailed dragonflies

These are medium-sized dragonflies with yellow-green and black markings. The eyes do not meet over the top of the head. They are restricted to slow-flowing rivers in Britain (but also occur in fast-flowing streams and lakes in continental Europe), with one resident species in England and Wales in the genus *Gomphus*.

Club-tailed Dragonfly
Gomphus vulgatissimus (Linnaeus)

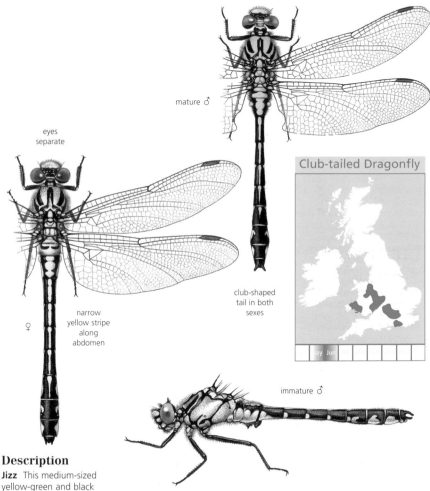

mature ♂

eyes
separate

Club-tailed Dragonfly

narrow
yellow stripe
along
abdomen

♀

club-shaped
tail in both
sexes

May Jun

immature ♂

Description

Jizz This medium-sized yellow-green and black dragonfly with a noticeably club-shaped tail is found along slow-flowing rivers or in adjacent woodland, although immatures can travel several kilometres from breeding sites. It has a low zigzagging flight and frequently perches on the ground, in low vegetation or in treetops.

Field characters Ab 32-37mm; hw 28-33mm. The immatures are black and yellow. When mature, the yellow changes to green, but in males the spots on the sides of abdominal segments 7-9 remain bright yellow, which contrasts with the green and black of the rest of the insect. The eyes in mature insects are dull

119

Gomphidae

green. This dragonfly is much more frequently seen on emergence, or as a teneral, than most species and a close approach is often possible; in this case, the separated eyes make identification easy. The larva is quite unlike that of any other British species, and the shape of the exuvial cases is diagnostic.

Similar species There are no really similar species. Mistakes are sometimes made by inexperienced observers who confuse Golden-ringed Dragonflies with Club-tails. Golden-rings are much larger; they are also black and yellow, but the yellow never changes to green; and the eyes are not separated. Occasionally, females and immature males of the Black-tailed Skimmer, which are also yellow and black, have caused confusion; these are the same size, but note the quite different pattern of markings and the unseparated eyes.

Status and conservation

The Club-tail is extremely local, but it can occur in very large populations where the habitat is suitable. It is known to occur on the mature stages of five rivers (including tributaries in some cases) which rise in the Welsh Uplands: the Dee, Severn, Wye, Tywi and Teifi. The populations on the Severn from its confluence with the Vyrnwy to the borders of Shropshire/Worcestershire are very strong. In southern England, the populations on the Thames are almost as strong and it occurs from Lechlade to below Windsor; it also breeds on some tributaries such as the Kennet and Loddon, but these populations are much smaller. It has a strong colony on the Arun in Sussex. The colony in the New Forest is probably extinct. Unless exuviae are looked for at the time of emergence, the presence of the species can be missed, and the Club-tail may still be under-recorded. It is found across Europe from France to Russia.

Threats to Club-tail habitat could come from water pollution, excessive dredging, and loss of woodland within easy reach of the river. Bankside treecover is usually present in the best sites and its loss could reduce valuable shelter. Emergent vegetation is not necessary, and this appears to explain why this species, unlike the White-legged Damselfly, has been able to cope with the tremendous build-up of pleasure-boat traffic on the Thames.

Ecology and behaviour

Habitat The Club-tail breeds in moderate to slow-flowing river systems in which there is sufficient silt deposited for the larvae to burrow, and bankside tree cover for adults.

The **larvae** are often commonest on meanders, where deposition of silt is greatest. The larval stage is believed to last 3-5 years. This is a spring species and **emergence** can begin on the Thames as early as 8 May, and about a week later on the Severn. Numbers emerging build to a peak around the end of May (early June on the colder rivers). Emergence is tightly synchronised and the majority of the population emerges within a week. Emergence starts in the morning from about 8.00am, numbers building to a maximum in early afternoon. In one survey, 36% of the day's emergence occurred between 1.30pm and 3.30pm, compared with only 6% between 7.30am and 9.30am. Emergence occurs fairly close to the banks, on any suitable supports: short grass, emergent vegetation and occasionally tree trunks. Bad weather causes reductions in the numbers emerging. In the same survey, during the peak at the end of May, only half as many emerged on rainy days as on fine days, and 54% of the 839 exuviae collected (throughout the emergence period) were females. The **flight season** lasts from early May until the end of June.

Most tenerals make their maiden flight about two hours after emergence. They flutter upwards, showing a strong aversion to water, and fly some distance from the water. Dispersal of teneral adults is widespread, and maturing specimens can be found feeding in clearings in woodlands up to 10km from the river. They also utilise the tree canopy more than most species, and this can make them difficult to observe.

Mature males return to the river about a week after emergence. They can be seen perching on exposed banks and bankside vegetation, especially where the flow-rate is minimal. The preference is for sections where there are steep banks and good tree cover. They are territorial, and fights take place over the water. There appears to be no interaction with other dragonflies at the water. Males can be seen searching for females, making large circuits of sections of the river, returning to the same spots. They fly very close to the water surface, often less than 30cm above it. Coupling is rarely seen, but mating pairs have been noted at least 5km from the River Severn and about 650m from the Thames. At the water, females appear suddenly from the treetops, flying rapidly above and dipping the abdomen several times in the water before disappearing. The eggs are spherical, and lack any mechanism to prevent them being washed downstream such as is found in many tropical gomphids (e.g. coiled filaments or gelatinous coatings). This correlates with their requirement for very slow-flowing stretches of water. There is no evidence of upstream migration of adults to compensate for downwash of eggs.

On the Continent, the species will breed in large lakes, especially where there is some wave action. In Britain, it occasionally breeds in ponds adjacent to those rivers which hold very strong breeding populations.

Graham Vick

CORDULEGASTRIDAE
Golden-ringed dragonflies

There is one resident species in the genus *Cordulegaster*. It is a large dragonfly, striped yellow and black, with green eyes which meet in a point on top of the head. It is usually seen patrolling upland and heathland streams.

Golden-ringed Dragonfly
Cordulegaster boltonii (Donovan)

Description

Jizz This is one of the largest British dragonflies. Males are frequently encountered flying leisurely, a few centimetres above small moorland streams. The flight is unidirectional. Adults may also be encountered away from water, hawking over moorland or along woodland rides, or hanging like a hawker dragonfly from ferns or the outer branches of trees.

Field characters Ab 54-64mm; hw 41-47mm. The thorax and abdomen are black with yellow bands, and the abdomen is slightly swollen at the tip. Adult males and females have green eyes. Females have a long pointed ovipositor.

Similar species This dragonfly is unlikely to be confused with other species on account of its large size and black-and-yellow banded pattern. However, immature Southern Hawkers, in which the abdominal markings can be also be yellow, may cause confusion. Golden-ringed Dragonflies may be distinguished from hawker dragonflies by the narrower eyes, which meet only in a point on the top of the head.

Status and conservation

The species is common in moorland and heathland areas of southern, western and northern England, Wales and Scotland. It is rare or absent in Ireland, eastern Scotland, the Midlands and eastern parts of England. It is found in central and northern Europe.

Although not seriously threatened throughout most of its range, the species may be excluded from conifer plantations where the scarcity of organic detritus, due to the erosive characteristics of forestry run-off, and the lack of emergent plants, as a result of excessive shading, reduce suitable larval habitats. Adults are also discouraged from such localities by the poor foraging conditions.

Ecology and behaviour

Habitat Larval habitats include small, often acidic, moorland and heathland streams or runnels in bogs, but not standing water. Such streams are usually unshaded by trees, but more open woodland streams will also support the species. Typically, breeding streams are less than 2m wide, and are often deeply cut and overhung with ferns, grasses and other emergent vegetation. During the summer, the water may be only a few centimetres deep and have a slow to moderate flow.

The **larvae** live partially buried in fine silt and detritus overlying gravel, with just the face and upcurved tip of the abdomen protruding. They have short legs, small protruding eyes, and a squat body, covered in fine hairs to which particles of silt adhere. Larvae may remain in the same position for several weeks, waiting to ambush prey that passes by. Development can be protracted in the cold, unproductive waters of northern and upland streams, taking 2-5 years.

Emergence occurs at night, usually on bankside vegetation (although larvae occasionally wander a considerable distance from the water), and is completed after 2-3 hours. Maturation takes about ten days, during which time adults feed in woodland or heathland. Adults will feed on fairly large insects, including other dragonflies, damselflies and bumble-bees. The **flight season** lasts from the end of May until September.

Males patrol long sections of breeding streams, flying a few centimetres above the water surface, and disappearing out of sight before returning several minutes later. The length of the patrol flight is governed by the density of males present on the stream, and males turn when they encounter another male. Occasionally they may pause to hover and investigate the bank or briefly perch on overhanging vegetation. Adult males do not defend territories but will clash with other males that they encounter. If a female is discovered, the male will carry her away in tandem and complete copulation perched in a tree, ferns or heather.

Females oviposit alone, usually during the morning, into the shallow margins of streams. The ovipositor is quite different in shape from that of other British dragonflies. It is long, straight and stout. This, together with the long abdomen, enables the female to thrust the eggs into the

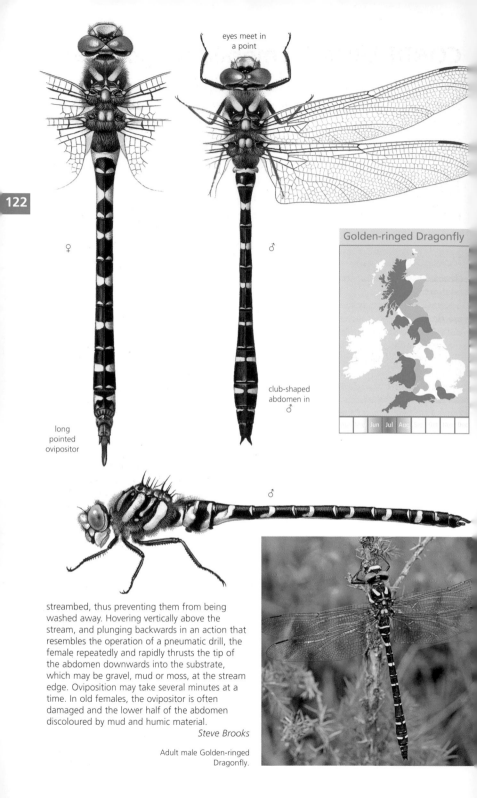

122

eyes meet in
a point

♀

♂

long
pointed
ovipositor

club-shaped
abdomen in
♂

Golden-ringed Dragonfly

Jun Jul Aug

♂

streambed, thus preventing them from being washed away. Hovering vertically above the stream, and plunging backwards in an action that resembles the operation of a pneumatic drill, the female repeatedly and rapidly thrusts the tip of the abdomen downwards into the substrate, which may be gravel, mud or moss, at the stream edge. Oviposition may take several minutes at a time. In old females, the ovipositor is often damaged and the lower half of the abdomen discoloured by mud and humic material.

Steve Brooks

Adult male Golden-ringed
Dragonfly.

CORDULIIDAE Emerald dragonflies

These are medium-sized metallic green dragonflies with a restless flight. They often hang down from branches when at rest and usually breed in standing water close to woodland. There are three resident species in the genera *Cordulia* and *Somatochlora*. *Oxygastra curtisii* formerly bred in this country.

Downy Emerald
Cordulia aenea (Linnaeus)

Description

Jizz Males are usually seen around the edges of tree-lined ponds. Their flight is fast and low, rarely more than a metre above water, and is reminiscent of a hawker dragonfly. The species rarely settles at the pond margins, but frequently hovers and clashes with other dragonflies, especially other male Downy Emeralds and chaser dragonflies.

Field characters Ab 33-39mm; hw 31-35mm. The general appearance is of a moderate-sized, compact dragonfly with an uptilted dark greenish-bronze, club-shaped (in the male) abdomen and bright apple-green eyes, with the sun glinting off the downy metallic green thorax. The distinctive green eyes do not develop until the insect matures; immatures have brown eyes.

Similar species The Downy Emerald resembles other emerald dragonflies, which are all metallic green and may occur together at sites in southern England or Scotland. The Brilliant Emerald frequently flies in more shaded parts of the pond than the Downy Emerald. To confirm identity, specimens should be netted and examined in the hand. In male Brilliant and Northern Emeralds the inferior appendage is unforked; the females of these two species have a vulvar scale which protrudes conspicuously from the abdomen in side view. The front and sides of the frons are yellow in the Brilliant Emerald but unmarked in the Downy Emerald.

Status and conservation

This species is local in the British Isles, and is mainly concentrated south of the Thames, but with scattered populations north to the Scottish Highlands and also in southern Ireland. It is largely confined to patches of mature deciduous woodland and will not readily leave the woodland canopy, making it a poor disperser. On the Continent, it occurs in western and central regions.

Loss of woodland ponds and nutrient enrichment, especially in East Anglia, may have resulted in range contraction. Dredging of woodland ponds is likely to eliminate the species by removal of the larval habitat. Excessive clearance of bankside trees will also have a negative effect by making the site less attractive to adults.

Ecology and behaviour

Habitat The larval habitat includes nutrient-poor, acidic (pH4.5) to slightly basic (pH7.5) sheltered woodland ponds, lakes and canals, usually with some sections containing overhanging trees and shrubs.

The **larvae** live on the bottom among coarse leaf-litter close to the water margin. They are not found among submerged aquatic plants and also avoid exposed silt or gravel and fine, well-rotted leaf fragments, where chaser-dragonfly larvae are often encountered. The larvae, which are marked with a distinctive black stripe on the side of the thorax, usually settle upside-down on the underside of large leaf fragments, just below the surface of the leaf-litter. It is during the night that larvae are most active and consume most prey. They are tactile hunters, and their ability to capture prey is not dependent on illumination. Water-lice, aquatic worms, midge larvae and alderfly larvae are abundant in this habitat and probably form a

Larva of Downy Emerald (photographed in May).

substantial part of the larval diet. Larval development takes two, possibly three, years.

Emergence of adults takes place throughout the morning and sometimes into the afternoon, and will continue in cool, overcast conditions. The emergence period lasts about two weeks and generally follows the first prolonged warm period in early May. Larvae use a wide range of bankside plants as emergence supports. Most emerge close to the water margin, but exuviae can be found up to 10m from the water's edge. Some larvae may climb 3m or more into trees and emerge at the tips of twigs. Following emergence, the maiden flight is directly upwards to treetop height and then away into the surrounding woodland. Mature adults return to the pond within about ten days of emergence. The **flight season** is from mid May to mid July.

Adults are often on the wing earlier and later in the day than other dragonflies, and continue to fly in cool, windy weather that will ground other species. Males patrol a zone, often a small bay, close to the pond margin and rarely cross open water in the middle of the pond. They also avoid areas of deep shade caused by trees with low over-hanging branches, as well as areas of dense emergent vegetation. The patrol flight is fast and close to the water surface, interrupted by frequent bouts of hovering. While occupying a territory, males will clash with other male Downy Emeralds and also with other dragonflies, especially Broad-bodied and

Four-spotted Chasers and tandem pairs of Large Red Damselflies, which they may mistake for female Downy Emeralds. Defending males almost invariably win these territorial combats. They sometimes share part of a pond with a male Emperor Dragonfly, but the two generally do not come into contact as the Emperor occupies the airspace 2-3m above that of the Downy Emerald. Any female Downy Emeralds that are encountered by a male are quickly seized and taken directly into the surrounding tree-tops. Tandem pairs form at the pond and the mating position is achieved during the nuptial flight. Mating may last at least one and a half hours.

Males seldom occupy a territory for more than 30 minutes, after which they suddenly depart for the surrounding woodland. During the peak flight season any vacant territories are quickly occupied by other males. The males periodically return to their original patrol areas, when vacant, throughout the day. In this way, a small part of the pond may be time-shared by several different males. The departure flight is usually high into the tree canopy; arriving males and females enter fast and low. Feeding rarely occurs at the pond. If prey is captured at the water, the adult will retire to the tree canopy to consume it. Feeding usually occurs in sunny woodland glades away from water.

Females are not accompanied by males during oviposition. They usually oviposit in shallow water among emergent or

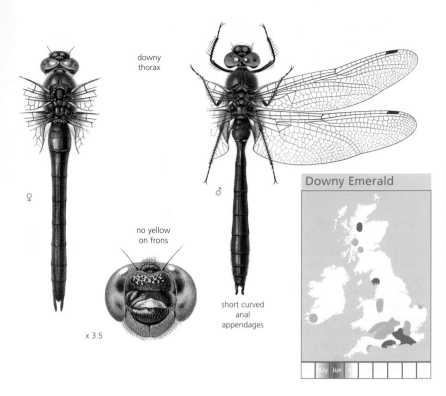

downy
thorax

♀

no yellow
on frons

x 3.5

♂

short curved
anal
appendages

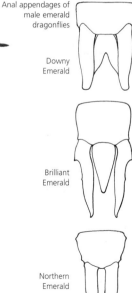

Downy Emerald

May Jun

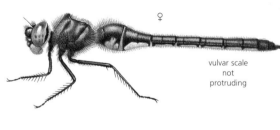

♀

vulvar scale
not
protruding

Anal appendages of
male emerald
dragonflies

Downy
Emerald

Brilliant
Emerald

Northern
Emerald

submerged vegetation in unshaded areas. Unvegetated areas and dense beds of emergent plants are avoided. Ovipositing females hover above the surface, rapidly tapping the tip of the abdomen into the water for several seconds. A clutch of about ten eggs is washed off each time. When males are present the females are secretive, but when males are absent they are more overt and will fly higher and further from the water's edge. Indeed, many females avoid the attentions of males by ovipositing early or late in the day, or during cool overcast conditions when male activity is at its minimum. At room temperature the eggs take 10-17 days to hatch.

Steve Brooks

Brilliant Emerald
Somatochlora metallica (Vander Linden)

Description

Jizz As with the Downy Emerald, males fly around edges of lakes and ponds, but the Brilliant Emerald flies faster and pauses less frequently to investigate shady nooks. Typically, they cruise at 0.8-1.3m above water, keeping 1-2m from the edge, and flying as much as possible under overhanging trees. Such deep shade is avoided by the Downy Emerald. They seldom settle near the water. Males swoop from the treetops, flying around the perimeter, without turning back and forth as frequently as the Downy.

Field characters Ab 37-40mm; hw 34-38mm. As in the Downy, the eyes are apple-green, but the abdomen and thorax are usually brighter emerald-green. However, this character is unreliable.

Similar species The Brilliant Emerald could be mistaken for either of the other two emeralds that share many of its localities throughout Britain. Both the Downy and the Northern Emeralds appear darker and less brilliantly metallic. The Downy flies with its 'tail' up; the Northern is smaller and more delicately built, and has a different habitat requirement (bog pools).

Insects should be netted to confirm identification. In male Brilliant Emeralds the anal appendages are diagnostic: the inferior appendage is unforked (forked in the Downy) and the superiors are gently curved when viewed dorsally, with a spine on each outer surface (unspined and calliper-like in the Northern). The head has more yellow than in the other emeralds, the yellow markings stretching across the frons. Females of the Brilliant can be distinguished by the large vulvar scale which projects perpendicularly and can occasionally be seen in flight. The Orange-spotted Emerald (extinct in Britain) looks similar to the Brilliant Emerald on the wing as the abdomen is held horizontally in flight, but the extensive yellow spotting on the abdomen is diagnostic.

Status and conservation

This nationally rare species occurs in two quite discrete populations. It is locally common in south-east England, occurring mostly on acidic soils, often, but by no means always, in pine woods. It is apparently expanding its range here, but populations could be adversely affected by dredging and excessive removal of bankside tree cover, a particular problem in waterbodies managed as fisheries, which support some of the strongest colonies. It also occurs extremely locally in the Scottish Highlands; strong populations are present here, but are possibly threatened by deforestation, leaving the lochs too exposed.

The Brilliant Emerald's curiously disjunct distribution may be the result of two separate colonisation events. The oldest may have occurred early in the post-glacial period, with the population retreating northwards during a warmer period, leaving the present isolated Scottish stock. The population in south-east England could have followed a more recent colonisation. This species is found in central and northern Europe.

Ecology and behaviour

Habitat This is predominantly a species of mesotrophic or often weakly acidic lakes. It avoids some of the small ponds at which the Downy Emerald can occur. There is usually tree cover around at least part of the lake, and woodland in the vicinity. Extensive emergent or floating vegetation may make the habitat unsuitable, as the amount of exposed water surface beneath the tree cover is reduced. In south-east England, this dragonfly also occurs in a few rivers and canals (e.g. Rivers Wey and Blackwater, and Basingstoke Canal) that are slow-flowing and lined with overhanging trees. Here there are extensive areas of large ponds and lakes in the vicinity, and these may support the primary populations.

The **larvae** occur on the lakebed, among dead leaves, twigs and sticks, avoiding bare sand and gravel. They are commonest in parts that are heavily shaded by overhanging trees. Development takes 2-3 years in England.

In Scotland, small pools are also avoided. Shelter is essential and breeding lochs are situated in hollows. Nearby tree cover is also essential, but the need for extensive margins

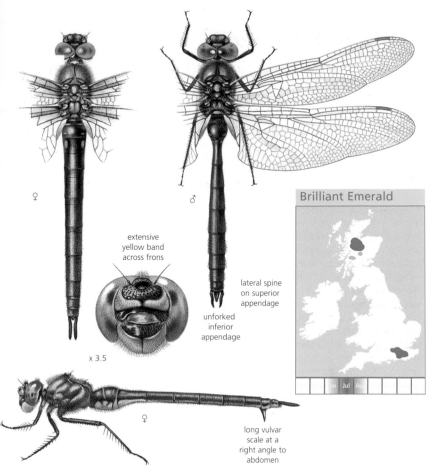

♀

♂

extensive
yellow band
across frons

lateral spine
on superior
appendage

unforked
inferior
appendage

x 3.5

Brilliant Emerald

Jun | Jul | Aug

♀

long vulvar
scale at a
right angle to
abdomen

of overhanging trees is less apparent than in England. All Scottish sites contain extensive *Sphagnum* moss margins.

Emergence takes place 3-4 weeks later than in the Downy, with a peak in late June. Adults usually emerge in the morning using bankside bushes and long grasses, but exuviae are also often found at up to 2m on tree trunks. Immatures disperse to surrounding woodland, and return to the lakeside as matures just as populations of the Downy are declining. In July, both species may be seen, but the **flight season** of the Brilliant continues into August and exceptionally into early September.

In good weather, adults fly between about 9.00am and 8.00pm, with successions of males flying around the perimeter of lakes. Females visit the water much less often, spending more time foraging in the tree canopy and in clearings. Feeding takes place

in surrounding woods; males rarely, and females never, take prey at the water. Females often come to water in overcast conditions or during early evening, in order to minimise male interaction. When a male seizes a female, the two fly away and coupling takes place in the tree canopy.

Egg-laying is unaccompanied. Females use the extended vulvar scale to place eggs in shady parts of the bank, among dense tangles of tree roots exposed at the water surface, or on the *Sphagnum* margins. They oviposit rapidly for several seconds before flying to another location to lay another batch. Eggs are sometimes laid above water, on vertical banks covered with *Sphagnum*, after the female first dips the tip of her abdomen into water. Sometimes the eggs are merely washed off the tip of the abdomen as she dips it.

Graham Vick

Northern Emerald
Somatochlora arctica (Zetterstedt)

Description

Jizz The Northern Emerald is a dark metallic dragonfly of bog pools, which it patrols at about 1m above the water. When feeding, it flies fast and straight at treetop height.

Field characters Ab 30-37mm; hw 28-32mm. This is a medium-sized, very dark green – almost black – dragonfly with shining green eyes and a characteristic shape in side view. In males, abdominal segments 1 and 2 and the base of 3 are swollen and appear to merge with the thorax, giving the impression of a very short abdomen and an enormous thorax.

Similar species The Northern, Downy and Brilliant Emeralds are similar in appearance but, unlike the others, the Northern is a bog-pool species. Its feeding flight tends to be at a higher level, and it is not found over open lochans. In the few areas in Scotland where suitable lochans and bog pools adjoin, all three species may frequent the same sheltered woodland glades. In the hand, the shape of the male anal appendages and the extent of yellow on the face are diagnostic. The superior anal appendages of the male Northern Emerald are shaped like callipers and are unspined, and the frons of both sexes has two separate yellow lateral spots; in the Brilliant Emerald the spots are connected by a yellow bar. The female vulvar scale is comparatively short and held parallel to the abdomen when compared with that of the Brilliant Emerald, in which it is held at a right angle. In the Downy Emerald the scale is short and inconspicuous.

Status and conservation

The number of 10km squares in Scotland in which the Northern Emerald has been recorded has doubled since 1982. This is entirely due to increased fieldwork and undoubtedly the species is still under-recorded. Indeed, its known range has recently been extended by the discovery of new Scottish populations to both the north and south. There is also an isolated population in south-west Ireland. The species is found in northern and central Europe and in mountain areas to the south.

In Scotland, there has been some loss of habitat resulting particularly from drainage and afforestation, although sensitive tree-planting, leaving the forest bogs untouched, could well prove to be beneficial.

Ecology and behaviour

Habitat The larval habitat includes bog pools with scattered cottongrasses (*Eriophorum*) among open forest, and similar pools on moorland adjacent to woodland.

The hairy **larvae** live among detritus in water up to 15cm deep beneath floating *Sphagnum* moss. In drought conditions, larvae have been reported surviving in semi-decomposed *Sphagnum* detritus some 30cm below the surface of the dried-out bog. Sampling for larvae is best done using a sieve or colander pushed under the *Sphagnum*, which is shaken to dislodge larvae clinging to the underside of the *Sphagnum*.

Both larvae and adults are elusive. For example, at Lochan Uath in Strathspey, some two man-hours' intensive searching produced just two larvae; during two visits in July, five exuviae were found, but no visiting odonatists have reported flying Northern Emeralds, despite easy access to the site. The population density is low in small bog pools. Sampling may produce dozens of Four-spotted Chaser larvae for every Northern Emerald. Few larvae emerge from any one bog pool. Eight exuviae were found in a 50m stretch of *Sphagnum*-covered roadside ditch beside Loch Maree. The following year the ditch was cleared out and deepened by a mechanical digger, but it was subsequently used as a breeding site by the Northern Emerald. On larger moorland pools with water of varying depth, larvae are found in the shallowest parts with the greatest *Sphagnum* cover. Larvae of other species, including Large Red Damselfly, White-faced and Highland Darters, and Common and Azure Hawkers, may be found in the same pool. Development of the larvae takes at least

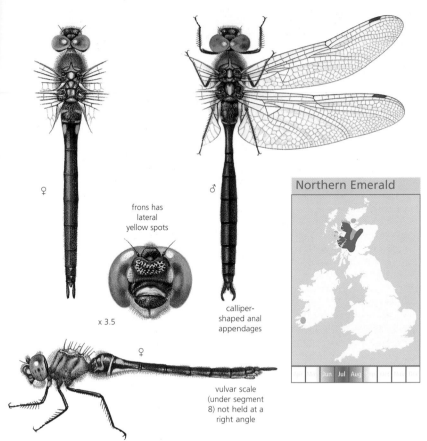

♀

♂

frons has
lateral
yellow spots

x 3.5

calliper-
shaped anal
appendages

♀

vulvar scale
(under segment
8) not held at a
right angle

Northern Emerald

Jun Jul Aug

two years. **Emergence** begins in late May, although the peak emergence is probably in early July, with adults still on the wing as late as 21 September. The **flight season** of the Northern Emerald is apparently a month longer than that of the other two emeralds in Scotland.

Exuviae are found about 5cm above water clinging to emergent plants, such as cotton-grasses. Emergence has been observed in the late morning in calm, damp conditions and usually takes several hours to complete. The maiden flight is into treetops.

Over the breeding grounds the males may patrol slowly, periodically hovering, at 1m or less above the wet bog, or swoop at high speed down, around and away. Aggressive interactions with other male Northern Emeralds are frequent. Rival males may clash and fly up to about 4m, then drop vertically downwards, whirling around each other in descending spirals before flying off in different directions. A male does not remain

long in one area, and soon flies off if the search for a female is unsuccessful. This is probably because breeding sites are often small and widely scattered. The presence of male Common Hawkers not only provokes aggressive clashes but also curtails the time spent by male Northern Emeralds at the pond. Eventually, however, another, or the same, male will return to a pool and repeat the process. When a male finds a female, the pair flies off in tandem into trees to mate. Copulation takes over an hour, and after-wards the female flies unaccompanied to a suitable oviposition site. When egg-laying, the tip of the abdomen is bent upwards and the eggs are washed off by repeated dipping into small light-reflecting areas of water overlying waterlogged *Sphagnum* or into small patches of open water between sundews (*Drosera*) and tussock clumps. The female regularly moves on to new oviposition sites and dips at intervals of 0.5-1.5 seconds.

Betty and Bob Smith

Orange-spotted Emerald
Oxygastra curtisii (Dale)

Description

Jizz A dark, medium-sized dragonfly the males of which patrol stretches of tree-lined rivers, streams and canals.
Field characters Ab 34-39mm; hw 32-36mm. The Orange-spotted Emerald, like other emeralds, is a metallic green insect. The body length is similar to that of a Four-spotted Chaser or Black-tailed Skimmer. At a distance, it appears dark. The spots which create the orange-yellow streak on the dorsal surface of the abdomen are obvious only when the insect is observed closely. In some individuals the spots are much reduced. The abdomen of the male is widened at segments 8 and 9 and so looks slightly club-shaped. Females have bands of saffron along the leading edges of the wings, and the wings of immature insects can also be tinged with saffron.
Similar species The Orange-spotted Emerald, now believed to be extinct in Britain, is very similar to the other emerald dragonflies which occur here. Its range overlapped with that of the Downy Emerald, whose males also have slightly club-shaped abdomens. In the Downy Emerald, however, the thorax is covered in buff hairs and the anal appendages are very different.

Status and conservation

This species was known for certain from only two localities in Britain: the Moors River in Dorset, near where the species was first discovered in 1820, and the River Tamar on the Devon/Cornwall border. It has not been seen again on the Tamar since its discovery there in 1946. It was a privilege for me to be introduced to the Orange-spotted Emerald in 1954 by the famous odonatist Lieutenant Colonel F C Fraser. It took us quite a time to find one! Later, in 1957, I saw the species again. I reckoned that only about 4km of the Moors River were suitable for it. In the 1.2km which I had inspected thoroughly, there appeared to be suitable habitat for only about six territorial males. The suitable habitat at the Tamar site is also very restricted. However, several tree-lined stretches of the rivers which rise in Dartmoor and of rivers in County Waterford and County Cork in Ireland appear suitable for the species, so an eye should be kept out for it in case it has been missed, or in case it recolonises the British Isles. It appears to have good powers of dispersal. Two or three insects which just conceivably could have been Orange-spotted Emeralds have been observed in recent years. On the Continent, it is restricted mostly to south-western Europe.

The species almost certainly became extinct in Dorset as the result of an accident which allowed sewage to enter the Moors River upstream of its habitat. If a new breeding site is discovered, great efforts should be made to prevent the river from being polluted. The species requires the shade of trees along the riverbank, but in Britain at least it probably also needed some stretches of water where males could patrol their territories in the sun.

Ecology and behaviour

The following description of the behaviour of the Orange-spotted Emerald is based largely on observations of A Heymer, made on the Rivière du Banyul in south-west France.
Habitat Males set up their territories in parts of rivers, streams and canals where water flows slowly and where at least part of the territory is shaded by trees or bushes throughout the day.

The **larvae** live in the mud or sand of slowly moving rivers or canals. There are very few records of breeding sites in static water. Larvae probably take 2-3 years to mature, or even longer. Some Orange-spotted Emeralds **emerge** on roots of trees just above the water, others up to 3m high on branches and tree trunks. In Britain the **flight season** was from early June to late July. On the Continent, adults have been observed from the end of May to the end of August.

Territorial males have a distinct flight pattern when patrolling their territories, making a very regular zigzag flight, raising

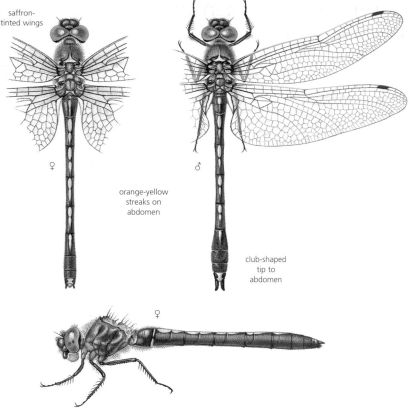

saffron-tinted wings

♀

orange-yellow
streaks on
abdomen

♂

club-shaped
tip to
abdomen

♀

the abdomen to an angle of about 30° from the horizontal at each change of direction. They usually fly about 20-30cm above the water surface. On fine warm days they are capable of patrolling their territories for a long time without pausing to rest. Territorial males are more active in the morning than in the afternoon. Heymer counted 35 males on a 7.5km stretch of the Rivière de Banyul. The beats of two males which I observed on the Moors River in England in 1957 were 10m and 22m long.

Female Orange-spotted Emeralds are quickly seized by males when they visit water. After an erratic flight the pair disappears into treetops to mate. The female returns to the river to oviposit unaccompanied by the male. She seeks shallow parts of the stream which are shaded by overhanging vegetation. She releases packets of yellow eggs by dipping her abdomen into the water. Away from water, adult and immature insects occur low down among bushes and crops, as well as high in the tree canopy. Adult Orange-spotted Emeralds can be seen feeding among bushes and trees and among crops bordering the river. Feeding is done throughout the day, but mostly away from the river, especially in the evenings, when Orange-spotted Emeralds feed on swarms of midges. In the morning they sometimes feed on White-legged Damselflies and other small damselflies. After feeding, adults roost in cover away from water. They perch with the abdomen hanging downwards. Sometimes several males can be seen perched close together as they warm up in the early-morning sun.

Much remains to be discovered about the biology of this local European endemic. It is possible that its behaviour may vary between different parts of its range. For example, I do not recall seeing patrolling males by the Moors River undertaking the zigzag flight described by A Heymer in France.

Norman Moore

LIBELLULIDAE Chaser, skimmer and darter dragonflies

These are small to medium-sized blue, red or yellow dragonflies. The eyes occupy most of the head. They have a darting flight and frequently perch (rather than hang) among marginal plants. They breed in the full range of aquatic habitats, except fast-flowing streams. In Great Britain and Ireland, there are ten resident species from the genera *Libellula*, *Orthetrum*, *Sympetrum* and *Leucorrhinia*.

Four-spotted Chaser
Libellula quadrimaculata Linnaeus

Description

Jizz This moderately sized dragonfly is usually seen perched on emergent vegetation surrounding ponds, pools and ditches. Aggressive, territorial flight is rapid, and males return repeatedly to the same perch. At other times they have a sustained gliding flight, and during the evening large numbers may congregate in swooping feeding swarms over water or in the surrounding countryside.

Field characters Ab 27-32mm; hw 32-40mm. Both sexes have a narrow, tapering dark brown abdomen with yellow sides, and with black at the tip. The wings are charac-teristically marked with broad, brown patches at the base and a smaller spot on the middle of the leading edge. Some indi-viduals have additional extensive dark marks near the wing tip; these are known as form *praenubila*.

Similar species The species has a passing resemblance to females and immature males of the Broad-bodied Chaser, but in the latter the abdomen is strikingly broad. It could be confused with the female or immature Black-tailed Skimmer but this species lacks any markings at the wing base.

Status and conservation

This species is widespread throughout much of Britain but absent from many parts of north-east England. It is common throughout most of its range, although in lowland England it is most frequently encountered at acid-water sites and is rare at base-rich sites. Found throughout most of Europe.

There appears to be no major threat to its conservation in Britain at present though it may be excluded from sites that become over shaded.

Ecology and behaviour

Habitat Occurs in a wide range of habitats, including heathland and moorland bogs, fens, canals and dykes, slow-flowing streams and even brackish water. It is often an early coloniser of newly flooded gravel pits and may breed in garden ponds.

The **larvae** live among well-rotted plant detritus, frequently in finer material than larvae of the Downy Emerald, from which they can be distinguished by the presence of a yellow fleck on the side of the labium. They take two years to complete development.

Emergence takes place on marginal emer-gent vegetation during early morning in late May and June. Immature and mature adults feed in woodland and heathland, often far from water. The **flight season** lasts through to mid August.

Sexually active males are highly territorial and aggressive. They adopt a vantage point among tall marginal vegetation, such as bare twigs and reeds, where they wait for the arrival of females or from which they launch frequent sorties to attack rival males and passing prey. Successful territory-holders are usually the most agile individuals, rather than the largest. At high male densities territories break down, and males may remain continu-ally on the wing, swooping in confused dog-fights. The male patrol flight is from about

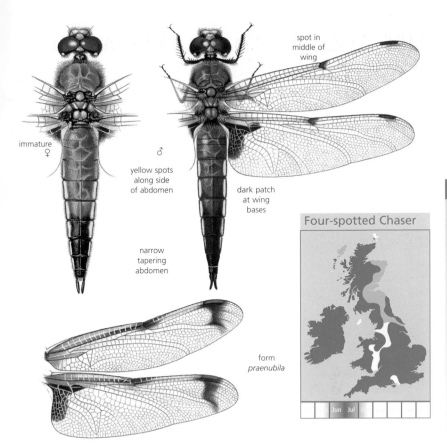

immature ♀

yellow spots along side of abdomen

♂

spot in middle of wing

dark patch at wing bases

narrow tapering abdomen

form *praenubila*

Four-spotted Chaser

Jun Jul

70cm above the water, and males are frequently captured as prey by Emperor Dragonflies, which patrol at a similar height.

Females spend much of their time away from water and are often seen perching on trees and bushes. When they do appear at the water to oviposit, they suffer continual harassment from males. Copulation is completed in flight and is brief, lasting 5-20 seconds. At high densities, males can be so frantic to mate that they will sometimes grasp female Broad-bodied Chasers.

Females oviposit by flicking eggs into the water or by dipping the tip of the abdomen. Oviposition sites are usually over submerged vegetation near the water surface, but open-water sites are also chosen. Females may oviposit alone, but usually the male hovers nearby on guard to chase off intruders. The male will not attempt to mate during oviposition but will try to mate again as soon as the female has finished. Oviposition is brief and is usually completed within 20 seconds.

The eggs are surrounded by jelly, which sticks them to submerged plants. They take about 29 days to hatch.

The Four-spotted Chaser is a migratory species, and vast swarms 500m long, 20m wide and 3-4m high, containing 2.5 billion insects, have been recorded in continental Europe. Migration is a cyclical event occurring every ten years or so. It is thought to be brought about by a combination of mass emergence, overcrowding and specific weather conditions, and is possibly triggered as a reaction to the presence of a parasitic worm. Swarming behaviour in Britain is uncommon, but the species is a wanderer and is often encountered far from breeding sites. The species is well adapted for cool climates, and its dark coloration, transparent cuticle and fine hairs on the thorax help to keep the insect warm. Its abundance on heathlands in southern England means that it is often preyed on by Hobbies.

Steve Brooks

Scarce Chaser
Libellula fulva Müller

Description

Jizz Scarce Chasers have a preference for basking on the tops of dense vegetation such as tall umbellifers. Males spend up to two-thirds of their time surveying their territories from vantage points overhanging slow-flowing rivers, making only short forays over the water. Their flight is bright, alert and darting, often pausing to hover.

Field characters Ab 26-29mm; hw 33-38mm. The vivid orange coloration and the dark bases to the wings of sub-adult males and females are highly distinctive. Mature females lose some of the brilliance of their immature colours, and very old females eventually attain a similar coloration to that of the Four-spotted Chaser. Mature males have a powder-blue abdomen with the last three segments black. Dark markings are often visible on the sides of the abdomen of males; these are mating scars, and are positionally peculiar to this species.

Similar species There are four chasers in which the males have a pale blue abdomen. The Broad-bodied Chaser and the Keeled Skimmer do not usually have a black tip. The Broad-bodied Chaser also has a wider, less tapered abdomen. On rare occasions, the Keeled Skimmer may have a dark tip to the abdomen owing to the rigours of mating, but the two are unlikely to occur in the same habitat. The dark wing base of the Scarce Chaser is the definitive character in separating it from both the Keeled and the Black-tailed Skimmers.

Status and conservation

Although locally abundant where it does occur, this species is scarce throughout its range in southern and eastern England, although new breeding colonies were recently discovered in Kent, and on the Wey in Surrey and Hampshire. Current populations appear to be stable and in some instances have expanded in recent years. It is widespread in western and central Europe.

There are four major conservation threats: the shading of habitat through the uncontrolled growth of marginal trees; over-abstraction of water, leading to low flows, higher water temperatures and deoxygenation; inappropriate river management, such as the removal of fallen trees and weed-cutting; and agricultural and industrial pollution, although the species appears to be relatively tolerant of this.

Ecology and behaviour

Habitat This is a species of river floodplains, water meadows and, occasionally, gravel pits, although breeding has not been confirmed in the latter. It has a preference for nutrient-rich slacks, backwaters and areas with prolific emergent vegetation and bushes, although heavily shaded areas are avoided. Breeding tends to be confined to areas of low current flow.

The **larvae** usually take two years to complete development. They occur in base-rich waters, inhabiting semi-decomposed vegetable matter where it has been trapped in the roots of aquatic plants and under the bankside in the lee of bends. They are not difficult to distinguish from other libellulid larvae, as the spines on the top of the abdomen are particularly visible and pronounced. They are opportunistic feeders, and the diet consists mainly of invertebrates.

The Scarce Chaser has a synchronised **emergence** which usually commences during the second half of May, but can be delayed because of adverse conditions. Emergence is usually completed by the third week in June, but in extreme conditions exuviae have been found at the end of July. Plants such as Common Reed (*Phragmites australis*) are preferred as emergence supports, the larvae climbing to 0.5-1m above the water and adjacent to the bank. Emergence takes place when the sun has warmed the area in the morning, and most maiden flights are completed by midday. Immatures bask on top of dense and soft vegetation, where full juvenile coloration is attained in a few hours. If disturbed they fly into the treetops, where most individuals complete maturation,

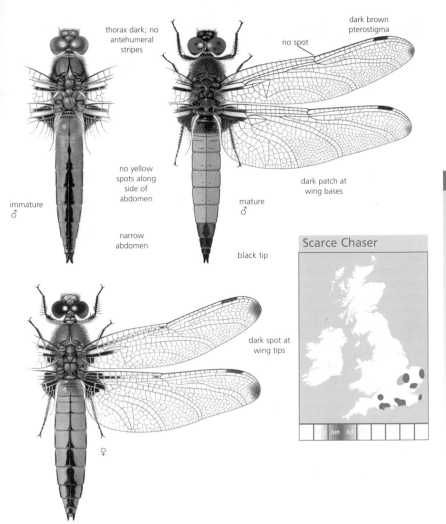

thorax dark; no antehumeral stripes

dark brown pterostigma

no spot

no yellow spots along side of abdomen

dark patch at wing bases

immature ♂

mature ♂

narrow abdomen

black tip

dark spot at wing tips

♀

Scarce Chaser

Jun Jul

although others may disperse a considerable distance. Maturation takes 1-2 weeks, during which time males develop a blue pruinescence on the abdomen. The **flight season** is short, lasting from the end of May to early August.

Mature males seldom establish territories until mid-morning, when they select a vantage point and make periodic flights over it. They are particularly attentive and will investigate any movement without straying far from the territory. On larger rivers, where management for fishing creates bays, each bay may be occupied by a single territorial male. On smaller rivers, where competition for sunlit areas is fierce, several males may occupy a small area with little visible aggression. Following mating and territorial clashes, males soon become scarred, with torn wings. Copulation usually takes place in the immediate post-midday period. It is prolonged, seldom less than 15 minutes, with the pair flopping down at ground level into vegetation. They are easily disturbed and may fly considerable distances before dropping down again.

The female lays her eggs by flicking her abdomen on to the surface of open water, often close to the bank, usually with the male hovering in close attendance. The eggs sink to the bottom and, being sticky, adhere to the substrate.

Dave Winsland

Broad-bodied Chaser
Libellula depressa Linnaeus

Description

Jizz This medium-sized dragonfly is usually seen over shallow, sunny ponds and lake margins during early summer. It frequently perches for long periods on vegetation, interspersed with bouts of rapid, direct flight.

Field characters Ab 22-28mm; hw 33-37mm. A bulky dragonfly with a characteristic broad, flattened abdomen, which in males is pale blue (yellowish-brown in females and immature males) with yellow lateral spots. The yellow spots make females and immature males look like gigantic wasps. Look also for the blue-green antehumeral stripes and the brown markings at the base of the wings.

Similar species Males are most likely to be confused with Black-tailed Skimmers, which often share the same localities, but in the latter the black-tipped abdomen is much narrower and the wings lack the dark basal spot. Scarce Chasers are also similar, but have a narrower abdomen with a black tip. However, these two species are unlikely to occur together, since Broad-bodied Chasers are rarely seen over riverine habitats. Four-spotted Chasers are similar in colour to females and immature males, but have a narrower abdomen and an additional spot in the middle of the leading edge of each wing.

Status and conservation

This species is widespread and common throughout southern England and Wales, and has expanded into the north of England in the last few years. It occurs widely in Europe north to southern Scandinavia.

The species becomes less abundant in ponds in late successional stages but can be encouraged by clearance of bankside vegetation. It is not endangered nationally and benefits from pond and lake creation, but it has become less common in Fenland districts owing to the loss of farm ponds.

Ecology and behaviour

Habitat Quickly colonises new or semi-permanent sites, including garden ponds. It occurs in a wide variety of standing-water sites, favouring small, open ponds and ditches, but also breeds in well-vegetated or even mildly polluted and brackish waters.

The **larvae** occur in shallow water and can be abundant in sunny ponds with sparse aquatic or bankside vegetation. They are rarely found in acid waters, canals and rivers. Larvae live partially buried in silt and fine detritus, with just the top of the head and tip of the abdomen exposed. Large larvae do not climb among submerged vegetation, although early-stadium larvae may occur in this situation. They are absent from areas of coarse stony substrate. The tips of the labial palps are more deeply serrated than other chaser larvae, but this can be difficult to see in the field.

Larval development is completed in 1-3 years. Despite the long development time, the larvae will persist in ponds that are dry for a short time during the summer, and probably survive buried in damp mud. Such ponds are usually devoid of submerged aquatic vegetation, but are generally open to the sun and experience low levels of dissolved oxygen. They may support large populations of the Broad-bodied Chaser but few other dragonflies. There are also records of larvae overwintering in dried-up pools.

Larvae entering the final stadium after July go into diapause, and emerge the following spring. This ensures that **emergence** is usually well synchronised and occurs over a period of a few weeks from mid May. Adults emerge during the early morning and use a wide variety of bankside vegetation as supports. Emergence takes 1-2 hours. Immatures disperse widely and are often encountered feeding alongside hedgerows well away from water. The species is a wanderer and is sometimes migratory. The **flight season** lasts until early August.

When mature males first arrive at the breeding site, they show no territorial behaviour but search the pond widely for females. After the first successful mating and subsequent oviposition, the male continues to guard the oviposition site and adopts this as his territory. The male then assumes a sit-and-wait strategy for females and overlooks

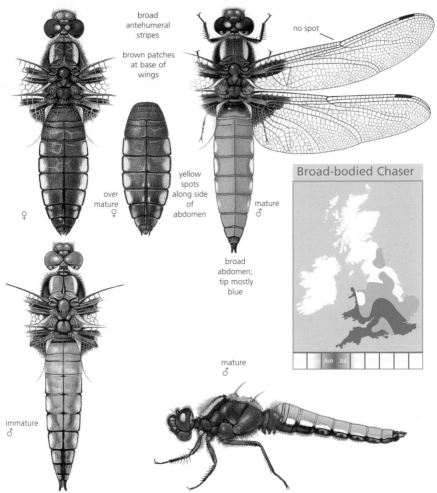

broad antehumeral stripes

brown patches at base of wings

no spot

over mature ♀

♀

yellow spots along side of abdomen

mature ♂

broad abdomen; tip mostly blue

Broad-bodied Chaser

mature ♂

immature ♂

Jun Jul

the territory from a prominent perch in an open, sunny position. He may occupy the same territory for at least two days, but if there are no subsequent matings at this site he will return to the wandering strategy. It follows, therefore, that wandering males either are unmated and inexperienced or are older males that have experienced low mating success. The male tenaciously defends his territory and wins over 90% of the battles against rival males. However, he may lose his dominance if he allows another male to mate in the same territory. This is because males have a marked increase in aggressiveness immediately after mating.

Females perch in vegetation and trees close to the waterbody and are often easier to approach than males. Males grasp females

visiting the pond to oviposit, and the tandem pair soars 2-3m into the air before assuming the wheel position. Copulation is brief, seldom lasting more than a few seconds. It is usually completed in the air, but in windy conditions the pair may settle. Males sometimes have difficulty in distinguishing females from those of Four-spotted Chasers.

During oviposition, the male guards the female by hovering close by. Oviposition usually occurs immediately after copulation but, when there is high male harassment, the female may depart and return to oviposit alone later in the day. Oviposition sites are in sunny areas where submerged water plants are at or near the surface. The female hovers a few centimetres above the water, periodically tapping the tip of her abdomen on to the surface. The eggs are washed off, and jelly which surrounds them absorbs water, swells and sticks the eggs to submerged plants. The time from when the male first seizes the female to the completion of oviposition may be as little as 2.5 minutes. The eggs hatch after 2-3 weeks.

Steve Brooks

Black-tailed Skimmer
Orthetrum cancellatum (Linnaeus)

Description

Jizz A fast, low-flying, highly active species which is commonly observed perching on open ground or on muddy banks, stones, dead trees and roads. At temperatures above 26°C, it will perch on low vegetation.

Field characters Ab 29-35mm; hw 35-41mm. Its size, clear wings and black-tipped blue abdomen (in males) are distinctive. Immatures and females have a yellow abdomen with two prominent longitudinal black bands on the upper surface. Older females become dark brown, occasionally with a grey-blue pruinescence. Older males commonly bear scratch marks towards the base of the abdomen on the dorsal surface, indicating that they have mated. The pterostigmata are black.

Similar species Mature males could be confused only with male Scarce Chasers, but these have dark patches at the base of the wings and are seldom seen at standing-water sites. Females could be confused with Club-tailed Dragonflies, which have superficially similar markings, but in Club-tails the abdomen is predominantly black with only a narrow yellow dorsal stripe and the eyes do not meet over the top of the head.

Status and conservation

This species is quite common in southern England, parts of Wales and central Ireland. There are indications that its range may be increasing, and it has recently been reported as breeding in Pembrokeshire and north-east England. The species has benefited from the increase in the number of flooded gravel pits in the last few decades, particularly in south-east England. Males require areas of bare ground on which to perch, so the species tends to become less abundant as water-bodies enter late successional stages, and bankside vegetation becomes more dense.

Ecology and behaviour

Habitat Found in lakes and slow rivers and also sometimes in marshes and small ponds, typically with exposed marginal areas with bare trampled soil or stones.

The **larvae**, which can be found in lakes and slow rivers and also sometimes in marshes and small ponds, are thickset and have short legs. They live partly or wholly buried in bottom debris, and development may take 2-3 years with 11-12 stadia.

Emergence occurs in the early morning from late May to July. Larvae may travel over 10m from the water margin if suitable emergence sites are not available. After emergence, tenerals fly a few metres and then hang vertically for some hours, before flying inland. The **flight season** lasts until early August.

They feed from perches on a variety of types of prey and sometimes show a preference for large items, taking butterflies, grasshoppers or damselflies as large as demoiselles. While feeding they return repeatedly to the same perch, where they often sit with their fore legs raised in the flight position, a position that enables the head and prothorax to swivel around to fixate visual targets.

Mature males acquire and retain territories which may occupy over 50m of a bank. They are very aggressive towards other males and commonly perch on the ground or low on vegetation at the water margin within their territories, from where they can scan a large area of water. They make frequent and extensive patrol flights over the water, commonly but briefly entering the territories of neighbours as they do so. Females spend most time away from water, feeding along hedgerows or in open ground. After arriving at an oviposition site, a female may be

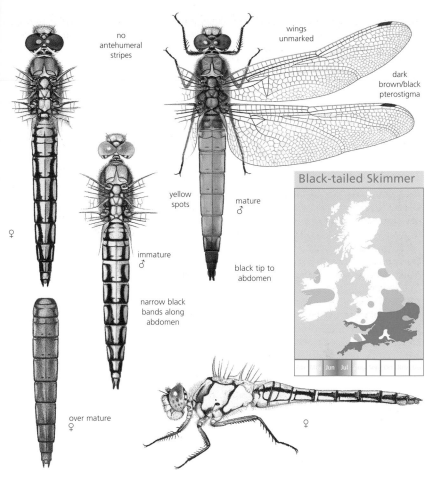

no antehumeral stripes

wings unmarked

dark brown/black pterostigma

yellow spots

mature ♂

black tip to abdomen

immature ♂

narrow black bands along abdomen

♀

over mature ♀

Black-tailed Skimmer

Jun Jul

♀

immediately seized by a territorial male, with copulation quickly ensuing, this usually taking place while perched in the male's territory but sometimes without alighting; it normally lasts only 20-30 seconds. Females oviposit by flying over the water, periodically dipping the tip of the abdomen into it. They are usually closely guarded by the male. If they select a single site for oviposition, the male may perch nearby. While dipping down to the water surface the female beats her fore and hind wings alternately (counter-stroking); but, as she rises, the wings beat together (parallel-stroking), which generates more power, and this may be followed by a brief glide before dipping down again. When the density of males is high and disturbances are frequent, however, females may oviposit by perching on surface vegetation and peri-odically rising up a few centimetres, then immediately settling down again, depositing a batch of eggs each time they do so. A male which captures an ovipositing female in flight forms a tandem and then may somer-sault with her in mid-air, an operation which flings out a small white object from the female, probably eggs from the vagina, thus freeing her passage for copulation.

Non-territory-holding males sometimes capture females away from water at feeding grounds and then copulate with them while perched. Such copulations may last up to 15 minutes and result in the removal of all the sperm of rival males from the female, before the male transfers his own sperm. Males holding territories also occasionally make such long-lasting copulations.

Peter Miller

Keeled Skimmer
Orthetrum coerulescens (Fabricius)

Description

Jizz This is a small, darter-like dragonfly with a preference for aquatic habitats in acid peat regions. This, together with the blue pruinescence in mature males and a slender, tapering abdomen, makes it rather unlikely to be confused with other species.

Field characters Ab 25-31mm; hw 28-33mm. Tenerals have yellow-tinted wings, whereas those of mature individuals are clear or slightly smoky. The body of immatures is yellow to light brown, and in older females it becomes dark brown. The male develops a blue pruinescence on the upper side of the abdomen which reaches the thorax only in old males, when it may become dark grey. The pterostigmata are bright yellow.

Similar species Mature males could perhaps be confused with other blue libellulids, but the Black-tailed Skimmer and Scarce Chaser both have a black tip to the abdomen, and in the Broad-bodied Chaser the abdomen is noticeably very broad and flattened. All three of these species are considerably larger than the Keeled Skimmer. Female and immature male Keeled Skimmers resemble darter dragonflies in size and general coloration, but can be distinguished by the prominent whitish stripes on top of the thorax and the lack of yellow on the side of the thorax. Immature male and female Black-tailed Skimmers can be recognised by the prominent black bands surrounding yellow spots on each side of the abdomen, which are absent in the Keeled Skimmer.

Status and conservation

Locally common in acid, boggy regions of south and south-west Britain and Ireland, this species is also found at several localities in northern England and Scotland, showing a markedly discontinuous distribution. It also occurs in west and central Europe.

The species is threatened by building developments, which are encroaching on its strongholds in the Dorset heathlands, and by peat extraction in other regions.

Ecology and behaviour

Habitat The Keeled Skimmer occurs at small rivers and streams, ditches and swampy pools in acid-peat regions, usually where there is *Sphagnum* moss. The **larvae** are often buried in the debris at the bottom. They probably do not require an acid pH, but exploit these habitats for other reasons, perhaps because of the relatively warm water, reduced fish predation or lack of competition from other dragonflies. Development takes about two years. Adults remain close to the habitat in which the larvae live.

Emergence starts at about 8.00am in warm weather, and tenerals fly a short distance away from water towards trees or bushes. The **flight season** lasts from early June to late August.

During feeding, individuals perch on the ground or, at higher temperatures, on low vegetation such as heather or bushes, often with the fore legs raised in the flight position, as in the Black-tailed Skimmer. After perching, the wings may be gradually depressed and twisted forwards so that their flat plane may lie at nearly 90° to the long axis of the body.

Mature males establish small territories, sometimes over 5m in diameter, perching on the banks of streams or at pools, or on emergent vegetation over swampy regions, periodically challenging intruders and making intermittent patrol flights, flying for about 4-18% of the time. Typically there may be about 15 territories per 100m of bank. They commonly encounter males of the Golden-ringed Dragonfly at stream habitats and sometimes interact strongly with them.

Most females approach the water around midday and may be instantly seized by territorial males. The pair then adopt the wheel (copulatory) position in flight. Copulation is normally completed after settling low down in vegetation, and it may last for as little as 1-2 minutes or be extended for over one hour. Copulation tends to be longer in duration when the male does not hold a territory, or if the sun becomes obscured by cloud.

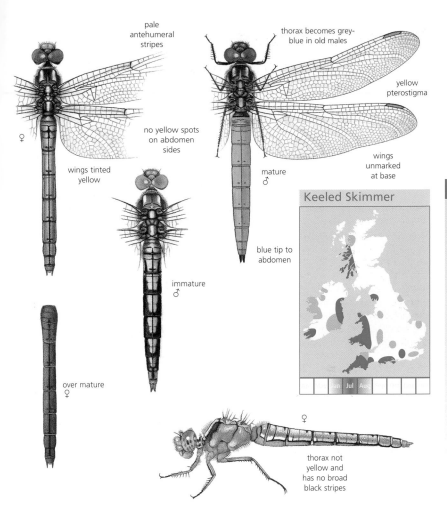

pale antehumeral stripes

♀

no yellow spots on abdomen sides

wings tinted yellow

thorax becomes grey-blue in old males

yellow pterostigma

mature ♂

wings unmarked at base

immature ♂

blue tip to abdomen

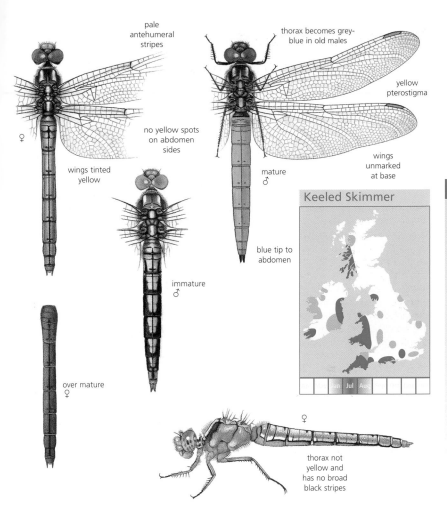

Keeled Skimmer

Jun Jul Aug

over mature ♀

♀

thorax not yellow and has no broad black stripes

Males unable to gain territories for themselves may fly through the territories of other males, or perch within them acting as satellites, occasionally catching a female unobserved by the territory-holder. A female in tandem with a non-territorial male is sometimes reluctant to initiate copulation, and this may induce the male to fly with her over streams or bogs, periodically dipping down to the surface, apparently demonstrating potential oviposition sites to the female in order to persuade her to accept copulation. This has been termed in-tandem courtship.

After copulation, the pair separates and the female usually remains perched close to the water (usually in the male's territory) for several minutes. The male perches close to her, occasionally even on top of her, but makes periodic flights over his territory. He may attempt to initiate oviposition by head-butting the female. The time spent resting by the female may be partly determined by the density of other males in the vicinity, the female perhaps waiting for an opportunity to oviposit without excessive harassment. Females oviposit by dipping down to the surface and scooping droplets of water containing eggs towards the bank or surface vegetation. Although the male remains on guard, flying or perching nearby, an ovipositing female is quite commonly seized by another male. Unguarded females are also frequently to be seen ovipositing alone.

Peter Miller

Darters – *Sympetrum* species

Darter dragonfly species are among the most difficult to identify. This group has a relatively large number of species that look superficially rather similar to each other. However, they do differ in details of the shape of the male and female genitalia. The illustrations below show these structures. The extent of the black line along the top and sides of the frons is also useful in separating some species, but it is difficult to see unless specimens are examined in the hand. If this character is applied uncritically it can lead to confusion as the length of the line is the same in several different species.

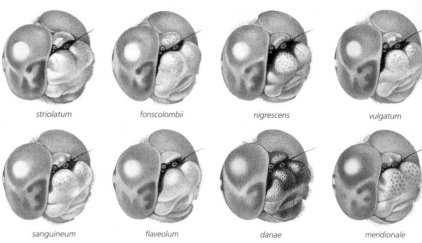

striolatum   fonscolombii   nigrescens   vulgatum

sanguineum   flaveolum   danae   meridionale

Male and female genitalia

females		males	females		males
vulvar scale		secondary	vulvar scale		secondary
side view	ventral view	genitalia	side view	ventral view	genitalia

danae

pedemontanum

meridionale

striolatum

fonscolombii

nigrescens

sanguineum

vulgatum

flaveolum

Common Darter
Sympetrum striolatum (Charpentier)

Description

Jizz The Common Darter is a small, restless dragonfly that regularly perches among bankside vegetation or (unlike most other darters) on the ground in cool conditions, often returning repeatedly to the same spot.
Field characters Ab 25-30mm; hw 25-30mm. Mature males have an orange-red abdomen. Immatures and females have a yellowish to light brown abdomen. Old females may become reddish. Look also for the black line across the top of the frons which is not continued down either side of the eye, and the outer sides of the legs which are striped with yellow.
Similar species At a distance, the species may be confused with the Ruddy Darter. In the latter, however, the legs are all black. The Ruddy Darter can also be distinguished by its smaller size, club-shaped abdomen and the deeper red of the males. The Highland Darter, found in parts of north and west Scotland and Ireland, is altogether darker but otherwise very similar to the Common Darter; its specific status is still in dispute. For differences between the Common Darter and rarer migrant darters close examination is required, see those descriptions and opposite.

Status and conservation

Common and sometimes abundant throughout England, Wales and Ireland and occurring sporadically in much of Scotland, this species is found throughout most of Europe, except for northern regions.

Behaviour and ecology

Habitat The Common Darter occurs in a wide range of waterbodies, from ponds and lakes to ditches and rivers, and will tolerate all but shaded or polluted sites, even brackish water.

For such a common species there have been surprisingly few studies of the behaviour or ecology of the larvae or adults.

Larvae can be found mostly in still water but also sometimes in slow-flowing canals and rivers, often among vegetation. Development lasts a year. **Emergence** takes place in the early morning and can occur as early as mid June to as late as the beginning of October. Tenerals and immature adults appear sometimes in large numbers on the margins of the larval habitats. The **flight season** in mild autumns has been known to last through until November or, in rare instances, December.

In warm conditions, the Common Darter perches high on the twigs of bushes and trees, and also on posts and barbed-wire fences, all of which are used as feeding perches. It is able to remain active at temperatures (below 12°C) which may be too cold for other species of a similar size. When cool,

it often perches in sunny spots on the ground, on rocks, on logs, or even on dark clothing.

Reproductively active males can be seen at ponds and lakes between about 9.00am and 3.00pm in the summer. On first arriving, they may make a series of dipping movements, like those of oviposition, possibly as a means of checking the water quality. They then commonly perch on the ground but later adopt perches on vegetation. The first male to arrive may be aggressive towards later arrivals, attacking them from below and chasing them off, but some males may be able to perch unobtrusively in the vicinity and a hierarchy may be established, with the first male remaining dominant. Males may spend much of the time on the wing when there are many other individuals in the vicinity, and feeding from a perch may also occur while they are at the water.

Females fly to aquatic habitats and either commence oviposition immediately or settle nearby after an inspection of the site. Males seize females in flight without courtship, although unwilling females can often escape. After a few seconds of tandem flight, the male translocates sperm to his secondary genitalia and the wheel position is adopted. Copulation is completed after perching and lasts 7-15 minutes, with the occurrence of prominent rocking movements by the male's anterior abdominal segments during the first few minutes. These may coincide with the displacement of rivals' sperm within the female. When copulation has finished, the pair may briefly rest in tandem and then fly over the water, dipping in various places, initially without contacting the surface. They may then hover over one site, which is sometimes close to submerged vegetation, dipping down repeatedly about once per second. Site selection and oviposition movements are believed to be under control of the male, and a male in tandem with a dead female may still make oviposition movements. Females are often seen to oviposit alone, doing so at a lower rate of dipping. Towards the end of oviposition, which lasts 3-6 minutes, the female raises her abdomen by 45°, inducing the male to release her, and she then flies rapidly upwards, sometimes with the male following. Alternatively, after being released, a female may continue oviposition, with the male still guarding and hovering close to her. Eggs laid in September or earlier may hatch after about two weeks, but those laid later enter a diapause and do not hatch until the following spring. After a male has copulated and flown off in tandem with a female, another male may then become dominant at the same site and the first male usually does not return.

Many darter species are well known for their migratory habits. It is likely that in good summers migrants arrive from the Continent to supplement indigenous populations of Common Darters, and movements in the reverse direction may also occur. It is not uncommon to see various-sized swarms flying unidirectionally in England during the late summer or autumn, which perhaps represents local migratory movements.

Peter Miller

Highland Darter
Sympetrum nigrescens Lucas

The validity of this taxon as a species distinct from the Common Darter has been questioned by several dragonfly specialists in recent years. Specimens resembling the Common Darter but with more extensive black markings, particularly on the side of the thorax and underside of the abdomen, have been referred to as the Highland Darter. Such specimens are generally restricted to north-west Scotland and western Ireland. However, the extent and intensity of the dark markings are variable, leading to ambiguity, and many specimens cannot be assigned to either taxon with certainty. It seems likely that the Highland Darter will prove to be a melanic colour form of the Common Darter.

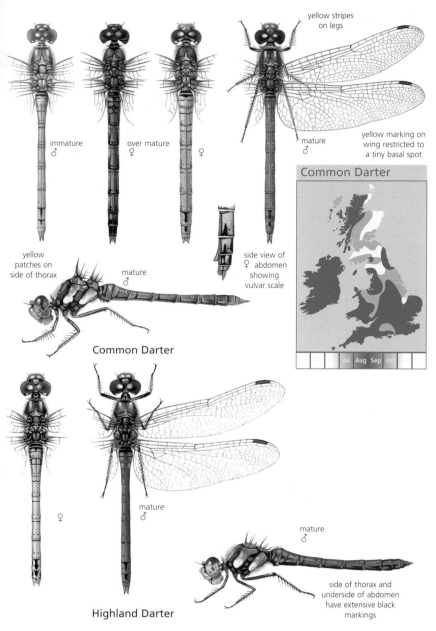

yellow stripes
on legs

immature
♂

over mature
♀

♀

mature
♂

yellow stripes
on legs

yellow marking on
wing restricted to
a tiny basal spot

Common Darter

Jul Aug Sep Oct

yellow
patches on
side of thorax

mature
♂

side view of
♀ abdomen
showing
vulvar scale

Common Darter

♀

mature
♂

mature
♂

side of thorax and
underside of abdomen
have extensive black
markings

Highland Darter

It is a common feature of many insect species that those individuals occurring at the northern extremities of a species' range exhibit dark colour forms. The dark colour may assist in maintaining high body temperatures in cold climates.

There are also subtle but inconstant differences in the structure of the male secondary genitalia and female vulvar scale, and some authors regard this as an indication that the Common and Highland Darter do not interbreed. DNA-fingerprinting of northern populations of the two taxa may help to resolve this taxonomic problem and establish whether or not they are distinct species.

Steve Brooks

Ruddy Darter
Sympetrum sanguineum (Müller)

Description

Jizz The male is a small, bright crimson darter often seen on a prominent perch among vegetation beside shallow, overgrown ponds, lakes or canals, frequently situated in woodland. Females are ochre and defend feeding perches on bushes and tall grass away from open water. The flight is distinctive: a bouncing and swinging movement, with longer periods of hovering than in the Common Darter.

Field characters Ab 20-26mm; hw 23-29mm. The mature male Ruddy Darter has a waisted blood-red abdomen and dark sides to the thorax (the sides may have yellow patches when immature, as in the Common Darter). The black line over the frons extends down the sides. Both sexes of the Ruddy Darter have entirely black legs, unlike other red darters which have a yellow stripe on the legs. The saffron wing colouring is restricted to a small area at the wing base. The wings acquire a golden hue with age, especially noticeable in bright sunlight. Some mature females acquire red coloration with advanced age.

Similar species This species is most likely to be confused with the Common Darter, with which it often shares a pond. However, that species has an orange-red straight-sided abdomen. The black line around the frons of the Ruddy Darter might lead to confusion with the rare Vagrant Darter, which is paler overall, larger, but also slightly waisted. The female Ruddy Darter lacks the black thoracic triangle of the female Black Darter.

Status and conservation

The British population is supplemented by regular Continental immigrations each summer; proof of breeding depends on finding newly emerged adults and observing oviposition. The resident population is strongest in south-east England, mostly up to the Humber/Bristol Channel line. It has been recorded from most of Ireland. The species appears to be expanding its range northwards, where it has been seen on the south Solway coast on the Scottish borders, and westwards at present and was not known from Ireland before the 1920s. It is found throughout Europe.

This species is vulnerable to excessive removal of emergent plants, and its requirement for shallow ponds means that it is vulnerable to drought, drainage and encroachment of terrestrial vegetation.

Ecology and behaviour

Habitat The Ruddy Darter prefers shallow, well-vegetated ponds, lakes, canals, boggy pools, ditches and occasionally streams, frequently situated in woodland.

The **larvae** live among the roots of emergent vegetation, particularly horsetails (*Equisetum*) and bulrushes (*Typha*). They are difficult to distinguish reliably from Common Darters and are dark greeny brown and spidery-looking. The life cycle is usually completed within a year. Larvae either hatch a few days after oviposition, or the eggs may diapause, if laid in late summer, and hatch in spring. Mature larvae complete **emergence**, which takes about two hours, a short way up a vertical plant stem in the early morning. Emergence is unsynchronised and occurs between late June and September. After the maiden flight, both sexes spend time feeding over bushes, long grass and marshy areas. Maturation is temperature-dependent but takes on average ten days. In males, the red coloration begins to spread from the tip of the abdomen and extends upwards with increasing exposure to sunlight. If the weather is good, the **flight season** may extend into late autumn, even after the first frosts. Late in the year, lack of food rather than cold nights may kill adults.

Both sexes, when feeding away from water, typically perch in trees and bushes facing towards an open space. The perch is in an area of abundant food and is left only to catch food or to chase away an intruder. The owner usually defeats intruders and returns to the same perch. Upper perches on the end of twigs are most favoured. The abdomen is held horizontally regardless of

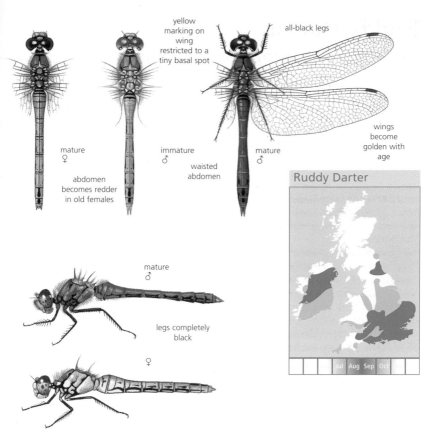

yellow marking on wing restricted to a tiny basal spot

all-black legs

mature ♀

abdomen becomes redder in old females

immature ♂

waisted abdomen

mature ♂

wings become golden with age

mature ♂

legs completely black

♀

Ruddy Darter

Jul Aug Sep Oct

the angle of the perch. The threat display is a movement of the wings upwards from the forward resting position, accompanied by a slight raising of the abdomen. This display is given on landing and whenever an intruder flies too near.

Mature males move to water in the middle of the day. They perch low, facing or parallel to the bank on a prominent perch such as a bush, twig or long grass stem, but not usually at the water's edge itself. If the air is cool, they may settle on bare ground or on a log to benefit from the reflected warmth. They do not remain at one particular territorial site but will chase other males that approach them, thus maintaining small exclusion zones around themselves. Tandem pairs are usually tolerated within this zone. They make frequent sorties to catch food and chase off rivals. If a female passes overhead, a male will pursue her and attempt to form a tandem by grasping her head with his claspers. Copulation is carried out perched among vegetation

and may last several minutes.

Following copulation, the pair remains in tandem and may pass over a large area in an undulating flight before the male finally selects an oviposition site. This may be over submerged plants, or among terrestrial vegetation at the water's edge, or in damp mud, which may become inundated during winter flooding. The male repeatedly swings the female downwards, and the eggs that accumulate at the tip of her abdomen are washed or flicked off. The eggs are drought-resistant and do not hatch until covered by water. If there is no harassment by other males during the initial stages of tandem oviposition, the male may release the female but continue to guard her by hovering close by. This is advantageous because of energy savings and because the pair is less prone to predation from frogs. Females may return to oviposit on their own, but for the rest of the time they remain away from water.

Andrew McGeeney

Black Darter
Sympetrum danae (Sulzer)

Description

Jizz This small darter dragonfly is usually seen in late summer. Its flight is erratic and of short duration, with frequent perching among vegetation near shallow, acid-water pools.

Field characters Ab 18-24mm; hw 20-26mm. Males have a waisted abdomen and are black when mature. Females and immature males are yellow, becoming olive with age; look also for the completely black legs and the black triangle on top of the thorax. Females have a small yellow patch at the base of the wing, but the pterostigma is black.

Similar species Mature males are the only black darter to occur in Britain, so are unlikely to be misidentified. However, emerald dragonflies may appear black in some lights, but, unlike the Black Darter, they seldom perch, and then they hang from vegetation after the manner of a hawker dragonfly. Female and immature male Black Darters resemble other darter dragonflies, but may be distinguished by the combination of small size, entirely black legs, black triangle on top of the thorax, and a row of three yellow spots enclosed within a median black stripe on the thorax side.

Status and conservation

The Black Darter is a northern species with a circumboreal distribution, and occurs in Europe, Russia and Canada. In southern Europe it is restricted to the Alps and Pyrenees. The species is widespread throughout much of Britain and can be abundant, especially in the north; it is local in southern Ireland and eastern and central England.

Although not threatened nationally, it has been lost from former breeding sites, especially in eastern England, following agricultural reclamation and drainage of heathland, and industrial-scale mining of peatlands.

Ecology and behaviour

Habitat The larval habitat includes shallow, acidic, nutrient-poor pools with abundant emergent vegetation on heathland, moorland and bogs. The adult is a wanderer and may undertake migratory journeys, and so is likely to appear far from water or in locations that do not support breeding populations.

The **larvae** are sprawlers and live on the bottom among *Sphagnum* mosses. They are able to survive temporary drying-out of the habitat by burrowing into damp moss which is protected from dehydration by a crust of dry moss above. Larval development occurs during spring and early summer and can be completed within two months. There are usually ten larval stadia.

Adult **emergence** is non-synchronous, and dispersal across the surrounding countryside does not occur until 3-4 weeks after emergence. The **flight season** is usually from mid July to mid September.

The species' black markings have a thermoregulatory function for cold conditions. Male flight activity occurs when the body surface temperature is between 20°C and 40°C, and the insect adjusts its body heat by perching at different heights. In very warm conditions the insect will point its abdomen vertically towards the sun (the obelisk position), thus reducing the surface area exposed.

Mature males are non-territorial. They frequently settle on the stems of marginal vegetation, or on rocks and bare ground, where they bask in the sun. Most pairs are formed during the morning, away from water, so females arrive at the breeding site already in tandem. Peak sexual activity occurs at midday, and unpaired males move to the pond in the early afternoon. By late afternoon sexual activity diminishes and feeding flights predominate.

Females are most active during late afternoon. They perch in denser vegetation than males so as to avoid male harassment. With clutch intervals of 3-4 days and 66-75% of females unreceptive on any particular day, they need to hide from males. By hiding, females ensure that they mate with males which are the most accomplished at searching to find them. Any females that are not mated during the morning move to the water during the afternoon. Their flight tends

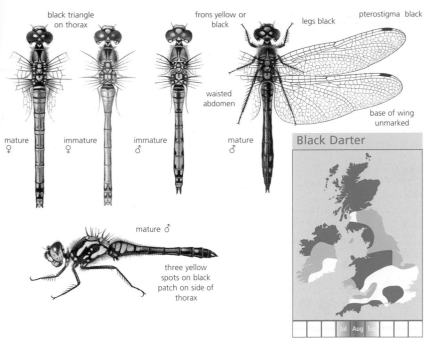

black triangle on thorax

frons yellow or black

legs black

pterostigma black

waisted abdomen

base of wing unmarked

mature ♀

immature ♀

immature ♂

mature ♂

mature ♂

three yellow spots on black patch on side of thorax

Black Darter

Jul Aug Se

to be fast and overt, thus attracting the attention of males. They are chased by several males, in a whirling pack of competitors, but will be mated only by the fastest. Copulation may takes 6-60 minutes, and is briefest at high temperatures and late in the day. Mated pairs perch on tall grasses or bushes near the breeding pools. Sperm competition is intense, and 95% of the eggs are fertilised by the last male. Males occasionally try to pair with female Common Darters.

The oviposition-site assessment flight is slow. Substrate selection is achieved visually, and a pair is attracted to areas where other Black Darters are already ovipositing. This indicates that predation risks are probably low, and there is also the flock effect: all the ovipositing pairs rise together if one spots danger. However, selection is also dependent on thermoregulation, and south-facing sites are chosen late in the season when the body temperature is low, whereas north-facing sites are preferred in early season when the body temperature is high. At high temperatures, site-searching and oviposition bouts are longer. The pair chooses wet substrates at the water-line as oviposition sites to prevent the eggs from dehydrating. Sites with *Sphagnum* are preferred but other

mosses are also used, as occasionally is plant debris, mud and open water. Areas with overhanging trees are avoided.

Oviposition always starts in tandem, and the period of tandem oviposition tends to be more prolonged at times of high male density. By adopting this tactic the male prevents other males from taking the female, but the chance of predation increases. Following a period of tandem oviposition, the pair may then separate and the female continues to oviposit with the male hovering close by, which reduces the predation risks. The male will react to a predator, thereby warning his partner to escape. To remove the eggs, the female flicks her abdomen or dips it into the water while the pair is in flight. The pair starts the dipping action about 30cm above water, but then makes contact with the water if not disturbed by predators or other Black Darter males. Lone ovipositing females tend to be more jittery than tandem pairs; they frequently change orientation and move from one *Sphagnum* patch to another.

Soon after laying, the eggs enter diapause and overwinter in this condition. Diapause is broken the following spring, and the larvae hatch after about three weeks.

Steve Brooks

Banded Darter
Sympetrum pedemontanum (Allioni)

Description

Jizz A small darter dragonfly with weak, fluttering flight, frequently resting among tall, dense herbage, where it can be surprisingly cryptic.

Field characters Ab 18-23mm; hw 21-26mm. Characterised by the narrow reddish-brown band in the outer half of all wings. Mature males have a broad, vivid blood-red abdomen, and a bright red pterostigma. In females and immature males, the abdomen and pterostigma are yellow-brown.

Similar species The species is smaller than most other darter dragonflies, and the brown wing band renders it unmistakable.

Status and conservation

A rare migrant to Britain, recorded for the first time in this country in 1995. In Europe, the species has a south-central distribution and is most frequent in hilly districts. However, it was recently discovered as a breeding species in The Netherlands and so may reappear in Britain.

Ecology and behaviour

This darter breeds in marshy meadows and swamps. Larvae complete development within a few months, and adults are on the wing from July. Oviposition is in tandem and occurs over dense aquatic vegetation.

Yellow-winged Darter
Sympetrum flaveolum (Linnaeus)

Description

Jizz A medium-sized darter dragonfly. Flight is strong and reminiscent of the Common Darter. This darter is often associated with dense marginal vegetation, but may be seen in fields and meadows or alongside hedgerows far from water.

Field characters Ab 22-26mm; hw 24-29mm. The abdomen of mature males is orange-red, but in females and immature males it is yellow-brown. It is characterised by a broad yellow-amber patch at the base of the wings in both sexes.

Similar species Similar in size, body coloration and habits to the other darters. However, the extensive yellow patch at the base of the fore and hind wings will serve to distinguish this darter, although this may not be apparent until the species is viewed closely. The Red-veined Darter has less extensive yellow patches at the wing bases, but in males of this species the wing-veins are red, and not yellow as in the Yellow-winged.

Status and conservation

The Yellow-winged Darter is an infrequent visitor to Britain, but when it does occur it may be present in large numbers. In some years (notably 1926, 1945, 1955 and 1995), coinciding with strong prevailing winds from the south-east in late July or August, the species may be superabundant and occur almost anywhere. In years following even these mass immigrations, however, established breeding populations are few and short-lived. This seems surprising considering that the species breeds in southern Norway, Sweden and Finland, where winters are considerably harsher than in Britain.

Ecology and behaviour

Larvae occur among aquatic vegetation or on the bottom of marshy pools, peat bogs and the weedy parts of lakes. Adult males perch on emergent vegetation or may congregate, sometimes in large numbers, in meadows away from water. Females oviposit in tandem among aquatic plants in shallow water at the water's edge, or even in damp hollows which become inundated during the autumn and winter.

Steve Brooks

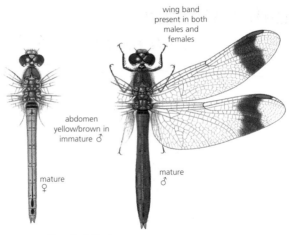

wing band present in both males and females

abdomen yellow/brown in immature ♂

mature ♀

mature ♂

Banded Darter

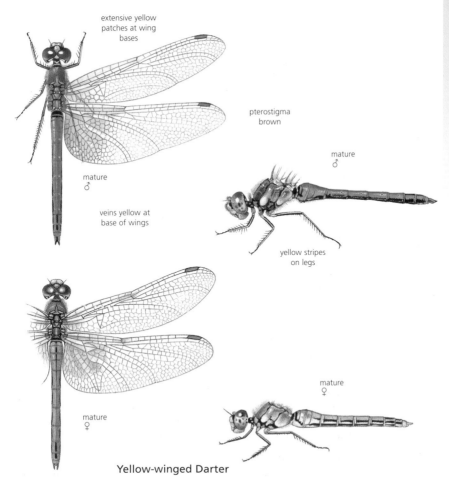

extensive yellow patches at wing bases

pterostigma brown

mature ♂

mature ♂

veins yellow at base of wings

yellow stripes on legs

mature ♀

mature ♀

Yellow-winged Darter

Red-veined Darter
Sympetrum fonscolombii (Selys)

Description

Field characters Ab 24-28mm; hw 26-31mm. A medium-sized darter dragonfly. Mature males have a brick-red abdomen; this is yellow-brown in females and immature males. The base of the hind wing usually has a yellow patch which rarely extends beyond the discoidal cell in the basal quarter of the wing. The veins in the basal half of each wing, adjacent to the leading edge, are conspicuously red in males and yellow in females. The pterostigma is pale yellow with black borders, even in mature specimens.

Similar species This species is similar in size, colour and habit to other darters, and is best distinguished by the red or yellow veins along the leading edge in the basal half of each wing. Note also the eyes in males, which are red above and blue below. Like the Vagrant and Ruddy Darters, the Red-veined Darter has a black line extending down the side of the frons.

Status and conservation

The species is a frequent migrant to Britain, being reported in most years and major influxes occurring in 1992, 1996, 1998 and 2000. Most often sighted in south-west England from July, following strong south-westerly winds, it has also recently been reported from southern Ireland. Occasionally breeds in England, but most populations succumb after a few years. There are currently breeding colonies in Kent and Cornwall that have been maintained over the last 3-5 successive years. The species is widespread throughout southern Europe.

Ecology and behaviour

Breeds in a wide variety of shallow ponds, lakes and ditches and will tolerate brackish water. Larvae live among aquatic plants and develop rapidly. In southern Europe, two generations can be completed in one year. Males are aggressively territorial. Females oviposit alone or in tandem.

Steve Brooks

Vagrant Darter
Sympetrum vulgatum (Linnaeus)

Description

Field characters Ab 24-28mm; hw 24-29mm. This is a medium-sized darter with unmarked wings. Mature males have a slightly constricted, red abdomen (less orange than that of the Common Darter); females and immature males have a yellow-brown abdomen. In female Vagrant Darters, the vulvar scale extends prominently at right angles to the abdomen; the vulvar scale is less prominent in other darter species (see page 142).

Similar species The Vagrant Darter is very similar to the Common Darter, from which it differs in having the black stripe extending down the side of the frons. In the Common Darter, the black band is restricted to the upper surface of the frons only. Note that this feature can be seen clearly only in specimens examined in the hand, and that the Ruddy and Red-veined Darters also have the black band extending down the side of the frons. In the Ruddy Darter, however, the legs are entirely black, whereas in the Vagrant and Red-veined Darters the legs are bicoloured black and yellow. Wing-veins are black in the Vagrant Darter but red or yellow in the Red-veined Darter, especially those in the basal half adjacent to the leading edge.

Status and conservation

The Vagrant Darter is a rare migrant to Britain, where it has been found flying in the company of Yellow-winged and Red-veined Darters in southern and eastern England. The

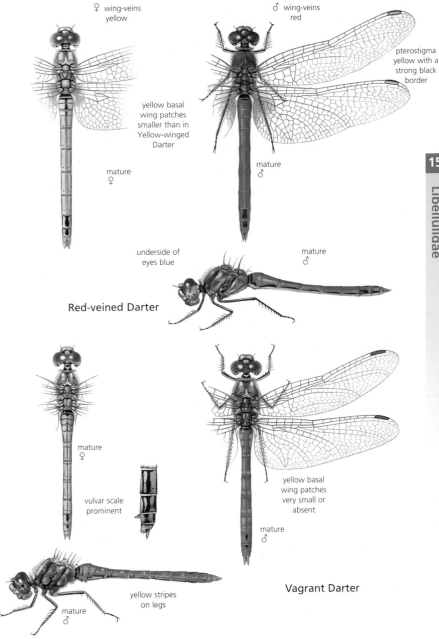

♀ wing-veins yellow

♂ wing-veins red

pterostigma yellow with a strong black border

yellow basal wing patches smaller than in Yellow-winged Darter

mature ♀

mature ♂

underside of eyes blue

mature ♂

Red-veined Darter

mature ♀

vulvar scale prominent

yellow basal wing patches very small or absent

mature ♂

mature ♂

yellow stripes on legs

Vagrant Darter

species is common and widespread in central and north-east Europe.

Ecology and behaviour

In Europe, this dragonfly breeds in a wide variety of standing-water habitats at altitudes of up to 2500m. Larvae occur among debris on the bottom. Adults are on the wing from late June. Females oviposit in tandem in shallow water at the edge of the breeding site.

Steve Brooks

Southern Darter
Sympetrum meridionale (Selys)

Description

Jizz A medium-sized darter dragonfly with strong flight. Frequently perching among tall vegetation or on bare ground.

Field characters Thorax yellowish or reddish brown with hardly any trace of black markings on the side. Mature males with bright orange-red abdomen. Immatures and females with yellow-brown abdomen. Legs yellowish brown with narrow black stripe.

Similar species Superficially similar to the other red darter species but can be distinguished by the almost total lack of black markings on the side of the thorax.

Status and conservation

This species has been recorded only four times in Britain. The most recent record was in 1901. Reappraisal of the records and re-examination of the specimens where available has led subsequent authors to doubt the authenticity of these records. The distribution of the species is centred around the Mediterranean.

Ecology and behaviour

Breeds in small shallow ponds with abundant vegetation. The flight period in southern Europe is between June and mid October.

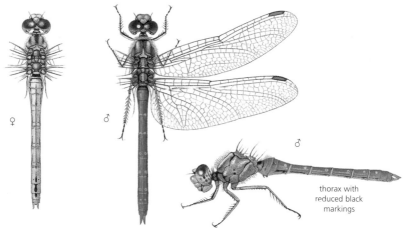

♀   ♂   ♂

thorax with reduced black markings

Scarlet Dragonfly
Crocothemis erythraea (Brullé)

Description

Jizz A large darter dragonfly with strong flight; pauses frequently to hover. It perches among tall vegetation or on the ground with wings swept forward and may be seen far from water.

Field characters Ab 22-29mm; hw 27-32mm. Mature males have a bright scarlet head, eyes and abdomen, with reddish-brown thorax. Immatures and females are yellowish brown, females becoming olive with age, with a row of pale yellow spots along the side of the abdomen. The abdomen is relatively broad and flattened. The wings are marked with a pale yellow patch at the base, which is larger in the hind wing than the fore wing.

Similar species The Scarlet Dragonfly resembles other darter dragonflies although it is slightly larger. The almost entirely bright scarlet body of mature males is unmistakable. The abdomen, which is broader than other darter dragonflies, is also a useful distinguishing feature. Note also that there are 9-11 complete antenodal cross-veins along the leading edge of the fore wing, whereas there are only eight antenodals in *Sympetrum* species.

Status and conservation

The Scarlet Dragonfly is a rare migrant to Britain with the first confirmed record from Cornwall in August 1995. The arrival of this specimen coincided with a large influx of migrant *Sympetrum* species. Since then the species has been recorded three more times, from Devon, Cornwall and the Isle of Wight. The species is common and abundant in southern Europe and is a well-known migrant, being able to travel hundreds of miles, and is frequently attracted to lights on board ocean-going ships.

♀ larger yellow patch at base of hind wings

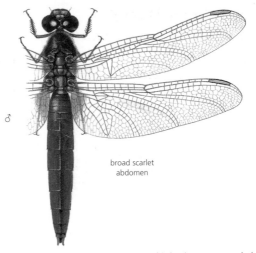

♂

broad scarlet abdomen

Ecology and behaviour
Breeds in a wide range of standing water habitats including brackish and moderately polluted pools. Larval development can be rapid in warm pools in Mediterranean regions and there may be two generations in one year. This leads to an extended flight season from April to November. Males are territorial. Mating is rapid and is usually completed in flight. Females oviposit alone or with the male hovering close in attendance.

Globe Skimmer
Pantala flavescens
(Fabricius)

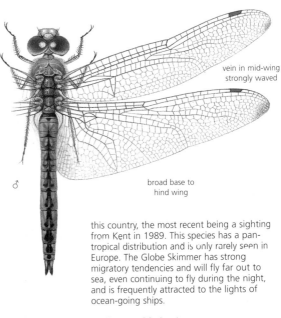

♂

vein in mid-wing strongly waved

broad base to hind wing

Description
Jizz A large yellowish-red libellulid dragonfly with strong, high gliding flight, rarely settling. Frequently observed far from water.
Field characters Ab 26-32mm; hw 38-42mm. Both male and female Globe Skimmers have a narrow, strongly tapering abdomen which is yellowish, becoming more olive in females or reddish in older males with a black mid-dorsal stripe. The base of the hind wing is noticeably broadened. The pterostigma is red-brown and the wing tips may be marked with a small yellowish-brown spot.
Similar species The species is distinctive and unlikely to be confused with any of the resident British species.

Status and conservation
A rare migrant to Britain having been recorded only four times in this country, the most recent being a sighting from Kent in 1989. This species has a pan-tropical distribution and is only rarely seen in Europe. The Globe Skimmer has strong migratory tendencies and will fly far out to sea, even continuing to fly during the night, and is frequently attracted to the lights of ocean-going ships.

Ecology and behaviour
Breeds in small, shallow, often temporary, pools. Larval development is rapid. Females oviposit alone by tapping the surface of the water with the tip of the abdomen. The species is gregarious and may form large feeding and migratory swarms. Feeding flight may continue beyond dusk.

Steve Brooks

White-faced Darter
Leucorrhinia dubia (Vander Linden)

Description

Jizz This is a small darter dragonfly inhabiting peat bogs. Mature individuals fly in an agitated, skittish manner. They frequently hover low over water and typically settle on bare patches of peaty soil and low vegetation close to the margins of bog pools.

Field characters Ab 21-27mm; hw 23-28mm. In flight, the body of the mature male appears dark, almost black, the red thoracic and abdominal markings having darkened with age. The characteristic white frons is very distinctive and contrasts strongly with the rest of the body. Over dark, peat-stained water, the pale veins give the vibrating wings a slightly milky appearance. Teneral males and females have yellow thoracic and abdominal markings but share the characteristic white frons.

Similar species The White-faced Darter is most likely to be confused with the Black Darter. Both species can appear together towards the end of the White-faced Darter's flight period (July). Although teneral males of the Black Darter may be confused with teneral males of the White-faced, the former does not possess the white frons or basal dark brown wing patches present in this species. For a positive identification, specimens should be examined in the hand.

Status and conservation

In the British Isles, the White-faced Darter is a rare dragonfly with a disjunct distribution within Scotland, England and Wales. The major strongholds for this species are in the Scottish Highlands. It has not been seen at its Surrey site for some years. In Europe it is essentially a northern species; in southern Europe it is rare and is generally restricted to suitable habitat in montane districts.

Regrettably, in England, the destruction of habitat through drainage, agricultural reclamation, peat extraction and afforestation has significantly reduced the number of breeding sites over the past 40 years. Fortunately, several important populations are now protected within nature reserves, where the creation and maintenance of pools and hinterland management are of considerable importance for their long-term survival.

On 'mosses' in central England, peat-cutting by hand in the traditional, low-intensity, piecemeal way has maintained a steady supply of suitable habitat for this species as cuttings are abandoned and replaced. A little-known but serious threat at one breeding site for this species was the commercial collection of moss from bog pools for the hanging-basket trade. Having passed virtually unnoticed, this practice was removing larvae along with their habitat!

Ecology and behaviour

Habitat Breeding sites are confined to acid, oligotrophic bog pools that support floating and submerged *Sphagnum* moss.

The White-faced Darter generally has a two-year life cycle, although some individuals may complete it in one or three years. The **larvae** can be distinguished from other darter larvae by the presence of dark stripes on the underside of the abdomen. They live almost exclusively among the matrix of floating and submerged *Sphagnum* moss within and fringing bog pools, but also occur among water-logged *Sphagnum* in depressions devoid of standing water. The larvae are active during the day and night, but consume most prey at night. Such activity would tend to make them vulnerable to fish predation, and the species is usually confined to pools that are too acidic to support fish.

Diapause in overwintering final-stadium larvae is triggered by shortening daylength and ensures synchronised emergence the following year. Adult **emergence** usually begins during the second and third weeks of May, and may continue into the beginning of July depending on latitude and weather conditions. Larvae generally select low emergence supports, most often 2-3cm above the water. Supports such as stems of cotton-grasses, heathers and rushes are frequently chosen, and it is not unusual to find several exuviae, some on top of each other, or even inverted individuals, on a single support. Emergence can continue on cool and cloudy

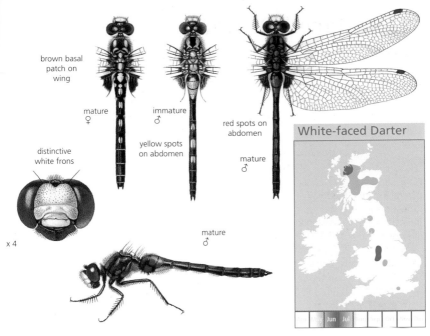

brown basal patch on wing

mature ♀

immature ♂

yellow spots on abdomen

distinctive white frons

x 4

red spots on abdomen

mature ♂

mature ♂

White-faced Darter

Jun Jul

days. There is, however, some evidence that the number of crippled individuals increases in these conditions. Most emergences take place between early and mid morning.

The maiden flight is directed away from water and is often short, perhaps only 2-3m, although subsequent flights are of longer duration. Tenerals tend to fly to the nearest suitable scrub or woodland in close proximity to the breeding site. The shelter, roosting facilities and abundant food found in such areas are particularly important. There is little evidence of any long-distance dispersal. Sites in open, windswept areas which are otherwise suitable for breeding are often ignored by this species. The **flight season** lasts until the end of July or early August.

The maturation period is temperature-dependent and may take 4-12 days in males and a few days longer in females. Once mature, males begin to hold territories, flying low over water. In hot weather, activity is reduced during the middle of the day. The territory is relatively small, and the species has been described as only mildly territorial. Interactions with other species rarely involve physical contact, but they will investigate and indulge in a short chase before returning. Away from water, males will bask on logs and bare ground and tolerate the presence of others.

Females are rarely encountered over water except during oviposition, since they prefer to perch in surrounding vegetation, trees and shrubs or to sun themselves on open ground. Copulation is often initiated over water, with the pair settling on the ground or on the stems and twigs of low vegetation nearby, and lasts about 30 minutes. Non-receptive females vibrate their wings and raise the abdomen at approaching males.

In most cases, oviposition occurs immediately after copulation. Females oviposit alone but are often guarded by the attendant male. The chosen oviposition site is among floating and waterlogged vegetation; *Sphagnum* moss and between the stems of cottongrasses are particularly favoured sites. The insect's perception of the bright reflections from exposed water around the floating moss appears to be important in the site-selection process. The very nature of oviposition behaviour in this species means that later seral changes in vegetation could modify and restrict the availability of oviposition sites. Although bog-pool habitat can be relatively stable in the north of the species' range, further south active management may be necessary to maintain or develop oviposition and larval habitat.

Bob Kemp

Further reading

d'Aguilar, J, Dommanget, J-L & Préchac, R 1986 (English translation) *A field guide to the Dragonflies of Britain, Europe and North Africa.* Collins, London 336pp
Pocket guide with general introduction and notes on identification, habitat, behaviour and distribution of each species. Illustrated with line drawings, distribution maps, colour paintings of adults and colour photographs depicting behaviour and habitats. Keys to adult genera and larvae at family level.

Askew, R R 1988 *The Dragonflies of Europe.* Harley Books, Colchester 291pp
Includes keys, distribution maps, brief biological notes and large colour paintings of adults and larval keys to all species occurring in western Europe. Large format.

British Dragonfly Society *Dig a pond for dragonflies*
Contains advice on pond creation and maintenance to attract dragonflies.

British Dragonfly Society 1993 *Managing habitats for dragonflies*
Includes advice on conservation management of wetland habitats for dragonflies. Aimed at countryside managers.

Corbet, P S 1962 *A Biology of Dragonflies.* Witherby, London (reprinted by E W Classey in 1983) 247pp
Seminal work on dragonfly biology including examples from Britain and the rest of the world.

Corbet, P S 1999 *Dragonflies: behaviour and ecology of Odonata.* Harley Books, Colchester 829pp
Comprehensive account of the lives of dragonflies, synthesising information gathered since 1962, written by the world's leading authority on dragonflies.

Corbet, P S, Longfield, C & Moore, N W 1960 *Dragonflies.* New Naturalist Series, Collins, London (reprinted in 1985) 260pp
Classic work on the biology of British dragonflies.

Fitter, R & Manuel, R 1986 *Collins Photo Guides – Lakes, Rivers, Streams & Ponds of Britain & North-West Europe.* Collins, London 382pp
Contains keys, biological notes, line drawings and colour photographs to assist in the identification of all groups of freshwater plants and animals. Pocket-sized field guide.

Gibbons, B 1986 (reprinted 1994) *Hamlyn Guide – Dragonflies and damselflies of Britain and northern Europe.* Hamlyn Publishing, London 144pp
Pocket guide including all the British species and many of the migrants. Includes general introduction, illustrated with colour photographs and line drawings.

Hammond, C O 1983 (2nd edition, revised by R Merritt) *The Dragonflies of Great Britain and Ireland.* Harley Books, Colchester 116pp
Keys to adults and larvae, distribution maps, brief biological notes and large format colour paintings of adults.

McGeeney, A 1986 *A complete guide to British dragonflies.* Jonathan Cape, London 133pp
Identification guide to the British species with brief biological and ecological notes, descriptions of adults illustrated with colour photographs, keys to adults and larvae illustrated with line drawings.

Merritt, R, Moore, N W & Eversham, B C 1996 *Atlas of the dragonflies of Britain and Ireland.* HMSO, London 149pp
Comprehensive distribution maps including records up to 1990. Colour photographs of selected species as adults and larvae, notes for each species on identification, ecology, flight period and status.

Miller, P L 1995 *Dragonflies.* Naturalists' Handbooks 7. Richmond Publishing Co, Slough 118pp
Concise, informative and stimulating account of biology and ecology of British species, also includes colour paintings of adults of selected British species and keys all to adults and larvae.

Powell, D 1999 *A guide to the dragonflies of Great Britain.* Arlequin Press, Chelmsford
Pocket guide written and illustrated in the style of a field notebook, with colour sketches of adults of each species and brief notes on behaviour.

Silsby, J 2001 *Dragonflies of the World.* The Natural History Museum, London 216pp
A family-by-family review of the world's dragonflies, with photographs and ecological and taxonomic overviews.

There are also a number of good quality regional and county guides available (e.g. Mendel, H 1992 *Suffolk Dragonflies.* Suffolk Naturalists Trust, Ipswich) covering many areas of Britain. You should enquire at your local museum or library for details of these publications.

Addresses

Organisations and museums

British Dragonfly Society, The Secretary, The Haywain, Hollywater Road, Bordon, Hants GU35 0AD

Contact the Secretary for details of the Dragonfly Recording Scheme which is currently co-ordinated by the British Dragonfly Society. Publishes a journal, newsletter and arranges regional walks and lectures.

Worldwide Dragonfly Association, I Haydn Avenue, Purley, Surrey CR8 4AG

The Wildife Trusts, The Green, Witham Park, Waterside South, Lincoln LN5 7JR

The county and regional Wildlife Trusts own and manage many reserves throughout the country, many of which are important for dragonflies.

Entomological book suppliers

E W Classey Ltd, PO Box 93, Faringdon, Oxfordshire SN7 7DR (tel: 01367 244 700)

Pemberley Books, PO Box 334, Hayes, Middx UB4 0AZ (tel: 0181 561 5494)

Pond nets

GB Nets, PO Box 1, Bodmin, Cornwall PL31 1YJ (tel: 01752 295407); e-mail gbnets@efe-uk.com

Marris House Nets, 54 Richmond Park Avenue, Queen's Park, Bournemouth BH8 9DR
(tel: 01202 515238)

Entomological equipment

Watkins & Doncaster, PO Box 5, Cranbrook, Kent TN18 5EZ (tel: 01580 753 133)

Checklist of Odonata of Great Britain and Ireland

Damselflies Zygoptera

☐ Beautiful Demoiselle *Calopteryx virgo*
☐ Banded Demoiselle *Calopteryx splendens*
☐ Emerald Damselfly *Lestes sponsa*
☐ Scarce Emerald Damselfly *Lestes dryas*
☐ Southern Emerald Damselfly *Lestes barbarus*
☐ Willow Emerald Damselfly *Lestes viridis*
☐ White-legged Damselfly *Platycnemis pennipes*
☐ Large Red Damselfly *Pyrrhosoma nymphula*
☐ Red-eyed Damselfly *Erythromma najas*
☐ Small Red-eyed Damselfly *Erythromma viridulum*
☐ Southern Damselfly *Coenagrion mercuriale*
☐ Dainty Damselfly *Coenagrion scitulum*
☐ Northern Damselfly *Coenagrion hastulatum*
☐ Irish Damselfly *Coenagrion lunulatum*
☐ Norfolk Damselfly *Coenagrion armatum*
☐ Azure Damselfly *Coenagrion puella*
☐ Variable Damselfly *Coenagrion pulchellum*
☐ Common Blue Damselfly *Enallagma cyathigerum*
☐ Scarce Blue-tailed Damselfly *Ischnura pumilio*
☐ Blue-tailed Damselfly *Ischnura elegans*
☐ Small Red Damselfly *Ceriagrion tenellum*

Dragonflies Anisoptera

☐ Azure Hawker *Aeshna caerulea*
☐ Common Hawker *Aeshna juncea*
☐ Migrant Hawker *Aeshna mixta*
☐ Southern Migrant Hawker *Aeshna affinis*
☐ Southern Hawker *Aeshna cyanea*
☐ Brown Hawker *Aeshna grandis*

☐ Norfolk Hawker *Aeshna isosceles*
☐ Emperor Dragonfly *Anax imperator*
☐ Lesser Emperor *Anax parthenope*
☐ Common Green Darner *Anax junius*
☐ Vagrant Emperor *Hemianax ephippiger*
☐ Hairy Dragonfly *Brachytron pratense*
☐ Club-tailed Dragonfly *Gomphus vulgatissimus*
☐ Golden-ringed Dragonfly *Cordulegaster boltonii*
☐ Downy Emerald *Cordulia aenea*
☐ Brilliant Emerald *Somatochlora metallica*
☐ Northern Emerald *Somatochlora arctica*
☐ Orange-spotted Emerald *Oxygastra curtisii*
☐ Four-spotted Chaser *Libellula quadrimaculata*
☐ Scarce Chaser *Libellula fulva*
☐ Broad-bodied Chaser *Libellula depressa*
☐ Black-tailed Skimmer *Orthetrum cancellatum*
☐ Keeled Skimmer *Orthetrum coerulescens*
☐ Scarlet Dragonfly *Crocothemis erythraea*
☐ Common Darter *Sympetrum striolatum*
☐ Highland Darter *Sympetrum nigrescens*
☐ Vagrant Darter *Sympetrum vulgatum*
☐ Southern Darter *Sympetrum meridionale*
☐ Red-veined Darter *Sympetrum fonscolombii*
☐ Yellow-winged Darter *Sympetrum flaveolum*
☐ Ruddy Darter *Sympetrum sanguineum*
☐ Black Darter *Sympetrum danae*
☐ Banded Darter *Sympetrum pedemontanum*
☐ White-faced Darter *Leucorrhinia dubia*
☐ Globe Skimmer *Pantala flavescens*

Index

Main entries are indicated by **bold** type.